D1095130

1P
~~1754~~
12.00

LARGE MAMMALS AND A BRAVE PEOPLE

Large Mammals and a Brave People

SUBSISTENCE HUNTERS IN ZAMBIA

By Stuart A. Marks

UNIVERSITY OF WASHINGTON PRESS
SEATTLE AND LONDON

This book was published with the assistance of
a grant from the Andrew W. Mellon Foundation.

Printed in the United States of America

Library of Congress Cataloging in Publication Data

Marks, Stuart A. 1939–
Large mammals and a brave people.

Bibliography: p.
Includes index.
1. Bisa (African tribe) 2. Hunting, Primitive—
Case studies. I. Title.
DT963.42.M35 639′.11′096894 75-26945
ISBN 0-295-95447-7

For my family

Preface

To consider the plight of a small group of hunters in Central Africa as they contend with continuity and change requires that the researcher be both modest and presumptuous—presumptuous in that on the basis of only fourteen months of study, he must attempt to analyze a highly complex and integrated system of thought and behavior; and modest in that any attempt at elucidation of an alien culture demands a complex indoctrination, a sympathy entailing the rejection of intellectual pride.

Moreover, to characterize an alien people with whom one has lived and learned is inevitably to reveal oneself. In some ways, my sojourn among the Valley Bisa was a personal quest for adventure, a search for manhood in the thicket of interdisciplinary research. At a deeper level there was a strong emotional impulse toward identification with hunters whose traditions are fading and a longing to understand the importance of my own past as well as that of other people. I do not believe the emotional motivation behind my research invalidates my findings. On the contrary, I believe no intellectual work is of value unless there is deep personal and emotional involvement.

From my mother's side I inherited an artistic skill which lately has gone undeveloped. An initial recollection is a response to nature as reflected in the colors of various birds and mammals and my attempts to capture some of their beauty in sketches. In addition to this artistic wish was the desire to possess these creatures. My father, a dentist, was reared on a farm in eastern North Carolina and had an ardent interest in sport hunting, to which I was introduced at an early age. When, in 1948, my parents became dental missionaries to the Belgian Congo (now Zaire) under the auspices of the Southern Presbyterian Church, my exposure to other cultures began.

There were many components of my education in the Congo. As a child, I was without the strictures of adult roles and through an easy association with the Congolese gained many subconscious but instructive insights into their culture. These insights proved a definite asset later in my study of the Valley Bisa, for the Bisa shared a similar cultural history and language with the Lulua of the Congo.

After finishing high school in the Congo, my inclinations led me to earn a degree in wildlife biology. I then pursued graduate education in animal ecology at Michigan State University, for I entertained hopes of eventually doing research for an advanced degree in Africa. The opportunity to return for research, however, was still a few years off.

When I accepted a temporary position as a biologist with the Alaska Department of Fish and Game and was stationed for a month and a half among the Eskimos of St. Lawrence Island, another facet of my background that had been dormant was awakened. For one with an emotional commitment toward wild mammals and their conservation, I found that I also had a strong social bias, engendered, I suspect, by the religious commitment of my parents and by my earlier upbringing in the Congo.

An important prerequisite in conservation, as in any field, is a knowledge of the subject. The main focus of research on wildlife has centered on its value as a resource. Such applied knowledge has been successful in maintaining and in some cases, increasing wildlife populations in many parts of the world. Without such pragmatic orientations among researchers, it is doubtful if some species of wildlife would have survived today. But such investigations examine only half of the picture, for their focal point is primarily on the utilized, and not the utilizer—man. The perception and use of wildlife in many cultures where it is a resource is different from that of the biologist. Such differences often lead to misunderstandings and naïve efforts on the part of many conservationists to implement programs that prove to be ineffective and unrealistic.

When I returned to Michigan State University during the winter of 1963 for graduate work, I had decided to undertake an interdisciplinary study of hunting in an African society. My graduate committee, composed of Professors George A. Petrides (Fisheries and Wildlife, Zoology), John E. Cantlon (Botany and Plant Pathology), Moreau Maxwell (Anthropology), and Charles G. Hughes (Chairman of African Studies, Anthropology), are due credit for their guidance when my own ideas were still in a formative stage. Under their guidance, I submitted a proposal to several Central African countries to study "traditional" patterns of hunting. Zambia's response was favorable and they suggested I study the Bisa in the Munyamadzi Corridor. Support from the Foreign Area Fellowship Program made further training in anthropology and language possible.

An NDEA fellowship during the summer of 1965 enabled my wife and me to study the Bemba language at Michigan State University under Professor I. Richardson and Mubanga Kashoki. These studies were followed under Foreign Area Fellowship Program sponsorship with a term of Nyanja under Dr. G. Atkins and two terms of Bemba under Messrs. Michael Mann and Grenson Lukwesa at the School of Oriental and African Studies of the University of London during 1965–66. In conjunction with these studies we attended courses and seminars in economics, political science, social anthropology, and African history at University College, School of Oriental and African Studies, and London School of Economics. Professor C. von Furer-Haimendorf, Drs. A. Richards, P. Gulliver, G. Kay, and Miss B. Ward were particularly helpful in clarifying my objectives before I began my field work.

During the nine months at the University of London, I read widely and struggled to obtain a clearer perspective of my proposed research problem. When I discussed my research with ecologists and conservationists I found them aloof and unfeeling toward problems involving people. Neither their knowledge of game nor their experience in Africa was of much help to me in understanding the predicaments of indigenous people. Even the best references available then on African conservation were written on a higher level and seemed to me to be too full of stereotypes of "poachers" to provide insight into what really had happened and was happening on the local scene. I found most social anthropologists in London equally parochial in their views. They suggested I confine myself to studies of social systems and kinship. I feel no qualms about my experiences with either orientation, for I learned something from my exposure to both.

My search through current literature also turned up the same dichotomy of interests and it became clear I would have to do the synthesis. The literature on African societies is enormous and I scanned many excellent and scholarly tomes. But the literature I reviewed lacked the one book I wanted to read. I decided to write such a volume—a book that would provide information on a group of hunters and their world. The formal concept behind this book is therefore an outcome both of my personal needs and experiences. In writing it, I unburden myself of a debt to the past.

Our project in Zambia was affiliated locally with the Institute for Social Research of the University of Zambia. Professor A. Heron, then director of the institute, was helpful in arranging for our initial contacts in Zambia and I wish to thank him for his continuing interest in this work. Many government officials resident in Lusaka who had visited the corridor or whose agency shared some responsibility for administration in the Luangwa Valley were generous with their time and furnished information about local conditions. Among these were Messrs. I. Makungo and H. Chipunga (Community Development); P. Hancock (Assistant Secretary for Community Development); C. M. N. White and

I. Mackinson (Zambian High Court); P. Greening (Department of Agriculture); N. Carr (former game ranger); and T. L. Fox-Pitt (former native commissioner at Mpika). I am extremely grateful to the Ministry of Lands and Natural Resources for its interest in my work and its suggestion that I study the Valley Bisa in the Munyamadzi Corridor. The Honorable Solomon Kalulu, then Minister of Lands and Natural Resources, took a personal interest in the project, and through his good office made cooperation with other officials and agencies possible. The staff of the Department of Game and Fisheries offered unfailing and courteous assistance. W. S. Steel, Director, and W. R. Bainbridge, Chief Game Officer, helped in many ways and materially assisted us in the field, as did L. D. C. Allen, Game Warden, Luangwa Command. W. L. Astle, ecologist in the Luangwa South Game Reserve, aided in identifying plants in the area. Dr. Donald Dodds and David Patton, wildlife biologists on assignment with FAO/UN Ecological Survey, encouraged us and assisted with the project. Thane Riney of the Forests and Forest Products Division of UNESCO, Rome, also gave us valuable advice.

The District Secretaries at Mpika, Messrs. Liambiye and Chitah, showed their concern and cooperation throughout our stay at Nabwalya. J. Ngulube, R. Simusokwe, S. Mwape, and A. Chileshye, teachers stationed at Nabwalya Government School, were helpful in interpreting the more esoteric phases of Valley Bisa life and language and in keeping records for us in our absences.

For their help and patience in interpreting phases of their culture, I am indebted to the Valley Bisa people living in the Luangwa Valley and their chief, Nabwalya (Kabuswe Mbuluma). They were hospitable hosts and tolerant of our inquisitiveness. Their sayings and behavior form the raw materials for much of this book, and I trust my writings do not betray their confidence nor invade their privacy. Toward this end, all names, lineages, and clan affiliations mentioned in the text are fictitious. My special appreciation goes to several individuals who must remain anonymous but whose close association enabled me to penetrate deeply into hunting lore and other phases of their society and culture. I wish to express my sincere appreciation to Dyson Luben, our research assistant, who, by his faithfulness, patience, and understanding, taught us much about present pressures on Valley Bisa society.

My field study and training at the University of London was made possible through a fellowship granted by the Foreign Area Fellowship Program. Without their generous support my research would not have achieved fruition. The initial draft of my manuscript was supported by a grant from the Research Foundation of Oklahoma State University. Their assistance is appreciated and gratefully acknowledged. The introductory and concluding sections of the manuscript and its final preparation for publication were aided by grants from St. Andrews Presbyterian College, Laurinburg, North Carolina. Mr. E. Schnell and Mrs. B. Haston, both of Stillwater, Oklahoma, prepared the figures from my original sketches. Tables 31, 33, 34, 37, 39, and 41; Figures 15, 17, and 18; and Appendix B appeared earlier in a slightly altered form in my article "Prey selection and annual harvest of game in a rural Zambian community," *East African Wildlife Journal* 11 (1973).

All or parts of the manuscript in various stages of writing were read and criticized by numerous people. I am extremely grateful for the valuable suggestions and corrections of J. Desmond Clark, W. Dillon, N. Egemonye, H. Guerry, J. Harris, L. D. Harris, D. McLean, D. Patton, T. Scudder, S. Siame, R. L. Smith, B. Stefaniszyn, and W. D. White. Subsequent research in Zambia during 1973 on hunting processes provided the opportunity to check the manuscript with the Valley Bisa. Through their help I have been able to correct some of my initial impressions which were misleading. With such benevolent assistance, persistent errors are my responsibility. Materials gathered during 1966–67 are the major source for the present volume and my use of the ethnographic present tense refers to this time period.

Finally, but most importantly, I wish to express my appreciation to my wife, Martha, who shared the excitement, hardships, and isolation of field work and the tribulations and revelations associated with preparing this manuscript. She cheerfully joined into all phases of my research and contributed many valuable observations. In addition, she accepted the menial chores of cooking, boiling water, and the many record-keeping chores of research in the field. She was an important source of moral support and a congenial companion under circumstances that were far from ideal. Furthermore, her presence did much to enhance our acceptability among those whom we studied. Since leaving the field, she has typed the numerous drafts of my manuscript and has offered many suggestions for its improvement.

The Valley Bisa whom I studied in 1966–67 and again in 1973 appeared to me to be on a threshold with the clouds of rapid change concentrating on their escarpment fringes. Much of their traditional culture probably has already or will soon pass from practice to the written page. Perhaps the observations recorded in this book may help their children understand some aspects of their past. I am grateful for their contributions to our knowledge of people as hunters in a transient world.

S. A. M.

Contents

Illustrations

MAP

FIGURES

PHOTOGRAPHS

Foreword

For more than one hundred and fifty years, white hunters have taken their toll of Africa's big game animals, and many are the volumes that have been written concerning their exploits. Some hunters were astute and assiduous observers of the animals they encountered and of the habitats in which they lived. Mostly, however, the interests of the authors of these books appear to have been dominated by their passion for securing record trophy heads, and all too often their books are either dull or nauseating records of butchery. Very few of these men, and occasionally women, took more than a passing interest in the role played in the indigenous communities by the hunters who served as their guides and trackers, and whose knowledge of animal behavior and skill in stalking and killing usually far outclassed their own. The indigenous hunters either remain anonymous or receive only cursory acknowledgment in these self-laudatory volumes. Fortunately, there are exceptions, especially among the nineteenth-century explorers, and, if it were not for the detailed, eclectic accounts left by these travelers, little would be known of the manner of life on the central plateau of Africa prior to the major social and economic changes that followed the establishment of colonial rule. The diaries of these explorers often contain a wealth of information on social and economic customs, but there is still little revealing any real appreciation and knowledge of the ways of the African hunter. In part, no doubt, this lack of interest is due to an overriding concern with trophies or the need to keep the cooking pot well filled, rather than with the manner in which the local hunters were able to achieve this. In part, also, it was due to the lack of opportunity for more than a casual acquaintance with the hunter, since any closer understanding would require full participation on the part of the observer and involve him in time-consuming and arduous hunting strategy.

Presumably for the same reasons, the conventional works of

professional anthropologists in Africa rarely contain more than a passing list of game animals and hearsay accounts of how they were hunted, together with a note, perhaps, on the significance of some of these animals for the people who used them. It has really only been within the last fifteen years—since it has become apparent from radio-metric dating methods that for more than nine-tenths of his existence man remained a hunter and food-gatherer—that an interest in learning about the hunting way of life has developed. To this end, highly successful studies of Kalahari Bushmen, Eyassi Hadza, and Ituri Pygmies have now been undertaken that have had great significance in the reconstruction of the evolution of human behavior. Although such investigations record behavior now much modified from that existing prior to contact with Europeans and already on the brink of extinction, they are quite crucial for what they reveal about the way hunters live and think. But today, studies such as those by Richard Lee and John Yellen of the Bushmen (Sari) and James Woodburn of the Hadze can no longer be repeated, so rapid and fundamental have been the changes enforced by well-meaning governments on the lives of these minority groups. The way of life described in these studies now belongs to the past.

It is true to say that we know even less about the role of hunting in the lives of the more settled food-producing populations of sub-Saharan Africa. It might be thought that hunting was of considerably less importance among hoe agriculturalists, and, while this is mostly true today, it was certainly not so in the past. Where the presence of the tsetse fly precluded the keeping of livestock, in particular cattle and sheep, and where traditional beliefs restricted the slaughter of cattle in the tsetse-free areas, a high proportion, often the greater part, of the meat consumed by central African villagers in the woodland savanna regions of the inland plateau was obtained by hunting.

White and black hunters with precision firearms, and government projects which were misguidedly thought to necessitate the eradication of game, have taken a drastic toll of the large game animals that one hundred years ago—indeed, less than fifty years ago—were spread in such great numbers throughout the tropical savanna. Today this game has practically disappeared from a very large part of the interior plateau and survives only in national parks and game reserves; but recent events show that even these are not the sanctuaries they were once believed to be. In contrast to this virtual annihilation, the traditional hunting methods using bows and arrows, spears, nets, muzzleloading guns, and traps usually cropped only the expendable surplus and brought about no significant reduction in the game herds; the annual number of kills of medium to large game animals that Stuart Marks recorded for the Valley Bisa is not appreciably different from that observed among present-day hunter-gatherers. Since the advent of the rapid-fire, high-precision rifle, however, there are pathetically few parts of the continent were it is possible to observe the traditional pattern of large animal hunting among any of the indigenous savanna peoples.

We are exceptionally fortunate, therefore, in having Marks's penetrating study of hunters among the Bantu-speaking Bisa peoples in the central part of the Luangwa Valley in eastern Zambia. This study area is uniquely situated in the corridor between two national parks, and it must be one of the few parts of the continent where documentation of some of the traditional behavior and beliefs connected with the hunting of such large animals as elephant and buffalo is still possible.

We are doubly fortunate in that Marks brings to this study the training of an ecologist as well as that of an anthropologist, a combination resulting in understanding of humans and animals alike. In addition to his formal training, the fact that he grew up in the African bush accounts in no small part for the success of his companionship with the Valley Bisa and his manner of relating the present to their earlier traditional patterns of behavior. His ecological background enables him to evaluate the way these Bisa hoe cultivators and hunters look at the different phenomena that make up their environment, and, as an anthropologist, he goes on to show the nature of their relationship with their habitat and the interaction between this environmental setting and their traditional cultural behavior.

It is no mean feat to have completed with such success a year's fieldwork in the Luangwa Valley where temperatures, humidity, and disease conspire to sap the energy of even the most ardent investigator. In addition to the conventional interviewing of informants in the villages, Stuart Marks also has had to spend long hours stalking with the hunters, joining them in their peregrinations through the hunting territory. Under such conditions and where it can be expected that two out of every three stalks will be unrewarding, the excitement of a kill can have been exceeded only by the exhilaration and satisfaction that follow the acquisition of previously unrecorded information.

Marks treats the hunting system of the Valley Bisa as an inseparable part of the whole culture system and shows how this relationship has changed and is continuing to change under the interplay of internal and external forces. His sympathy for and understanding of the beliefs and rituals of the hunt, and of the social and economic status of the hunters and the variety of techniques they use to exploit a major food resource, help to fill what was a serious gap in our knowledge of the hunter's role among the swidden, or slash and burn, agriculturalists of the central plateau lands. In addition, Marks's study goes beyond the empirical and forms a link with prehistory enabling archaeologists to perceive better the extent to which game and, in particular, the large animals were a major resource for the earlier Iron Age population of farmers as well as for their hunting and gathering ancestors for more than two million years during the Pleistocene. Precisely documented evidence on seasonality, location of kill sites, distances, numbers, techniques of stalking, butchery, distribution and preparation of meat, and disposal of waste are but some of the data set out in this book that are especially significant for the paleo-anthropologist. "Unlike zoological studies of predators where explanations of selectivity are sought in the behavior or morphology of the beasts, studies of hunting by humans must take into consideration the cultural and technological orientation of their respective groups." For one who spent twenty-three years investigating the past and studying the material culture of the present-day peoples of Zambia, the appearance of this volume is an occasion for much satisfaction. It is not difficult to see that it can become the basis for the first meaningful reconstruction of prehistoric hunting patterns in Africa's savanna woodlands.

Stuart Marks's close and warm relationship with his Bisa hosts brings to this book a depth of appreciation and understanding that is often missing from the formal anthropological treatise. Here the relationship that exists between the adaptiveness of a human population and the resources on which it depends for survival can be seen clearly. But the projected movement of the population of the Luangwa Valley to the plateau threatens to terminate the way of life described in this book, and, should this exodus come about, Marks's volume will be one of the few remaining records of and memorials to a brave people.

J. DESMOND CLARK
University of California
Berkeley

July 1975

LARGE MAMMALS AND A BRAVE PEOPLE

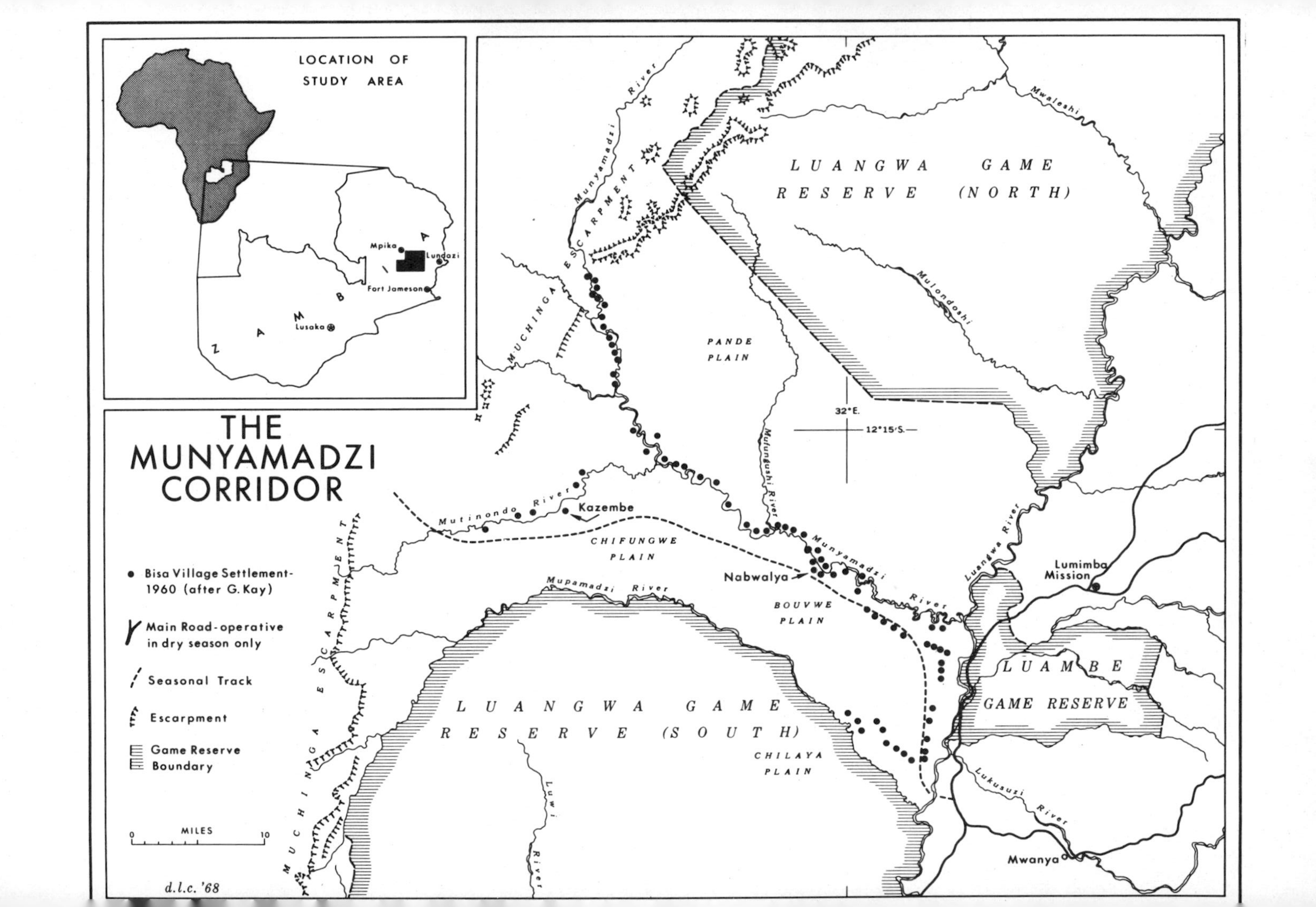
LOCATION OF STUDY AREA
Mpika
Lundazi
Fort Jameson
Lusaka
Z A M B I A
THE MUNYAMADZI CORRIDOR
Bisa Village Settlement-1960 (after G. Kay)
Main Road-operative in dry season only
Seasonal Track
Escarpment
Game Reserve Boundary
MILES
0
10
d.l.c. '68
LUANGWA GAME RESERVE (NORTH)
LUANGWA GAME RESERVE (SOUTH)
LUAMBE GAME RESERVE
MUCHINGA ESCARPMENT
Munyamadzi River
Mwaleshi
Mulondoshi
Mufungushi River
Luangwa River
Mutinondo River
Mupamadzi River
Luwi River
Lukusuzi River
PANDE PLAIN
CHIFUNGWE PLAIN
BOUVWE PLAIN
CHILAYA PLAIN
Kazembe
Nabwalya
Lumimba Mission
Mwanya
32°E.
12°15'S.

I

Preliminaries and Introduction to the Study

RESEARCH ITINERARY

I ARRIVED in Zambia on 17 June 1966 and spent the subsequent three weeks in Lusaka making contacts with officials, gathering firsthand accounts of the study area, and in general acquiring the necessary supplies and information for the journey into the Munyamadzi Corridor (see map, p. 2).

Two routes provide access into the Munyamadzi Corridor. Both are negotiable by four-wheel drive vehicles during the dry season. One route leaves the Lundazi–Fort Jameson (now Chipata) road south of Luambe Game Sanctuary and crosses the Luangwa River at Chibindi pontoon. Access into the corridor by this route is relatively easy since there is no precipitous descent of the escarpment. The other route runs east from the Great North Road along the plateau, descends the Muchinga escarpment (a drop of over two thousand feet in 2½ miles), crosses the Mutinondo River and then follows a bush track below the string of villages on the Munyamadzi River to the chief's village at Nabwalya. This was the route my wife and I chose initially.

During the late afternoon on 13 July we descended the escarpment and hurriedly pitched our tent on the outskirts of a village on the Mutinondo River. As the sun set, we were abruptly introduced to the sounds of our new environment. Mice entered our tent, scampering over the boxes and cots, always finding something to chew.[1] Hyenas visited the village during the night and we followed their wanderings by listening to the sound of their loud rising barks. Our initial impressions remain vivid for we slept little. On 15 July we drove the twenty-four miles to Chief Nabwalya's

1. Scientific names of mammals and birds identified in the text are given in Appendix A.

village, for it was the environs of the chief's village which were to become the focus of our study.

During the subsequent months we made a few trips to Chipata and Lusaka to purchase supplies, but in early November we left our vehicle with friends in Chipata. We immediately returned to Nabwalya where we remained until we emerged at Mpika on 14 January 1967 after a five-day hike. We spent 14 January to 10 April in Chipata and Lusaka, organizing our notes and reading the materials at the National Archives of Zambia and the files in Game Department offices. Our intention was to return to Nabwalya in mid-March, but floods in the Luangwa and its tributaries prevented our return until 10 April. Carriers met us at Mwanya and we began the three-day trek to Nabwalya.

The face of the land which we entered after crossing the Luangwa had gone through a complete metamorphosis since our departure in January. Grasses were extremely high along the river, and their towering heads obscured many of the landmarks with which we had become familiar. The Land Rover track was overgrown with grasses and would be cleared before the first Land Rover could pass through. Most villages were abandoned and overgrown with grass for the Valley Bisa had forsaken their villages and taken up residence in their fields.

When the Land Rover track was cleared toward the end of May we walked to Mwanya and returned to Nabwalya with our Land Rover. We left the Munyamadzi Corridor for the last time on 8 August 1967 and departed from Zambia on 25 August 1967. This description covers fourteen and one half months in Zambia, ten of which were spent in residence at Nabwalya.

THE MUNYAMADZI CORRIDOR AND STUDY AREA

The country in which the Valley Bisa live consists of an irregular rectangle lying between about 12° and 12°40′ south latitude and between 31°30′ and 32°15′ east longitude. Lying across the Luangwa Valley, the Munyamadzi Corridor is approximately forty-five miles long and twenty-five to thirty miles wide and contains some thirteen hundred square miles. The northern and southern boundaries of the corridor are the southern limit of the Luangwa Valley North Game Reserve (now Luangwa Valley National Park) and the northern boundary of the South Game Reserve, respectively. The corridor's eastern boundary is the Luangwa River, which forms the political division between Zambia's Northern and Eastern Provinces. Physical and environmental conditions on either side of the river are much the same, and inhabitants, whether Valley Bisa or not, share a similar culture and remain closely related. In the west, the precipitous Muchinga escarpment forms a natural barrier which encouraged the isolation of the Valley Bisa from their ethnic stock on the plateau.

I employ the term Valley Bisa to distinguish the Bisa inhabiting the Luangwa Valley from those settled on the plateau, whom I call the Plateau Bisa. Both Bisa originated from the same stock, but distinctions between them, based upon the different environments which each now occupies, appear to me valid, for those inhabiting the Luangwa Valley today see themselves as somewhat different from those inhabiting the plateau. They inhabit a different environment, grow different staples, have different problems, and speak a modification of the tongue spoken by the Plateau Bisa. Plateau lands are dotted with development projects, schools, churches, and hospitals, but the valley has remained a "backward pocket," surrounded by game reserves, cut off by the escarpment, and has hitherto encouraged few development projects by the government. Such disparities cannot be easily overlooked by the Valley Bisa. The abrupt Muchinga range has been an effective topographical and ecological barrier slowly isolating and molding two different peoples and cultures, in a process which had its beginnings long before the turn of the present century.

The land traditionally ruled by the Nabwalya chieftaincy is called Chitaba. In 1966, Chief Nabwalya's village was located along the Munyamadzi River at approximately 31°58′ east longitude and 12°23′ south latitude. It was in this village that my wife and I settled for our research.

Within the chief's village, the Zambian government maintains a boarding school, and it was in the dormitory section of the school grounds that we initially pitched our tent and later constructed our small hut. Here both teachers and students were helpful to us in making the necessary adjustments to valley life. Thus our main study area became the thirty square miles of land centered on the chief's village. Within this area resided some 244 adults scattered among 21 villages and settlements. Also here could be found samples of the major habitats of the valley floor and representative species of mammals.

My study was limited in that it was concerned mainly with a group of hunters inhabiting Valley Bisa villages confined to the center of the Munyamadzi Corridor. Yet this limitation was an inevitable necessity. Because of the national emergency existing at the time of our study between Zambia and Rhodesia, gasoline was severely rationed and expensive when obtainable. These restrictions limited the use of our vehicle during the dry season to infrequent journeys to nearby towns for purchasing supplies and to other areas of the corridor accessible by bush track. From November to June, travel by vehicle within the corridor was impossible because of flooded rivers and the moist clayey soils. At this time, maneuverability was restricted to foot travel or bicycle. In my opinion this restraint worked to our advantage and made us more dependent upon Valley Bisa hospitality than might otherwise have been the case. Therefore we decided to make an in-depth study of one area as an aid to structuring more general observations made elsewhere in the corridor. Schoolteachers stationed at two other sites in the corridor kept observations on Valley Bisa activities. I made visits to other sections of the corridor when possible. The material on Valley Bisa culture and hunting rituals applies to all sections of the corridor, but some components of my study, such as amount of time expended in hunting, quantities of meat consumed, and prey selectivity, probably do not. Naturally, I am reluctant to overgeneralize from my narrow base.

Hunters whom I wished to study were not easily distinguished from the rest by their profession, and because of their past experiences with Europeans were more aloof with strangers than were most men. As usual, the first few months on the local scene were spent in identifying individuals and their roles. Gaining and maintaining the confidence of hunters was a continuous process.

Since I view myself as a generalist concerned with synthesis, and my research as interdisciplinary between anthropology and ecology, something should be mentioned about the kinds of data employed. I began this venture to describe and survey, rather than to test a hypothesis or theory, although in the process of collecting and organizing my materials I have used ideas and theories from both disciplines. My analysis of the social field of hunters and the interpretation of their behavior, rituals, and cosmology are handled within the context of social anthropology. In my discussions of these topics, I have drawn upon the analytical tools and insights provided by A. R. Radcliffe-Brown, M. Gluckman, E. E. Evans-Pritchard, V. W. Turner, J. Beattie, M. M. Douglas, and others. On the other hand, data on the interactions between hunters in their predatory role with game, and the behavior and population structure of game are described in terms of animal ecology.

Methods employed to acquire background knowledge of the Valley Bisa are those generally adopted by anthropologists. I learned the language and my firsthand knowledge of Luba and my academic exposure to Bemba and Nyanja languages were indeed helpful. I observed everyday life in villages, gardens, and the bush, and continually questioned the Valley Bisa on what I was told or had observed. I attended ceremonies and funerals. I drew up genealogies of villages and made a census of those within the boundaries of the study area. Later, I took another census in conjunction with a questionnaire on marriage arrangements, labor experience, and prohibited meats. I recorded detailed life histories of fourteen men. Before and after the field work, I read the available manuscripts written about the Bisa and their neighbors. All these activities were an empathetic exploration of Valley Bisa life.

The primary method of data collection was active participant observation. This involved living in the community, having few outside necessities, and participating in the daily life of the community. While an anthropologist can never become a full-fledged member of the community which he purports to study, he can do much to minimize his conspicuousness that will establish rapport and assure him a more normal role in that society. The evaluation of an outsider by members of a community clearly becomes more favorable in proportion to his willingness to live by and accept their way of life. For my wife and me, this involved living in a hut, doing our own chores without a domestic, remaining in the area during part of the rains, participating in village activities, eating their food and sharing ours. In addition, we refused all roles commonly assumed by outsiders, such as curing the sick and serving as teachers.

The first two or three months of the field period were given over largely to participant observation with few focused interviews. Our main concern was to establish rapport with the residents in as an innocuous way as possible. We surveyed and mapped villages, constructed genealogies, surveyed fields, made reconnoitering trips around Nabwalya, and spent immeasurable time explaining our activities to local residents. Our primary concern at this time was getting our activity survey under way.

Initially, we kept diaries on the activities of the inhabitants of five villages and on seven households in two of the larger villages. After three months, when activities in all villages proved to be repetitive, the households surveyed were cut to a more manageable number so our assistant could gather more information on fewer individuals. Thus, we kept diaries on all residents of three villages and on seven households in two other villages from 24 August 1966 to 8 August 1967. In addition, we noted the relish dishes eaten by each individual at the main meal of the day and additional pertinent comments about village life.

My observations resulted in the compilation of approximately one thousand typewritten pages of field-note material plus supporting data. I divided these notes into two parts: recorded interviews with individuals, and random notes in which I kept observations on Valley Bisa activities and plant and mammal life.

I noted and organized my observations on plant and mammals according to procedures standard with field biologists. Plants of interest were collected while fertile, were pressed, and later were identified by W. L. Astle and confirmed by the herbarium in Salisbury, Southern Rhodesia. I recorded the indigenous names of these plants and their uses, if any, in magics, rituals, and medicines. Unfortunately, some plants used in rituals were never seen by us in flower and consequently are not designated by their scientific names.

Whenever possible, I made classification counts of all ungulates and noted the relative numbers of males, females, and young in each group. My observations on game in the study area were made in conjunction with my outings with hunters on foot. Generally, I classified all single mammals and small herds encountered by sex and age; larger herds of impala, for example, were estimated, and if possible I noted the number of adult and subadult males present within the herd. Large herds of buffalo were not sorted into sex and age categories. Observations on the population structure of game encountered in the corridor, but outside the study area, were made mainly from a slow-moving vehicle.

Determining the sex for ungulates in which males bear horns is a relatively easy matter, provided herds are not large and the observer has the opportunity to scrutinize all members. Where the two sexes are irregularly and unevenly spread over an area, biases occur if each sex is not sampled to the extent which it is represented in the real population. I was able to study game and its movements only in relationship to hunters and their movements. Since each hunter had his individual routes and patterns of hunting, and since I accompanied different hunters throughout the year, I feel my estimates of the game population are representative for the study area.

For most species, adult males are heavier in weight than females. Since I weighed none of the mammals killed, I use the weights obtained by Robinette (1963) in Zambia, and Sachs (1967) in East Africa, to estimate the mean adult weights for each of the major species (see Appendix B). However, live weights are not a measure of edible meat, for much of this weight is in the form of nonconsumables such as bone, skin, hooves, and the contents of the stomach and alimentary tract. To convert live weights to the weight of a dressed carcass, animal husbandrymen use the term *carcass yield*, or the weight of the dressed carcass expressed as a percentage of live weight (Ledger 1963:29). Although it is my impression that the Valley Bisa utilize a higher percentage of live weight of each carcass than do Europeans, for lack of a more appropriate estimator, I use the conversion factor of carcass yield to estimate the amount of usable meat for each game species.

For most species, size differences are readily apparent between newborn and first-year mammals (calves) and adults. In my analysis, I use the term *yearling* for a species between its first and second year, and *subadult* for one slightly smaller than adult size. To compute adult male: adult female:immature ratios, all individuals not listed as adults of either sex are included in the immature group.

For the males of horned species, individuals were usually sorted into three or more classes based upon length of horns in comparison with the length of ears. Unlike antlers, horn growth is continuous during the life of the individual, although in later life, wear at the tips prevents additional increments in length.

For dead herbivores, the amount of wear on permanent dentition is normally a reliable index of age at death. Since I possessed no jaws of known-age mammals to establish age classes, wherever possible, I sorted the kills of carnivores and hunters into three broad classes, which I defined as follows:

1. Slight wear: little or no wear on permanent teeth, all cusps sharp. Such individuals were thought to be subadults or adults in their first year of breeding.

2. Medium wear: wear on crests of middle cheek teeth, and on some crests dentine is visible. These were considered adults in the prime of life.

3. Heavy wear: incisors worn even, molars and premolars with considerable wear on most crests, some of which are worn smooth. These mammals were thought to be past their prime.

In this book I discuss the major components of hunting patterns recorded for the Valley Bisa. My focus is on the hunter in that society; however, in describing his role it is also necessary to portray the wider set of social, cultural, and environmental systems within which the hunter operates. These systems and their interactions are diagrammed in Figure 1.

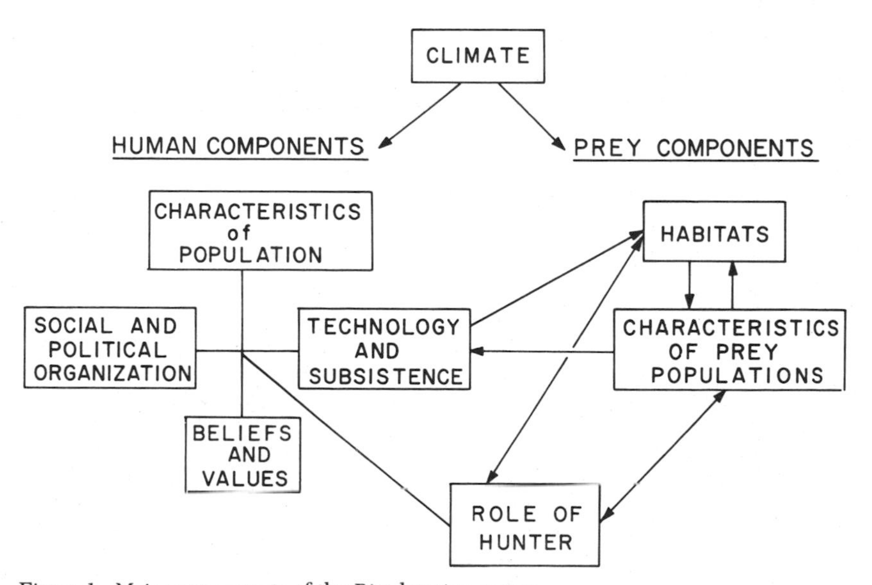

Figure 1. Major components of the Bisa hunting system

Part One

THE CULTURE AND SOCIETY OF THE VALLEY BISA

II

History and Population Characteristics of the Valley Bisa

> This land is closed.
> Let us return to our homeland, to peace.
> Bisa Song

VALLEY BISA HISTORY

Bisa Origins and Migration

LIKE many ethnic groups inhabiting modern Zambia, the Bisa had their origins in the Lunda–Luba empire formerly situated in the southcentral Congo. The Bisa say that it was from this empire, called "Kola" and ruled by Mwata Yamfu, that their ancestors came, and that disputes arising from land scarcity led to their emigration.

According to Thomas (1958), the emigration by the Bisa from Kola occurred about 1650, but it was not until early in the eighteenth century that the Bisa emerged as a distinct ethnic unit. Undoubtedly, these emigrations occurred in small groups and were a gradual process, with independence and autonomy coming after the Luapula River was crossed. During these migrations, certain lineages emerged as leaders and subordinated the others in their vicinity. Thus, among the Bisa, the "Ngona" (mushroom) became the clan of Bisa chiefs, and the "Ngandu" (crocodile) became the dominant clan among their sister group, the Bemba.

According to the Valley Bisa, the emigrating groups of their own ancestors and those of the Bemba were together until they crossed the Chambezi River. It was here, while the group paused before crossing, that the Bemba built a fish trap and caught a crocodile. When the Bisa found a ford and crossed, the Bemba remained to investigate and consume the crocodile. Bemba traditions relative to their separation from the Bisa are recorded in Brelsford (1956) and Thomas (1958).

From the Chambezi, the Bisa traveled to the plateau near Mainza Hill, said to be near the headwaters of the Mutinondo and Mupamadzi rivers, and settled there. It was from Mainza Hill, with its easy descent into the valley along the water course of the Mupamadzi, that some Bisa left the plateau for residence in the valley below. Bisa settlement in the Luangwa Valley was in itself a gradual process. I collected no material which would indicate that the Bisa had to conquer any lands west of the Luangwa River, but wars on the plateau with the Bemba at times undoubtedly did much to accelerate Bisa settlement in the valley.

The Luangwa Valley was known to the Bisa as a hunting territory before permanent settlement there took place. Seasonally, groups of specialized hunters descended the escarpment and established temporary hunting camps (*muzaza*). Such transitory settlements would include several hunters, a supporting staff of carriers, and perhaps their wives.

Later, permanent settlements were established. In 1798, Lacerda stopped at a Bisa village near Pande Plains to solicit carriers, and in 1825, the Portuguese acquired a plot of land east of the Luangwa for the purpose of furthering the ivory trade with the Bisa. Marambo, as this settlement was called, never achieved this purpose and was abandoned a few years after its establishment—a result of bad timing and management. At the time, the Bisa were engaged in wars with the Bemba and were not actively trading.

The capture by the Bemba of the important Chibwe salt pans and Bisa land on the plateau forced many Bisa to take refuge in the Bangweulu swamps and in the Luangwa Valley. Some found refuge in the caves and hollows of the abrupt Muchinga escarpment. These caves, subsequently stocked with provisions, were to provide subsistence during further raids by the Bemba and Ngoni. In response to recurrent raids by their powerful enemies, the Valley Bisa never cultivated large gardens, and thus the European explorers who visited the Luangwa Valley in the latter half of the nineteenth century found it difficult to obtain grain from the valley's inhabitants.

Toward the end of the nineteenth century, agents of the British South Africa Company arrived in the valley to administer the lands over which they had acquired authority. They represented a powerful external force whose influence manipulated and remolded traditional institutions to satisfy the demands and fit the needs of the new colonial administration.

The Valley Bisa Under the Colonial Administration

Agents of the British South Africa Company had little knowledge of alien languages, customs, and history, and this inevitably made their administrative tasks susceptible to misunderstandings and misjudgments. Yet their sense of, and belief in, their "civilizing mission" was so strong that they became ruthless in establishing control and in attempting to reshape traditional institutions. As elsewhere, their written records were to become the cornerstones in administrative decision making affecting Bisa life in the Luangwa Valley. From the beginning there was little in Bisa traditional political and social organization to recommend it to European minds. Tribal wars and the slave trade had to be stopped and all phases of tribal life were to be subordinated under the supposed superiority of the new system which the Europeans were to create. A political hierarchy was established from the Europeans down to the villagers with a recognizable and coherent chain of authority and rank. This meant that Europeans had to identify and use individuals who were friendly and open to their ideas and manipulations. It was impossible for these administrators to realize why their sweeping innovations were so strenuously resisted, for their plans were to run counter to some basic values and traditions of Valley Bisa life.

The establishment of an administrative post at Nabwalya, manned by Europeans, placed new demands on the Valley Bisa, but it also offered new opportunities. Because communication between the distant state posts was essential, conscription for road building began in 1903 with the construction of a road connecting Nabwalya with Mpika and Fort Jameson. In the same year, recruitment began for the mines on the Copperbelt and in South Africa.

New laws, based upon foreign premises, expressed European concern for plant and animal life. For example, in 1906, the new government prohibited the pollarding of trees to arrest the destructiveness inherent in the shifting system of agriculture (*chitemene*) and to prevent the disintegration of village life. Yet no alternative was proposed and in 1909, the ban on *chitemene* had to be lifted. Traditional hunting practices were also subject to new regulations. An entry in the Mpika District Notebook in 1907 reads: "Convictions for breaches of the game regulations were frequent, especially in the matter of game pits."

Simultaneously with the prohibition of the traditional system of agriculture, the government decreed the abolition of *mitanda* ("field huts") and the amalgamation of villages of less than twenty huts with larger ones. Thus, the administration began its attempts to reorganize valley social and political life into a pattern which was more orderly and understandable to European minds. According to the administration, it was impossible to administer the area properly "with the natives living all over the place." The administrator's model was to have large villages connected with wide paths along which government caravans could travel swiftly and safely between villages. The authority of the administration was repeatedly flaunted in spite of harsh punishments.

Residence in *mitanda* was in part necessity, and in part preference. With large mammals inhabiting their immediate vicinity, the Valley Bisa spent the majority of their time during the growing season residing in their fields and guarding their crops. Damage to cultivated crops, mainly by elephants, was recognized in government reports, but the government also noted that *mitanda* were the initial stage in the founding of new villages.

The preference for small villages where one is surrounded by closely related kin and friends is a typical pattern in many Central African societies in the recent past. The preference for small settlements is reinforced by the ambition of most adult males for the respect and recognition that comes with becoming the headman (*mwine muzi*) of his own village. In answering my query as to why it was necessary to live in small settlements, some informants said that sorcerers worked easily and effectively in large settlements whereas in smaller scattered settlements their work was much harder. Large settlements spawn social unrest on many fronts and in one sense accusations of sorcery are reflections of deeper underlying social tensions (Middleton and Winter 1963; Marwick 1965).

While the administration occupied its post (*boma*) at Nabwalya, it was possible to maintain some control over the settlement and life of the Valley Bisa. However, in 1908 the Luangwa River was made the eastern boundary of an enlarged district, and Nabwalya *boma* was abandoned for the more hospitable site of Mpika atop the Muchinga escarpment. Once the administrative presence shifted from the valley to the plateau, the problem of small settlements became a recurrent one. Somewhat earlier, the administration found it impossible to check the movement of individuals and settled upon counts of huts to assess whether or not its minimum village size was being maintained.

The 1930s saw sweeping changes in administrative policy. Under the principles of indirect rule, more authority and judicial power were returned to local chiefs; chiefs were given authority over local courts and local matters, including movement and settlement. But the government insisted that chiefs implement their regulations on minimal village size. District boundaries were realigned to conform more with the territories occupied by tribal units and the number of chiefs recognized by the government was reduced.

About 1940 when the Luangwa Valley Game Reserves were established, the few inhabitants of those areas were encouraged to leave and settle elsewhere. Although these game reserves displaced few inhabitants from their land, the Bisa have been concerned with the restrictions the reserves place on their choice of habitable sites and movements within the valley, and the rigidity with which its boundaries have been enforced. Since the creation of these game reserves, the Valley Bisa have been confined to the narrow neck of land between the two game reserves known as the Munyamadzi Corridor.

POPULATION CHARACTERISTICS

Population Estimates for the Munyamadzi Corridor

Population estimates for the Luangwa Valley began in 1910. Prior to that date the Munyamadzi Corridor was sparsely populated, according to early explorers, who encountered few settlements between the Luangwa River and the Muchinga escarpment. For the fifty-three years during which there are population figures, the Bisa population in the Luangwa Valley shows a steady increase (see table 1). For several reasons, these figures should be looked upon as an indication of population trends rather than as a complete census.

TABLE 1

POPULATION ESTIMATES OF VALLEY BISA FOR 1910–63

Year	Adult Males	Adult Females	Male Children	Female Children	Total Population
1910	2,124[1]		1,420		3,544
1912	2,165		1,512		3,677
1918	758	1,285	975	794	3,812
1921	670	1,142	959	891	3,662
1928	1,001	1,642	1,079	1,038	4,760
1934	735	1,028	829	889	3,481
1953	543	1,340	1,284	1,099	4,266
1963	848	1,376	1,696	1,863	5,783

Note: Figures include all of the Luangwa Valley section of Mpika District. Information abstracted from district traveling reports and Mpika District Notebooks.

1. Figures for 1910 and 1912 do not distinguish between male and female populations.

In the first place, itinerant officials were in a poor position to assess the number of inhabitants within a village, for the accuracy of these figures depended upon the cooperation of and rapport with the local people. The initial tallies were probably accurate, but as new demands were pressed by the administrators, local cooperation diminished. Lacking local cooperation, administrators increasingly relied upon counts of huts, for once constructed these endured for several years and provided a means for comparison from year to year.

Secondly, the Valley Bisa, a population in flux, have never been a homogeneous group. To be sure, the chiefs belonged to the Ngona clan, but those under them were a mixture of lineages which moved about as circumstances dictated. During the early part of this century, population movements were mainly out of the valley, stimulated in part by opportunities for employment elsewhere and by recurrent famines within the valley. It is impossible to assess the impact and magnitude of these emigrations on population structure. Superimposed on population flux at the local level was the shifting of district and provincial boundaries by the administration. Since the Valley Bisa population has been distributed in the past among three separate districts, changes in administrative boundaries make it difficult to assess which portions of the population figure for each district were Bisa.

With the creation of the Luangwa Valley Game Reserves about 1940, the population of the Valley Bisa under the jurisdiction of Mpika District has been stabilized to those inhabiting the neck of land between the two game reserves. Emigrations from this corridor continue to occur, but it is my impression that these are no longer of the same magnitude as earlier.

Population Density

The Munyamadzi Corridor contains approximately 1300 square miles of land in which there are some 175 miles of perennial streams. If this area of land surface is divided into the population figures for 1953 and 1963, the population density is 3.3 and 4.4 people per square mile for each of these two years, respectively (see table 1). However, human settlement is not randomly dispersed throughout the corridor, for a locality near a year-round supply of water is critically important. As a consequence, most settlements and gardens occur within one mile or closer of a permanent water source. Thus, the pattern of land use corresponds with the course of the major streams (see map). For this reason, the area within one mile on either side of these perennial streams (i.e., 350 square miles) is a better measurement upon which to compute population density. Dividing population figures by this smaller area, we see that population density in 1953 was twelve people per square mile, and in 1963, was seventeen people per square mile. Along the river, settlement occurs in clusters interspersed by stretches of uninhabited country.

Dynamics of Population and Settlement Pattern at Nabwalya

In common with many rural areas in Zambia, the human population around Nabwalya, the chief's village, changed in composition throughout the period of study as individuals left or returned to their respective villages. In addition several villages shifted their sites or split, so that the configuration of villages when my study began in July 1966 was noticeably different from that in August 1967 when the study ended.

Most villages and settlements are small and contain few dwellings (mean number 8.5 huts). Those on the study area are no exception. The number of adults on the study area in August 1966 (see table 2) shows an uneven sex ratio of 51 adult males per 100 adult females. Another census conducted in June 1967 reveals a ratio of 53 males per 100 females (see table 3). The 1963 government census for the corridor tabulated an adult ratio of 62 males per 100 females. Comparison of the government census with those I recorded at Nabwalya suggests that a greater percentage of adult men from the environs of the chief's village were away involved in urban employment than for the corridor as a whole.

TABLE 2

POPULATION AND NUMBER OF REGISTERED FIREARMS IN VILLAGES AND SETTLEMENTS IN STUDY AREA (AUGUST 1966)

Name	Adults Male	Adults Female	Children[1]	Registered Firearms[2]
Kabimba	3	5	13	2, 1 shotgun
Chongo	2	6	6	3
Chikwinda	2	4	7	2
Kanelli	3	3	...	2 rifles
Chibeza	2	3	7	0
Chibulu	3	8	16	1
Nabwalya	8	20	44	5, 1 rifle, 2 shotguns
Mponde	2	6	7	1—destroyed by fire 1967
Chigone	2	5	9	0
Chipi	3	6	8	1
Mukupa	6	8	12	3
Yudah	2	3	5	0
Chando	10	14	24	2 (1 non-functional)
Soma	1	2	1	0
Chibale	15	21	37	2
Jamesi	4	11	21	3
Kala	5	12	...	2
Munyobe	3	8	...	0
Chinka	3	11	...	2
Sumailande	1	2	5	0
Mark	2	4	...	1

1. Children tallied in villages where genealogies made.
2. Information from tax assessor's records. Numbers refer to muzzleloading guns unless otherwise noted.

TABLE 3

ADULT AGE STRUCTURE IN ENVIRONS OF NABWALYA, (JUNE 1967)

Age	Male	Female
19–24	8	28
25–29	7	21
30–34	6	17
35–39	8	14
40–49	14	12
50–59	11	12
60+	5	7
Total	59	111

This uneven sex ratio is only a temporary distortion since most young and middle-aged men are away working in urban centers. My survey shows that 92 percent of all males interviewed on the study area had held a job outside, and that a higher percentage had at least visited a city. For men, migration to the cities begins in their late teens when they usually accompany an older person on his return to town. In this sense migration is directional, for an individual migrates initially to urban centers in which he has relatives and these assist him, when possible, in acquiring employment. Men return to the valley at infrequent intervals, but they are not likely to settle for long periods in the valley until after their middle years. Neither are they likely to return to the same job or the same city, for most enter the job market as unskilled workers and accept employment where they find it. Most men return for longer periods of residence in their valley villages when they are about forty years of age.

The experience of urban life among adult women, on the other hand, is more limited. My survey shows that only 30 percent of the adult women surveyed had ever been outside the valley. And of these journeys, most were for the purpose of visiting relatives or offspring, and were of short duration.

Polygamous marriages are common (see table 4), and divorce is readily obtained. The summary of cases for 1966 and 1967 (see table 5) gives some insights into the common civil and criminal cases tried at the local court. But other cases may be heard in the chief's compound including the more serious allegations and accusations of sorcery. So this summary reflects only those impressions which the community itself permits to be shown to the outside world and does not necessarily mirror the deeper latent tensions and hostilities among individuals and groups.

TABLE 4

MARRIAGES AND DIVORCES FOR ADULT MALES IN STUDY AREA

	AGE CLASS		
Number of Marriages	20–30 Years	30–40 Years	40+ Years
1	13	3	4
2	3	6	7
3	...	5	12
4+	...	...	4
Number of Divorces			
1	7	7	6
2	1	1	3
3	...	...	...
4+	...	...	1

TABLE 5

COURT CASES HEARD AT NABWALYA LOCAL COURT

Statute	Type of Case	1965	1966
Civil	Divorce	12	13
	Adultery	4	4
	Domestic Disputes	6	2
	Debts	6	2
	Abusive Language	...	5
Criminal	Faunal Conservation	6	13
	Arms and Ammunition	...	1
	Assaults	8	7
	Threats, etc.	3	8

Infant mortality is high. To aid in determining the extent of infant mortality, I asked sixty-eight adult females, who had produced three or more children, to list all of their offspring both dead or alive. This tally showed an infant mortality rate of 39 percent, and the percentage was slightly higher for males than for females. This high rate is suggestive rather than definitive, since the women may not have listed all miscarriages, stillbirths, or deaths which occurred soon after birth. The Bisa name an infant only after it shows promise of survival. The death rate among infants of less than one year of age was greatest in the hot, humid season just prior to the inception of the rainy season. At this season many adults also fell ill. When a mother's health is poor, the chances of her newborn offspring surviving are also poor, although this seasonal pattern probably varies from year to year, especially if there are epidemics or famines at other seasons.

The kaleidoscopic movements of village sites and fields within the study area for seventeen years are given in Figure 2. Villages and fields shifted from the Munyamadzi River during the 1950s to Bemba stream and then back to the river in the 1960s. According to informants, floods in the river during the late 1940s and early 1950s gave impetus to this shift away from the Munyamadzi. During my study, several villages moved their locations and three villages split. In 1967, Chongo and Chikwinda, two villages north of the Munyamadzi shifted their sites east nearer the river to the middle of their fields. Following the 1967 harvest, Munyobe, Chinka, Sumailande, and Mark, located in 1966 along Bemba stream east of Mupete lagoon, moved to the river slightly east of the study area.

Soon after our arrival in 1966 a small matrilineal segment split from Chibulu and established a settlement, Yudah, three miles east of the parent village. Culminating many years of dispute in which sorcery was implied with his maternal uncle, the chief constructed a new residence on the Mupamadzi River some eight miles from his former site. When his new capital was complete in November 1966, the chief and a few of his

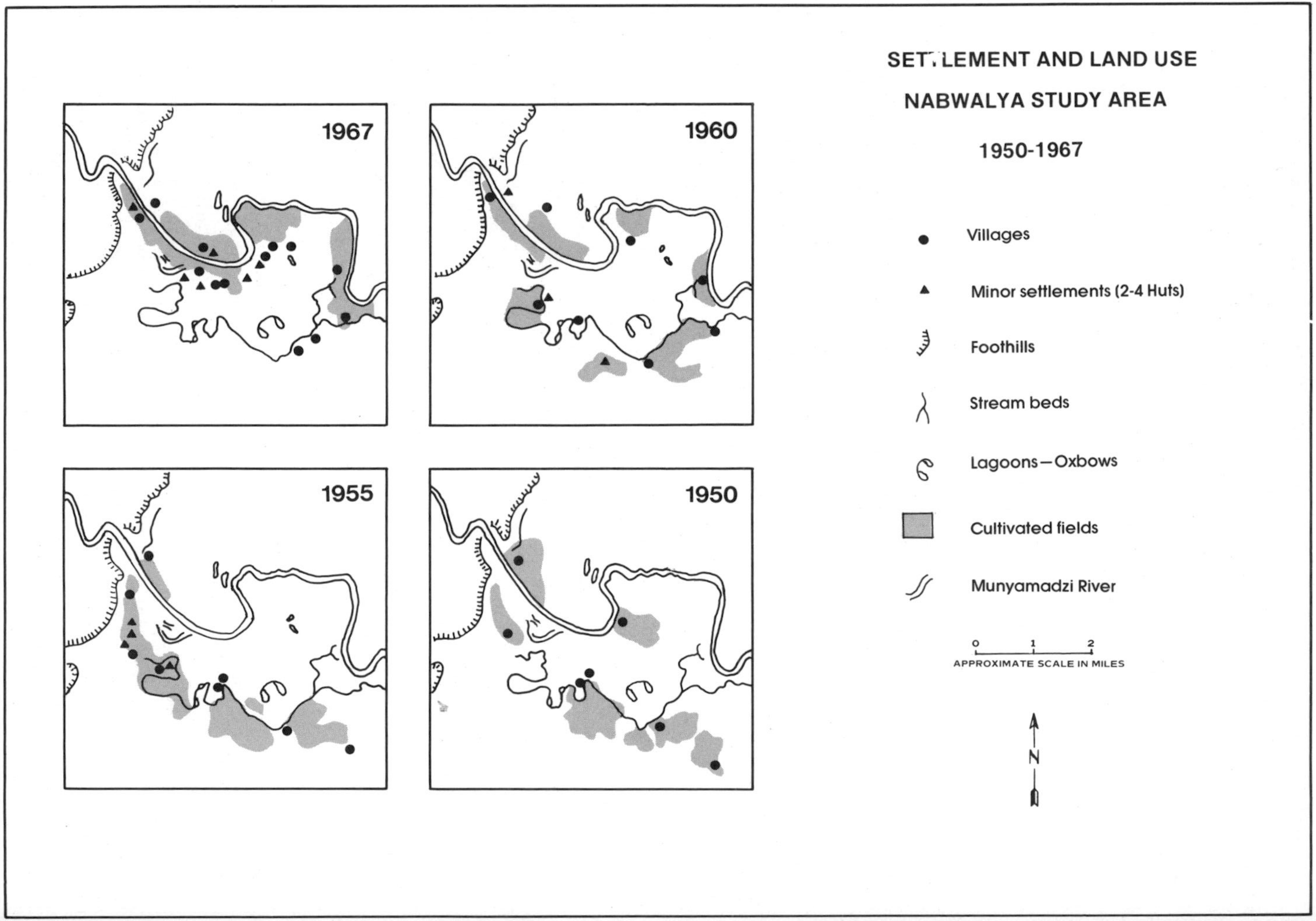

SETTLEMENT AND LAND USE
NABWALYA STUDY AREA
1950-1967

1967

1960

1955

1950

Villages

Minor settlements (2-4 Huts)

Foothills

Stream beds

Lagoons—Oxbows

Cultivated fields

Munyamadzi River

0 1 2
APPROXIMATE SCALE IN MILES

N

wives and councilors left for his new residence. Residents of the chief's village, who elected to remain on the Munyamadzi, stayed at the old site throughout the 1966–67 rainy season but constructed three separate settlements after harvesting their crops in June 1967.

Considering the widespread locations of villages along the river, it was necessary to limit the range of villages surveyed in my study. Therefore, I have intensively surveyed the block of villages and settlements from the base of Ngala and Chongo hills to Jamesi village, located three miles to the east (table 2).

Included in this area were two nonindigenous settlements—those of the game guards, and those of the teachers at the government school and court officials. Neither the guards nor teachers were Valley Bisa, and as outsiders, their interests and activities differed from the local resident population. The game guard post was located on top of Ngala ridge at the site of the abandoned government post. Their role as the protectors of game and prosecutors of hunters effectively separated them from residents. Departmental policy was to keep the game guards aloof from local concerns, and individuals were shifted frequently in location to avoid involvements on the local scene. Part of their work involved the killing of elephants raiding fields or granaries, and through this they contributed substantially to the total meat supply of local villages.

In a similar fashion, the school teachers and court officials were often excluded from local affairs, although their role as agents of change among residents should not be overlooked. In 1966, there was one head school teacher and two assistants in residence at Nabwalya. In January when the school year ended, these were replaced by two resident families and two assistants. A tax assessor and court clerk were also in residence near the school.

III

Social and Ideological Organization

> I am the son of an elder, do not debase me. I had a father who bore me. I was a pigeon playing on the roofs.
>
> Bisa Song

SOCIAL AND POLITICAL ORGANIZATION

Clan and Matrilineage

As is the case with many neighboring ethnic groups, the Valley Bisa are matrilineal in matters of descent, social status, inheritance, and succession. Each individual belongs to a matrilineal descent group, all members of which are descendants of the same founding ancestress traced back through the oldest living member of the group. The Valley Bisa use the term "*lupwa*" for this group, which is composed of related people who have the right to inherit property from each other and to choose a successor to fill a vacant position created by the death of one of its members. Members of this group accept responsibility for each other, and the men of the group may inherit each other's widows.

In addition, all individuals belong to a clan (*mukowa*); this affiliation is inherited from one's mother (*mukowa wapachifulo*). When asked the name of his clan, a Valley Bisa is likely to give the name of his father's clan, for he is also known as a "child" of this clan. He calls all members of his father's clan "father" (*bena tata*), although this group is not responsible to the same extent for him as are members of his mother's clan. An individual is also linked to a group called "grandparents" (*bena shikulu*), who include his mother's father, father's father, and members of his grandparents' clans.

Clans are exogamous and marriage to a cross-cousin (mother's brother's daughter or father's sister's daughter) was preferred for the first marriage in the past. To marry, a Bisa man usually resides initially in his wife's village (uxorilocal) for a period of service to his in-laws is part of the marriage contract.

Because of the principles of matrilineality and initial uxorilocal marriage, women are the core of localized descent groups and villages. The relevant grouping among the Valley Bisa is the group of sister siblings with their descendants and their uterine brother (born of the same mother) as the village headman. And it is such a group of uterine sisters and their brother, who has left his village of marriage, which forms the core of most villages.

Village Organization and Headmanship

As in many Central African societies, most inhabitants within a village are related in some way to their village headman. The Valley Bisa speak of villages as belonging to particular lineages—that of the village headman and those belonging to his matrilineal group. Valley villages, for the most part, are small and composed of close kin. Villages are named after their founding headman, and successors to the position inherit the name of its initial headman. By the rule of matrilineal descent, the headman's descendants belong to his wife's lineage and may not succeed to his title; yet while the headman lives they are linked to the matrilineal core of the village through its headman. A deceased headman should ideally be succeeded by his brother, then by his maternal nephew, and finally by his maternal grandson. But succession does not always follow this pattern. As they point out, succession to the headmanship is dependent also upon personal qualifications, age, and residence. Men out of the village, residing in their wife's village or on migrant labor, may be passed over for someone who is resident in the village but of inferior genealogical rank to those absent. The new headman succeeds to his predecessor's name and may inherit (*kupianyi*) his wives and any symbols of office such as a spear, gun, or ax. In the past the new headman also succeeded to a perpetual relationship within the political hierarchy under the chief. Richards (1950) suggests that the inheritance of personal property among the Bemba and Bisa is not an important determinant of kinship sentiment among males. Instead, the possibility of succession to office and positions of authority among one's matrilineal kin is an important aspiration for most men, although there are signs that this is beginning to change in the valley as it has elsewhere in Zambia.

Value and prestige are attached to the headmanship of a large village. A large village is identified with its headman and he is credited with the values and understanding which are necessary to hold many people together. But disputes crystallize about leaders of subordinate lineage sections who aspire to leadership. As a village grows in size, members polarize around factional leaders, who, if their following is sufficiently large, may wish to leave the village and set up their own village. The headman and the men resident under him in his village share the same system of motivations and values so that within any village there is a tension between the will and wish of the headman to retain all his relatives together under his charge and the motivations of certain leaders of subordinate lineages to depart and build villages of their own (Mitchell 1949). Although there are not many large villages in the corridor, the values deemed inherent in headmen of large villages are those which are extolled by elderly men. Deceased headmen are remembered for their harmonious attributes, and when a new headman succeeds, he is instructed: "When a person makes trouble, make peace; if the dead headman had not made peace, we would not still be together in a group."

The headman is responsible for discipline and attends small disputes. Since most residents have kinship ties with the headman, he is involved closely with the struggles between groups and persons within the village. Rendering impartial decisions under such conditions is difficult, and the headman may assemble his neighboring headmen to listen to the discussions and aid in making judgment. Disharmony within the village and tension between its component groups are often reflected on the surface by charges of sorcery. The headman is susceptible to the charge by his subordinates of using sorcerer's techniques to acquire his desires. On the other hand, most headmen assert that their role makes them especially vulnerable to sorcery by others. Villages may change in size and composition at any time; yet radical changes in both size and composition most frequently occur when a village shifts its site or upon the succession to office of a new headman.

The headman's authority is derived mostly from his position as head of his matrilineal descent group. In this capacity he is the ritual intermediary between his living matrikin and those members of the descent group who, upon death, become spirits. It is the headman who performs first fruits (*kupepa*) ceremonies for the whole village and makes arrangements for building and maintaining the spirit huts (*mfuba*) on the edge of the village. It is also the headman who chooses the new site for the village. Headmen say good soil (*vyonde*) close to permanent water is the most important criterion when prospecting for a new village site; yet the headman solicits ancestral help when making or sanctioning this choice. The headman is said to protect his village both from wild animals and sorcerers by magical means (*nshipa*).

Two basic principles determine residency and affiliation within villages: uxorilocality and matrilineal descent. Men leave their villages to marry. Uxorilocality is the initial principle in fixing the residence of married men, and for their initial marriage men must reside in their in-laws' village for an indefinite period. Only after several years of residence there, the birth of one or more children, the payment of a traditional fee, and the consent of their in-laws are young men able to determine their village of residence. Influential and older men in their subsequent marriages are apparently not so encumbered, but are expected to divide their time among the villages in which their wives reside. Husbands marrying into a village are called *bena buko* and have few rights in their wife's village, for matrilineal descent identifies a man with his mother's lineage. These principles of village organization are illustrated in the genealogies and the histories of three villages which follow.

Village Structure and Composition

The village is the significant local unit found in most Central African ethnic groups, for it is within the framework of the village that cooperation in production, social activities, and competition normally takes place. Yet the site and composition of the village are both susceptible to change. Members may withdraw and create temporary settlements, or remain in their field huts during disputes, but usually return to their village upon the resolution of the controversy. Villages shift their sites as soils in the vicinity are exhausted, water pools dry, or the site is deemed unsuitable for other reasons. However, most shifts in site are over short distances.

The Valley Bisa use the same term *muzi* for a semipermanent settlement of almost any size, although small temporary or unregistered settlements are also called *chitente.* Small settlements of one to three huts are normally within hailing distance of larger villages and most are located on the margins of their fields. Typically a village consists of a small cluster of huts under a headman who protects the residential area with magic (*nshipa*) and serves as the spiritual intermediary between the spirits and his group. Villages which have had two or more headmen also have spirit huts (*mfuba*). Smaller settlements characteristically have neither *nshipa* nor *mfuba.*

Each hut within a village is the private quarters for a family, consisting of a man, his wife, and small dependent children. Unmarried daughters of puberty age or older reside with an unmarried aunt, widow, grandmother, or by themselves. Once boys are capable of keeping up with others their age and older, they construct a hut of their own. Huts are little used other than as sleeping quarters and for storage, as all domestic activities, except during inclement weather, are performed either outside in the open areas around the hut or in the shade of its veranda. In the past, according to the Valley Bisa, the government enforced the construction of both kitchens and pit latrines within the villages. Today few huts have adjacent kitchens, and the Bisa perceive no advantage in having pit latrines.

Most villages are composed of the descendants of a single ancestress and their spouses, and within a small or new village no male matrilineal descendant may be resident. The genealogical structure of such a village is normally a matrilocal extended family. In larger and older villages, the genealogical structure is more complex and composed of a matrilineal core and several related groups. The social composition and complexity of Bisa villages is largely a function of the stage of growth and relative age of the village, as has been described by many students of Central African societies (Turner 1957; Stefaniszyn 1964a; Kapferer 1967). Within the study area, villages could be classified into one of three groups based upon their relative stage of growth. A representative of each group is described below.

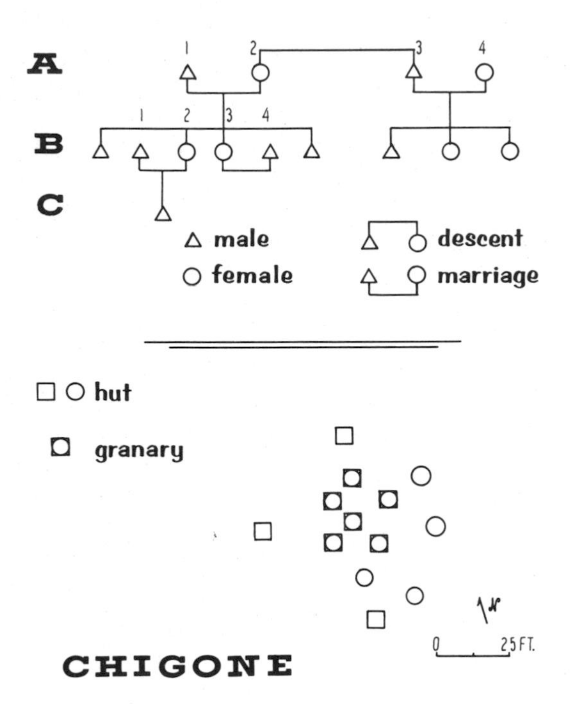

Figure 3. Genealogy and morphology of Chigone village

Chigone village (fig. 3) belongs to the Mbo lineage and its structure is representative of a recently separated settlement. Its genealogical structure is simple and is representative of six other settlements in the study area. Its headman (A1) was a court messenger and resided previously in the chief's village. In 1965 he obtained permission from the chief to establish a settlement of his own with the proviso that he settle in the vicinity of the court. Chigone insisted there was no dispute between him and the chief; he only desired his own settlement. By constructing his own settlement he was able to gain some independence but was still dependent upon the chief.

From the genealogical outline given in Figure 3, it can be seen that the residents of Chigone village are the headman (A1) and his wife (A2), originally from the headman's father's village, two twin daughters (B2, B3) and their spouses, and a brother of the headman's wife (A3), his wife, and three children. The elder son of the headman was away for schooling in Lusaka. An additional hut was occupied during the dry season of 1966 by a sister of A1 and her spouse, but their residence was transient. Her husband returned from work on the Copperbelt, and after harvesting her crops she joined him in another village. Later, this vacant hut was occupied by a school teacher and then by a local court clerk. A3, B1, and B4 were away most of the year working on the Copperbelt. The parents of A4 were residents in the chief's village.

During the rains the residents of Chigone, with the exception of A4, cultivated land about a mile east from their settlement. A4 cultivated her crops with those of her parents, and her field hut was located about one quarter mile west of the settlement along the river. Not all granaries in the settlement belonged to its residents, for two large granaries belonged to residents of the chief's village whose fields were adjacent to the settlement. Since their fields were nearby, arrangements were made with the headman for the safekeeping of their grain. A third granary was owned by the parents of A4.

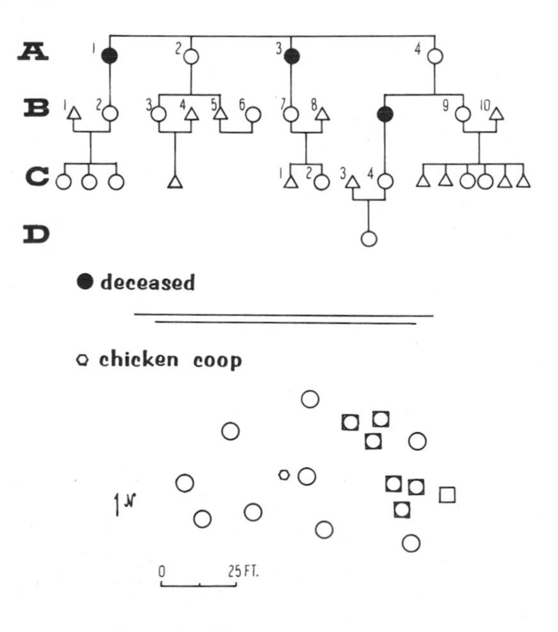

Figure 4. Genealogy and morphology of Mukupa village

Mukupa village (fig. 4) belongs to the Kani lineage. It is structurally larger than Chigone and represents a type of village from which related groups have recently split. Mukupa was first entered in the district registry in 1914. At that time it was a much larger village, and since the 1930s six villages had split from it. In structure, it is similar to three other villages on the study area.

Mukupa, B5, now elderly and ailing, had left the valley in his earlier years for two trips to gain employment in towns. Both excursions were brief. Now he was reportedly senile and spent most of his time in another village into which he had married. He had three sons by his wife in Mukupa; all of these were married and living uxorilocally. His two daughters had died while still children.

Most of the other residents were elderly and the men spent much of their time away from the village. B1, B4, B5, B8, and B10 had wives in other villages. B10, a headman of a much larger village some two miles away, occasionally spent a night in Mukupa village. B1 returned from a job in Kitwe early in 1967 and spent half his time with another wife resident in a village across the Munyamadzi River. After divorcing his first wife, C3, a young man in his late twenties, had recently married into this village.

A maternal uncle of Mukupa returned in 1964, after a twenty-year absence on the Copperbelt. Mukupa had inherited the title of headman since the dead headman's brother was on the Copperbelt. Senior in genealogical rank, yet younger (by some fifteen years) in age, the uncle claimed he was not respectfully treated by his nephew. In 1965 he and his sisters withdrew from the village and cleared land elsewhere for settlement and cultivation, but this split was not sanctioned by the chief, who prevailed upon the uncle to return closer to Mukupa where he could assume responsibilities for the village when the ailing Mukupa was away.

Mukupa village had been in its present location since 1958. The age of the village was apparent from the number of fruit-bearing trees scattered among its huts and the state of disrepair of many of its huts. Four huts collapsed during the rains of 1967 and had to be rebuilt. The activities of these villagers during twelve months are diagrammed and discussed in Chapter Four.

Chibale (fig. 5) is one of the oldest and largest Bisa villages in the valley. It was registered in 1900 when records of villages were first made. Chibale belonged to the Nguni lineage, and it is said that their ancestors were among the first to enter the valley, together with those of the present chief. At any rate, the site of their village has always been in close proximity to the chief's village, and its current location was on a site occupied by a former chief's village. The present headman (B10) had been a court assessor for eleven years, but there was reported dissension between him and the chief.

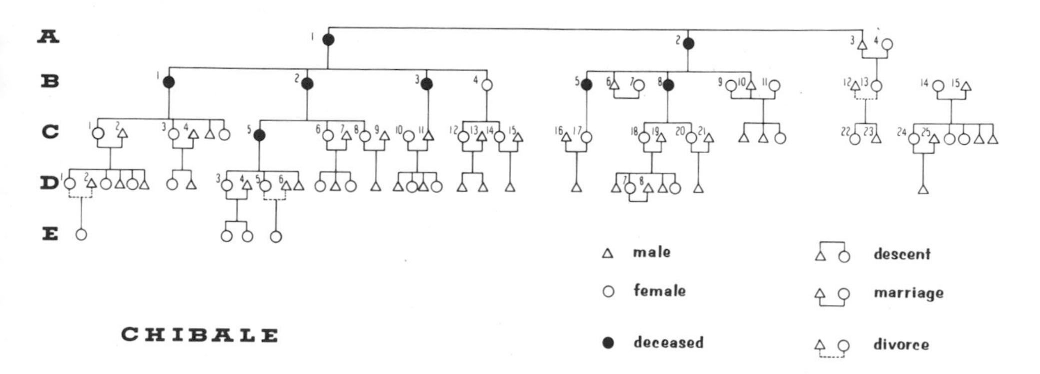

Figure 5. Skeleton genealogy of Chibale village

The village had been located at its present site since 1960. Some of its past history was written in the mounds of the sites the village formerly occupied. An old village site (*cibolyia*) dating to the late 1930s contained forty-four hut mounds. In 1951, a large group of matrikin withdrew leaving a core of only twenty-seven huts on the next site. In 1966, Chibale village contained twenty-five huts and showed imminent signs of further splitting.

From December 1966 to March 1967 four deaths occurred which became the focus of discussion and discontent among residents. In December alone, a two-year-old son of C24 and 25, and an infant son of C12 and 13 died; these two misfortunes sparked discussions on their cause. Some accused the headman of sorcery in killing the members in his village. Others voiced the opinion that it was Ngona spirits, who controlled the site upon which the village was located, whose afflictions now reflected their disapproval of deteriorating relations between the chief and their village headman. In one year, four divorces occurred and these young men felt the headman had used magic to disrupt their marital relations. In addition, the village headman was accused by some of discriminating credit practices between his close and distant relatives in the operations of his store.

After the 1966–67 harvest, Chibale, in preparation for relocating his village, constructed huts on a site closer to the river. He was joined in construction by A3, B6, C19, and D8. C16 and C21 were away in town, but it was likely that their spouses would shift to the new site as soon as houses were built for them. Descendants of A1 and B14 remained in the old village site despite coercive action by the village headman. In August 1967 when I departed, these two sections were still living in the old village site and remained undecided as to their eventual plans.

Genealogically, Chibale village was not complex, for most of its residents were the descendants of two deceased sisters A1 and A2. B14 was the wife of a former headman but was not inherited by the present headman. She had decided to remain in the village because her daughter was married to C11 and she had few friends elsewhere. B9 and B11 were seminal sisters, born to the same father. Chibale had inherited a wife, B9, from his predecessor.

A village and a settlement in its vicinity had their genesis within Chibale village. The headman of the village remained a close associate of Chibale who was married to his two sisters B9 and B11. Then in 1966 a section of a minor lineage withdrew under a diviner. This diviner, an elderly man suffering from "swollen legs," was married to a clan sister of the headman, but it is said he withdrew because local residents had accused him of sorcery. He was joined by his mother's sister, a widow, and temporarily by another elderly couple whose wife, A4, was reported to despise the machinations within the larger village. Her husband, A3, a maternal uncle of Chibale, joined this breakaway group while its headman was away on the Copperbelt.

Chieftainship

The Ngona are the traditional rulers of the Bisa. Until their number was reduced by government decree, the Luangwa Valley west of the Luangwa was populated by a number of Ngona chiefs, some of whom were subordinate to Nabwalya.

Succession to the office of chieftainship is based upon matrilineal descent within the Ngona clan. Within the broader clan was a smaller lineage in which succession was stabilized after a few generations. Formerly, rank was based upon close kinship to the chief and these, of either sex, were entitled to special respect.

In the past, the chief maintained a "spiritual" monopoly over the land and its products. Men approached the chief and were given land upon which to settle, and the chief's village was the focal point for external trade and contact. It was the chief from whom traders, strangers, and travelers sought permission to pass through his land, hunt his game, or trade with his people. His bargaining position was enhanced economically through his rights to tribute and his control over ivory, slaves, salt, skins, and the other valuable resources within his territory. Politically, the chief's position was secured by the number of his followers and through marital ties and alliances with neighboring chiefs.

The relationship between the chief and his people was one of mutual independence although both shared a common system of values. The people provided the chief with tribute both in work (*mulaza*) and in produce (*mutulo*), and they staffed his army and caravans. The chief provided protection, both physical and ritual; was the final arbitrator in their disputes; and dispatched those accused of asocial crimes. In addition, the spirits of dead chiefs were believed to control the well-being and fruitfulness of the land and were approachable only through their living descendant.

In the past, certain large mammals—eland, lion, and elephant—were identified with the chieftaincy, and when killed on the chief's land parts of these mammals had to be sent to the chief as "tribute of allegiance." The chief's right to receive tribute in the form of game formerly rested essentially on his power to exact it, and failure of a hunter or a group to send appropriate tribute was construed as an act of rebellion.

In time, under both colonial and independent governments, many of the traditional relationships between the chief and his people were undermined. The chief's control over settlements was taken away by the early colonial government which initially stipulated minimal village size and granted permission for village movement. Later this authority was returned to the chiefs under the principle of Indirect Rule. Natural resources now belong to the government: ivory, lion, and leopard skins are delivered to the government post (*boma*), instead of to the chief's compound (*musumba*). Tribute in labor, meat, work, and grain is stopped. This tribute is replaced, in the Bisa's eyes, by government taxes and by game and trade licenses. The chief receives a small stipend and has become largely dependent upon government for his position and status. As a consequence, the interdependence with his people is weakened, for it is necessary for the chief to act upon and enforce decisions made by an alien administration whose values and goals may not be understood or appreciated by his people.

Yet in certain aspects the Nabwalya chieftainship remains strong. Since accusations of sorcery are not tenable through government courts, the chief is often the one to adjudicate these claims. Belief in his spiritual control over the fertility of the land and its products remains viable. Eland, lion, and elephant, traditionally associated with the chieftaincy, still retain some elements of that former association.

BELIEFS AND COSMOLOGICAL CONVICTIONS

Probably because of their remoteness from urban centers and the inhospitable valley conditions which have hitherto made long-term residence by Europeans improbable, the Valley Bisa have been able to preserve many features of their traditional beliefs. Despite the slow rate of contact prior to 1966, it was apparent that subsequent years would bear the marks of increasing changes. Signs were eminent that the independent Zambian government was no longer willing to permit a small isolated pocket of people to go their own way as had the colonial government. The government has proposed on many occasions that the Bisa be removed from the valley and resettled on the plateau where appropriate government services could be provided. Further, the safari and tourist industries in the valley were beginning to boom. To insure the future of these developments, the government solicited the assistance of ecologists, biologists, and economists from the United Nations. As these studies continue, it becomes obvious that traditional patterns and orientations of subsistence-based economies will become incompatible with modern strategies of conservation and management. Nonetheless, in 1966–67 the traditional system of beliefs was sufficiently viable to enable me to observe many rituals and discuss the meanings of these with informants.

Among the Valley Bisa, traditional and European beliefs are held in a somewhat different amalgam by all adults, dependent upon the extent of his or her exposure to outside influences. Christian doctrines and their spectrum of influences are seen predominantly among the younger men, the majority of whom have spent several years in external centers and have been exposed to several years of formal education. For this reason and perhaps because it was traditionally so, Bisa beliefs are generally characterized by a lack of rigidity. Yet certain patterns do emerge and it should be understood that these allow rather wide limits of expression and extent of belief.

At the level of belief, the "traditional" system has five main components: (1) belief in the existence of a supreme being, Muzili Mfumu; (2) belief in the existence of ancestral spirits, who possess the power to withhold or bestow upon their living descendants the desirable things of life, as well as the existence of other spirits; (3) belief in certain supernatural impersonal and unrelenting forces which afflict an individual or an innocent person should an individual vary from prescribed patterns of behavior at specified times; (4) belief in the power of certain plant or animal substances which when properly prepared can be used for good or harm; and (5) belief in the antisocial and destructive power of sorcerers.

The Nature of the Supreme Being

The Valley Bisa say that Muzili Mfumu (Lord of the Earth) created the world and all therein. Traditional myths relative to this creative process have now been supplanted by an indigenous interpretation of the Book of Genesis. But the Bisa maintain that upon the completion of his creative role, Muzili Mfumu withdrew and is no longer directly approachable by living man.

Muzili Mfumu is but one of the names ascribed to the Supreme Being. This name connotes both his creative and sovereign roles. The Bisa are conscious of his many activities, and his additional names seem to refer to these other roles. In creation myths the sun and moon are subordinate deities which quarreled. These quarrels led to their separation so that the sun shines during the day for men and the moon provides light for the animals. The anger of God is heard in thunder (Kalumba) and his promises are seen in the rainbow (Mukolamvula). Leza and Mulungu are additional names. The name Leza is used by the Valley Bisa in pronouncing an oath or curse. To remove such a curse, one must bathe using a wild shrub, *muti waku Leza (Cassia peteriana).* Lucele Nganga, a mythical being, appears in both Bemba and Bisa traditions, but his place among supernatural beings is not clear.

Mulenga is a deity confined to the natural world where he occasionally vents his wrath and kills whole herds of buffalo or other mammals. The Bisa say they know Mulenga has been active when they come upon whole herds of dead mammals for these are healthy (fat) when killed, so they must have been killed capriciously by Mulenga. A middle-aged Bisa explained Mulenga in the following manner: "Mulenga is a *chibanda* [evil spirit]. Sometimes spirits of the dead arise from the ground and kill children. Mulenga is not such a spirit, but has been created (*chiapangwafye*). He moves with the air or wind. Often he moves in cold air, and when he goes there all the trees will get dry and die. Such cold air affects animals and trees but does not affect people's lives."

The rinderpest which decimated the valley's population of some ungulates toward the turn of the last century is attributed to Mulenga, and many remember stories of this carnage from their parents. Occasionally, unexplained deaths still occur among mammals.

The pattern which emerges is that the Supreme Being is omnipotent and is the creator, but is far removed from the daily affairs of men. But the Bisa are reminded of his power and presence in the occurrence of certain natural phenomena and in their dependence upon the vagaries of climate.

The Spirits of the Ancestors

Muzili Mfumu, the creator and controller of the universe, is approachable mainly through the ancestral cult. The spirits of one's ancestors are considered to reside with Muzili Mfumu and in their capacity as spirits may influence him to produce circumstances favorable to their living descendants. Thus, when a Bisa seeks supernatural aid from Muzili Mfumu, his prayers are directed to his ancestors, who in turn approach Muzili Mfumu. This hierarchy is not necessarily expressed in all Valley

Bisa rites. In some instances, it would appear that the ancestral spirits themselves are capable of granting requests rather than serving as intermediaries.

Ancestral spirits form an extension of the Bisa social structure and are believed to interact continuously with their living descendants. As Marwick (1965:65) points out, the term ancestor as applicable for a matrilineal society needs clarification. Within a matrilineal society, one is not concerned for the most part with lateral but with collateral ancestry. A man's closest and most influential ancestral ties are with senior collateral kin such as his mother's brother or mother's mother's brother. On occasion he may also address his deceased father's spirits, for such spirits are regarded as benevolent though less influential.

An individual, before undertaking a difficult journey or making an important decision, may invoke the spirits of both his mother and father. Thus, a headman of a new village which he had just founded called on ancestral help with the following words:

> *Bata* [name], *Bama* [name], *musalila. Napata imwe mipashi yanji. Mwamona mpano apo naikele. Ndokwenda vye umutende.*
>
> [Spirits of my father and mother, I surrender to you. I beseech you, my spirits. You see me here where I stand. May I live a healthy life.]

But in a corporate ceremony a headman of a village which has endured for two or more generations calls only upon the spirits of his deceased predecessors who were headmen. Such a ceremony is performed on the edge of the village each November or December. Here the men clear an area and construct a small spirit hut (*mfuba*). In the ground beneath the straw roof, a hole is dug for each deceased leader of the matrilineage. The women brew beer (*bwalwa bwamipashi*) and grind sorghum flour as an offering. Then the village headman as titulary head of the matrilineage calls each collateral ancestor by name in the following manner:

> *Ba* [name], *muleefwaya ubwalwa? Nabikamo ubunga nobwalwa. Muleefwaya nsaka? Tuaimaka. Tuamubikila akasalu akabuta.*
>
> [(Name), do you want beer? I have placed both flour and beer. Do you wish a shelter? We made one. We put a white cloth on top.]

The beer and flour are poured into the hole by a grandson and granddaughter, respectively. Offerings by grandchildren are in keeping with the Bisa tradition of amiable relations between alternate generations.

The Bisa distinguish two kinds of spirits, *chibanda* and *mupashi. Chibanda* is an evil, troublesome, unpredictable, uncontrollable, and haunting spirit. Good and benevolent events are believed caused by the action of *mipashi.* Afflictions may be caused by good spirits, but these relent when ancestral names have been remembered and an offering of beer and flour dedicated to them. An elder distinguished between the two spirits in the following manner:

> You can tell whether it is a *mupashi* or a *chibanda* when a person becomes sick. You go to a diviner and ask him to tell you frankly the cause of the sickness. So after using all sorts of magical powers, the diviner comes back and says, "It is that father or mother or maternal uncle or grandmother or your brother who died but to whose name beer has never been brewed in remembrance of his good works." Now when people come and brew beer they do so in remembrance of that particular person whose name was given by the diviner. Then the village headman says, "This beer we have brewed in your name so help us." If the sick person recovers, it is said that he was afflicted by a good spirit (*mupashi uusuma*). But if the sick person does not recover when the offering is poured, we know that he is afflicted by a *chibanda*.

The Bisa say that if a person dies feeling an injustice, his shade will be revengeful and haunting and may afflict others besides his relatives. Valley Bisa funeral rites are not elaborate, but any wish of the deceased expressed in words either before death or through dreams after death should be fulfilled. The brewing of funeral beer, *bwalwa bwa chililo*, made in remembrance of the deceased follows his burial and all adults who knew the deceased well are invited to partake of this beer. *Bwalwa bwa bupianyi*, inheritance beer, is brewed and consumed only by the family of the deceased. At this time another person assumes the deceased's role among his matrikin.

Ancestral spirits normally manifest their interests and concerns negatively. Shades cause affliction for two reasons: (1) neglect in performance of obligations owed the spirits, and (2) default of kinship obligations. The spirits are entitled to receive offerings and sacrifice both before and after each year's harvest.

Through such social institutions as inheritance, the living incur tangible debts from their forebears who have become ancestral spirits. In passing on a gun or spear, assembled matrikin invoke its previous owner's name to secure his blessing and help for the one assuming his social position. In this manner the weapon is placed in the custody of a surviving member of the matrilineage but the individual inherits not only a weapon but also the responsible position as hunter for his nonhunting relatives. In his capacity as hunter, it is assumed that ancestors protect him while he is afield and enable him to kill game. In turn, upon his return to the village after a successful hunt, he should distribute his kill to those dependent upon his skill. Failure in his obligations toward kin is believed to be reflected in the hunter's lack of success or misfortunes in the bush, which in turn are said to reflect the withdrawal of ancestral aid.

The second type of ancestral affliction is wrought upon those who fail in their performance of kinship obligations. Their affliction for the most part is reserved for individual acts which seem to deny the validity of their kinship with others (Gluckman 1965).

Gluckman also suggests that ancestral cults control relationships between kin in another manner. Offerings and sacrifices must be made when amicable relations exist between assembled kin. For to propitiate spirits in times of social stress and disharmony is to spoil the sacrifice and endanger those assembled. Such beliefs suggest that until minor groups are sufficiently independent to seek ancestral aid alone, they should maintain amiable rapport with other members of the matrilineage. Yet, the ancestral cult and its attendant rites do not obscure social conflicts. Conflicts in avowed principles remain, but the validity of those principles governing social organization is elevated to a mythical plane beyond scrutiny.

In its domestic posture, the ancestral cult is concerned with lineages and the maintenance of social order, but in its public aspect, it is concerned with chiefs and their lineages. An Ngona chief is described as having a "great spirit" (*mupashi mukulu*) and as being the "owner of the land" (*mwine chialo*). The spirits of dead chiefs are believed to survive as a guardian presence over their successors and become tutelary deities over the land. In these capacities they are said to control the fertility of crops and animals.

Spirits of dead chiefs are believed capable of reincarnation as lions. Lion claws and teeth placed in a chief's grave are the "activating particles" necessary for this transformation. In 1966, after many years of bitter fighting within his lineage on the Munyamadzi, the chief built a new compound some eight miles away on the Mupamadzi. A few months after the chief moved, a pride of lions troubled villagers living in their field huts along the Munyamadzi. These returned to their villages for protection and summoned the chief back from the Mupamadzi. The chief addressed his spirits with the following words:

> *Namona mwebene bachialo. Ndi nekumusungila ichialo chienu. Ndi nakuya kupapatile mumfuba zenu tuamuimakila. Amuli nimwe muikekalo pansi uko mualala. Abantu imibili ikofina. Mukobatinya mu chialo chienu, tabakosanguluka.*

> [I address you, the owners of this land. I am entrusted with your land. I will be worshipping in your *mfuba* that we built for you. If it is you, sit down where you have slept (where you were buried). People are going heavily with fear. You are frightening them in your land. They are not going happily.]

Shortly after this address the lions left the area. It was said that these "spiritual" lions were protesting the deteriorating relationships between the chief, his relatives, and people along the Munyamadzi.

The chief is still believed by some to control access to game inhabiting his territory. *Chialo chikokalipa* ("the land has become angry [hot]") was an expression heard in reference to the difficulty encountered by government officials and others attempting to secure game without first requesting permission from the chief. Its reference was that ancestral spirits had withheld game from those who denied the spiritual sovereignty of the chief over these animals.

In addition to ancestral spirits, the Bisa believe that certain individuals may become spirit possessed and on these occasions are capable of forecasting events or dispersing medicines to others. I heard the Valley Bisa refer to such individuals as *chipao* or *ngulu*. Possession takes place in late evening, and catharsis is accompanied by loud drum beating and dancing.

According to the Bisa, the bush is full of spirits and each extensive tract of bush is inhabited by many kinds. Individuals possessed or "caught" by such spirits behave in strange ways and may be relieved of these spirits and treated by individuals who have been similarly possessed and treated in the past. Of concern to hunters is the belief in haunting shades (*vibanda*) which inhabit some of the larger game.

Mystical Powers

In addition to their beliefs in a creator deity and ancestral spirits, the Bisa believe in the existence of supernatural and impersonal forces that react to inappropriate human actions and behaviors. The rules of living with which these powers are concerned refer mostly to productive and reproductive activities: hunting, cooking, birth, and death. In approaching each of these activities or crises, an individual should be mindful of a host of rules, the violation of which brings misfortune. It does not matter whether the violation is intentional, for invariably the response is mystical sanctions either immediately or subsequently. To describe the effects of these sanctions, the Valley Bisa use the term "*midulo*" (state of being cut).

They speak of an individual as "hot" or "cold" when he stands on the threshold of an important stage in his life cycle, is engaged in a hazardous undertaking, or has transgressed against norms. In such a state he becomes potentially dangerous to other individuals, whose state is described as the opposite value, until his condition is rendered normal through ritual cleansing. Central in this belief is the idea that contact with one who is ritually impure or dangerous (*mubishi*, "raw"; *kubangama*, "hot") afflicts a guiltless, susceptible (*kutalala*, "cold") person. The innocent party becomes "cut" across the chest and "cut off" mystically from the rest of his social group.

Neophytes and mourners are "cold" and taboos are imposed upon them and their kin. At her first menses, a girl (*chisungu*) is described as "cold" (*kutalala*), and she is excluded from contact with others besides her sisters, mother, or grandmother. Only they can prepare her food which must be served with particular roots, for ordinary food is "hot" and contact with it would kill her. Only after the cessation of her first menses and following a purification ceremony may she reenter the "hot" social scene of the village. When her husband or child dies, a woman becomes "cold" or "raw" and potentially dangerous to others in her village. Taboos are imposed on her behavior but are lifted following a ceremony (*kuteka inongo*) at the edge of the village.

Pregnant women were referred to as "hot" if married or "cold" if unmarried. In her "cold" state an unmarried woman must prepare her food herself and upon her delivery both she and her baby are ritually cleansed. A man should refrain from adultery while his wife is pregnant, for both she and her child are described as "cold" and adultery makes him "hot." Subsequent contact with his wife may either kill their child, cause his wife to die in labor, or make her labor difficult.

A menstruating woman is "hot" and must avoid preparing food for others at this time. Salt is a seasoning which makes food "hot." It is avoided at ceremonies or in food consumed before undertaking a journey or hazardous task.

Marwick (1965) points out that although it appears a supernatural sanction operates to uphold such traditional norms, the real sanction is a secular one. For breach of taboo does not necessarily affect only the transgressor but may also cause suffering to some innocent party.

Magical Substances

One of the more esoteric uses of resources is to be found in their employment as magic. As has been suggested by Evans-Pritchard (1937), I assume that magic has morally neutral attributes which can be manipulated for legitimate or illegitimate purposes. The Bisa differentiate between these uses of magic as *muti* or *bwanga*. *Bwanga* normally refers to magic of a sinister or evil nature. *Muti*, a common term for tree or bush, refers to the more legitimate use of magic for protective, assertive, creative, or healing purposes (Cory 1949).

The Bisa regard magical substances as a source of power and success, such that given the right ingredients and know-how, an individual may achieve almost anything through their use. Prescriptions are considered essential adjuncts to authority and their possession represents the success which one has achieved in his endeavors. The kinds of ingredients prescribed and the dosage are adjusted to both the status and personality of the individual.

The chief is acknowledged to have access to the most powerful magics. Likewise, many elders and village headmen are knowledgable about a variety of such substances. Magics are important accessories in most rituals although their use is not confined to them. As in many Central African societies, ritual and magic of various kinds play an important part in maintaining identities between generations and social strata in society. Skills in work, lovemaking, hunting, and fishing are often ascribed to the possession of magical substances and people are concerned to acquire these commensurate with their achievements.

Magic is commonly composed of two kinds of ingredients. The first part is selected from parts of trees or shrubs, usually roots or bark. These ingredients usually represent the animal or person for which the magic is prescribed, but for these ingredients to become effective, most require additional activating agents (*vishimba*) of human or animal origin. Generally, incantations or words are said to initiate the magic or to invoke the help of latent powers within the substances. Prohibitions are prescribed with every magic, and neglect of these prohibitions may account for failure in their efficacy.

Sorcery

Beliefs in sorcery are an integral part of the traditional cosmology in that they are one of several supernatural reasons for misfortunes. At the center of the "traditional" system was the diviner who apportioned blame for misfortune among sorcerers, ancestors, and spirits. With the subsequent weakening of the other elements in the traditional system, sorcery seems to have become a major cause for calamities of many sorts.

The Bisa do not make the classical distinction between a witch, as an innately mystical and evil person, and a sorcerer, as a person who consciously acquires and practices evil magic (*bwanga*) against others (Middleton and Winter 1963). Their term "*bulozi*" encompasses elements of both witchcraft and sorcery, and the practitioner of this evil craft is the *mulozi*, which can be most appropriately translated as sorcerer-witch. Since the most frequent idea expressed when the term *mulozi* is used is of someone who through jealousy inflicts others or who inappropriately connives to get ahead, I use the word sorcerer as an appropriate abbreviation.

A *mulozi* is an evil person, different in orientation from normal human beings, and symbolically represents all that is selfish and antisocial in man. Characteristics attributed to sorcerers are stereotyped, and when I pressed for details in addition to the normal list, informants were often affronted and typically exclaimed, "How should I know what sorcerers are? Ask them!" Traits of sorcerers upon which most agree are that they are active mainly at night and go about naked. They transgress against basic societal norms such as incest; they eat human flesh, and their victims for the most part are those to whom they are matrilineally related. The bush is their main sphere of influence. There they are drawn into alliances with familiars such as hyenas, jackals, ant bears, and owls which attack people or their property. Sorcerers belong to necrophagous guilds whose members share their kills. Such traits represent an inversion of normal behavior.

Techniques employed by sorcerers include making concoctions to kill or harm specific individuals. These include bodily excretions, fingernails, hair, or sand from the intended victim's footprint; placing magics within the victim's beer or food; employing an animal familiar to harm specific individuals; eating their victims alive; and attacking the victim in his sleep. The Bisa say they can identify sorcerers by their menacing and abusive language particularly noticeable at beer parties; their obvious prosperity and wealth which results from their magical stealing of crops and other things; their fatness caused by consumption of human flesh and using the spirits of others to work their fields at night; and their extrasensory perception which enables them to know immediately when and where a death has occurred. The precautions taken against these mystical evildoers are many and varied and include magical substances, which function as "sorcerer alarms" to awaken the intended victim in the presence of his tormentor, magic to render one's hut invisible at night, and charms placed on grave sites to protect corpses from consumption by sorcerers. The traditional method of sorcerer identification was the poison ordeal.

The Bisa maintain that sorcery has increased since the arrival of Europeans and their suppression of the poison ordeal. Sorcerers are held responsible for a variety of misfortunes including prolonged or unexplained illness, death, loss of property, miscarriages and stillbirths, mental disorders, and disturbances in normal social relations.

Accusations and suspicions of sorcery reflect deep underlying tensions in local communities, and informants recognize that certain relationships produce social friction and that persons occupying these roles are likely to practice sorcery against one another. Sorcery is most effective at close quarters and the matrilineal descent group is recognized as its natural and primary arena. Members of local descent groups desire prestige, power, and influence which comes to those who enjoy many dependents and assume the few statuses and prestigious roles which their society offers. Competition is especially keen since aspirants for these positions must vie with their own brothers or nephews for favors and recognition from other kinsmen which they all share in common. Normal judicial procedures are denied these kinsmen and the Valley Bisa are aware that competition over social positions and arguments over inheritance of property are conducive to accusations of sorcery.

Just as spirits are ambivalently conceived depending upon their nature, so too supernatural powers to which specialists have access may be employed either beneficially or destructively. I encountered no self-confessed sorcerers, but in a society where possession of magic is tantamount to power and influence, the line between a man of prominence and his magics and a sorcerer is a very thin one. Knowledge of magics and their successful deployment is ambivalent, and familiarity with white magic implies knowledge of its counterpart, black magic.

A number of studies (Middleton and Winter 1963; Marwick 1965; Gluckman 1965) show the important implications of sorcery beliefs for small-scale societies in which the more important methods of social control utilize their beliefs in mystical agents. Such beliefs sanction the general code of morality and influence individuals to suppress their feelings of open hostility toward each other. Moreover, these beliefs act as a conservative force against outside pressures of change. The mere thought of being labeled a sorcerer discourages some innovations and preserves the general contours of the society, while at the same time increases its resistance to outside influences. Sorcery beliefs comment upon the evil side of human existence which arises from the inevitable failures of some to live up to society's norms and ideals. The evil desires harbored by some are linked causally to the personal misfortunes of others for which there are no apparent reasons. For just as communal ancestral rites emphasize group unity and solidarity, sorcery accusations dramatize the inevitability of strife in relationships among people.

IV

Technology, Subsistence, and Seasonal Activities

> Nature unfettered and unrestrained is there on all sides. The tropical beauties of the Luangwa, the majestic masses of the Muchingas, the monotony of the great plains . . . all sink into one's very being after a few months of wandering in that land of wild beasts and uncivilized men, where the vegetation has run riot, and the great mammals which the Creator put on this earth roam free and wild.
>
> Owen Letcher (1911)

TECHNOLOGY AND ECONOMY

Material Culture and Subsistence

MATERIAL culture is an integral component of man–resource interactions. The Valley Bisa, befitting their relative isolation, possess a material culture that has remained relatively simple, yet contains admixtures of both traditional and modern artifacts. Some of these are pictured in Plate 1. Handicrafts, pottery, woodwork, tools and traps are similar to those described for the Ambo (Stefaniszyn 1964b), but in recent years household utensils of European manufacture have replaced many traditional wares. Local stores, scattered among the villages in the corridor, are seasonally stocked with soap, kerosene, cloth, salt, matches, razor blades, pots, saltpeter, and other externally manufactured commodities. By 1967, thirty-three stores had been registered for the corridor in the tax assessor's records.

Hoe and ax blades, two versatile implements, are available in local stores, but handles are fashioned from local woods. Iron blades may be fitted into different handles depending upon their use. Embedded in a knob at right angles to its long handle, a hoe (*luze*) is used for digging and turning soil. However, with the blade set in the end of the handle so that the axis of the blade is the same as that of its handle, the implement becomes a shovel (*nchindwe ya luze*). Depending upon its angle of insertion, an ax blade becomes an ax (*nzembe*), a lathe (*mbazo*), or a hole digger (*nchindwe*).

Plate 1. An assortment of Bisa implements and utensils. Assembled in the foreground are traditional wares; in the background are a few articles of European manufacture.

Plate 2. A Bisa blacksmith and his accouterments.

Plate 3. "Chando (left) paused at a *musebe* tree and showed his son where to remove sections of the bark. Initially, he took the inner bark from the side where the afternoon sun was shining."

Plate 4. "We went first to the trunk, where we all stooped to the ground. . . . We were instructed to spit in the trunk." Note that Chando holds portions of the magic in his hand.

Members of both sexes fish, although with different methods. Groups of women and children fish along the rivers and depressions with baskets (*luanga*) and plunger cones (*chivwavo*). Men catch fish with hook and line (*ndobo*), spears (*misumbu*), and cone traps (*mono*) placed at intervals in a weir.

In contrast to fishing, hunting is exclusively a male occupation. In the past, game was taken in a number of traps and pits but these now are rarely deployed openly. Bows and poisoned arrows, formerly widespread, are rarely seen. These have been replaced by muzzleloading guns, many of which are of local production or repair (plate 2). Hunters manufacture their own powder, firing caps, and shot, which contribute to the overall inefficiency of their weapons. Accessory weapons are axes and spears (*mikondo*), although the latter for the most part remain in the possession of elderly men.

As if reflecting the insecurity of the alien migrant economy in which most men have become involved, the Valley Bisa have retained subsistence-wise much of what was "traditional." The principle mode of subsistence is agriculture. Their agricultural cycle mirrors the rainy season with clearing and planting at the beginning of the rains and reaping before and during the cold season. Generally, rainfall is sufficient for agriculture, although crop success is dependent upon the timing and duration of the rains. Local crop failures reflect vagaries of rainfall, and more regional droughts are not uncommon. The basic instruments employed in agriculture still remain the ax, used for initial clearing of field plots, and the long-handle hoe, used for turning the soil. Both sexes assist in agricultural chores, but if a woman's husband is away, she clears, plants, protects, and harvests the crop herself with what assistance she can muster. Occasionally large work parties of nonkin are compensated with beer, salt, or soap.

Agricultural staples on heavy alluvia are several varieties of sorghums and maize. Varieties of pumpkins and cucumbers are usually planted together with these staples and their stalks furnish support for the climbing vines. Scattered patches of groundnuts, finger millet, rice, sugar cane, cowpeas, cassava, beans, rice, and tobacco are also planted.

The size of household plots varies from year to year as new land, if available adjacent to the plot, is cleared. Twenty-two fields which I measured along Kapola lagoon in 1966 varied from 0.7 to 2.1 acres.

Abundant wild mammals and periodic flocks of grain-eating birds and population cycles of small rodents and insects are problems with which valley agriculturalists must contend. Agricultural loss attributable to each of these varies from year to year. Valley Bisa strategy for protecting growing crops and stored grains is mirrored in their seasonal settlement patterns. Village morphology reflects a protective format with granaries towards their center surrounded by individual huts (Figures 3 and 4). During the growing season, small villages are temporarily abandoned while their inhabitants are devoted to crop protection. Individual households move to the areas which they have cleared for cultivation, and during the rains they reside in huts surrounding their planted fields. When crops are harvested and stored they return once again to the villages.

Despite these protective arrangements the annual crop loss to big and small mammals and birds is considerable. A phrase current among Europeans was that valley residents planted at least three seeds in each hole "one for the elephant, one for the guinea fowl, and one for themselves." To estimate the damage to ripening sorghum just prior to harvest, I sampled ten tenth-mil-acre plots in six fields on 29 April 1967. The number of sorghum stalks in each field and the damage attributed to mammals and birds varied, as is shown in Table 6. Yields reflect variations in site fertility and the number of years under cultivation. Fields A, L, and W were in their first year of cultivation. My samples show, with one exception, that damage attributable to game at this stage was not appreciable. Most loss came subsequent to this date, for harvest is a slow and lengthy process lasting a month or two from the time the tall grain stalks are laid on the ground to the time the grain heads are deposited in village granaries. Standing grain is unavailable to rodents, but from the time the stalks are laid on the ground (*kutoba masaka*) preparatory to harvest, grain stocks are subject to increasing devastation by rodents and insects. My observation that proportionally more grain is consumed and spoiled each year by rodents than all other types of mammals and birds combined is not a new view, for many game rangers have complained in their reports about the unjust slaughter of big game to appease villagers. But

TABLE 6

YIELD AND MAMMAL DAMAGE TO BISA SORGHUM FIELDS ALONG KAPOLA LAGOON (29 APRIL 1967)

Field	Acres	No. of Sorghum Heads Examined	Estimate of Total Stalks in Field (in 1,000's)	% of Total Sample Damaged	No. of Plots Containing Mammal Tracks[1]
A	1.9	70	133.0	3.6	5
D	1.8	53	95.4	6.4	1
F	1.5	34	51.0	5.3	3
L	1.5	62	93.0	12.8	2
O	1.3	44	57.2	4.3	0
W	2.0	66	132.0	3.5	5

1. Includes elephant, hippo, impala, waterbuck, and puku.

one should not belittle the occasional depredations by elephants or herds of buffalo which can devastate a sizable field or a granary.

For the Valley Bisa, the main meal and normally the only one of the day consists of two main articles of food. *Nsima*, the main constituent, a stiff doughlike porridge made from sorghum or maize flour and hot water, is consumed with a relish (*munani*) dish, a preparation of vegetables or meat braced with groundnuts and/or sauces. The relish dishes have one main constituent, either meat or vegetable, and each of these was recorded in the diary kept on each household in three villages (see table 7). The amount of relish dishes varies from season to season. On occasion during the hot, dry season no meals are prepared, and at other times and for different reasons women prepared two meals. Although no meals were weighed and therefore have no quantitative value, they do illustrate some aspects of Valley Bisa diets which may be compared with observations tabulated in a similar fashion in other parts of Central Africa (Thomson 1954; Scudder 1962; Kay 1964). By comparison, the Valley Bisa consume a higher percentage of wild meats at all seasons as a constituent of their relish dishes than do any of the above groups. Also note the importance of noncultigens (wild vegetables); these form the main constituents of Valley Bisa relish dishes for six months of the year. The importance of gathering among woodland savanna cultivators is discussed by Scudder (1971).

Because of the tsetse fly, the Valley Bisa keep no domestic animals other than a few dogs, semiwild cats, chickens, ducks, and pigeons. Most of these domesticates receive little care, although magical substances are believed necessary to make ducks and pigeons proliferate. There is a growing market for selling grain to government employees stationed temporarily in the valley. In addition chickens, ducks, and tobacco are hawked in Chipata and Mpika and to visiting government officials in the valley.

THE SEASONS AND ASSOCIATED EVENTS

The tempo and pattern of human, animal, and plant life within the Luangwa Valley are strongly affected by seasonal changes. According to the time of year, both the temperature and amount of rainfall vary, as shown in Table 8. These physical variables affect the vegetation, which in turn determines the movements of game and the agricultural activities of the Valley Bisa.

The Valley Bisa distinguish four seasons, two of which (*mibundo* and *mainza*) are associated with the rains. The dry season is subdivided into "windy" (*mwela*) and "hot" (*luzuba*) periods. *Mibundo* is a transitory interval associated with the uncertain beginnings of the rains in late October or November. Rainfall within the valley varies between different regions on the same day or even during each month and year, but gener-

TABLE 7

MAIN CONSTITUENTS OF VALLEY BISA RELISH DISHES RECORDED IN THREE VILLAGES, 1966–67

Village	Main Component of Relish		August–October		November–January		February–April		May–July	
			Total Dishes	% of Total	Total Dishes	% of Total	Total Dishes	% of Total	Total Dishes	% of Total
Mukupa	Cultivated vegetable	Fresh	37	10.5	160	18.4	293	40.8	668	55.4
		Dry	...		...		...		90	
	Wild vegetable		147	42.0	500	57.6	231	32.2	104	7.6
	Wild meat	Fresh	69	46.6	116	23.7	93	27.0	178	36.6
		Dry	94		90		101		323	
	Domesticated meat		3	0.9	2	0.3	...	...	4	0.4
Chigone	Cultivated vegetable	Fresh	35	18.0	119	28.3	237	37.4	155	38.5
		Dry	2		...		...		35	
	Wild vegetable		79	38.3	172	41.0	169	26.7	54	10.9
	Wild meat	Fresh	56	42.2	54	30.2	80	31.2	117	48.8
		Dry	31		73		118		124	
	Domesticated meat		3	1.5	2	0.5	30	4.7	9	1.8
Chipi	Cultivated vegetable	Fresh	33	16.0	75	17.1	192	40.9	196	37.3
		Dry	...		...		...		...	
	Wild vegetable		70	34.0	218	49.8	106	22.6	42	8.0
	Wild meat	Fresh	33	49.0	60	32.9	57	33.4	114	53.2
		Dry	68		84		100		166	
	Domesticated meat		2	1.0	1	0.2	15	3.2	8	1.5

TABLE 8

WEATHER DATA AT NABWALYA VILLAGE

	TEMPERATURE (degrees F.)				Precipitation		Cloud Cover
Month/Year	Average Max.	Average Min.	Highest	Lowest	Rainfall (in.)	No. days of rain	(No. of cloudy days)[1]
August 1966	90.1	61.7	98	53	0.00	0	5
September	96.9	68.5	105	58	0.01	1	3
October	102.2	75.0	110	70	0.89	2	4
November	99.2	74.7	109	69	2.80	16	22
December	95.3	72.8	107	69	6.48	20	25
January 1967	90.3	71.5	98	68	5.73	20	27
February	91.0	71.3	98	68	8.25	18	25
March	88.8	70.8	98	68	9.04	20	29
April	92.0	71.1	98	68	2.69	10	15
May	89.5	66.9	97	60	0.83	4	11
June	87.2	62.4	92	56	0.04	1	11
July	86.4	58.7	92	50	0.00	0	8

Note: Zambia temperature measurements taken in the shade of a hut veranda at six feet above ground level.
1. Defined as over 60 percent cloud cover at any time during day.

ally the predominant portion of the rain falls from December to March. Their name for this season, *mainza*, literally means "rain." Following the termination of the rains, the temperature drops sharply in the evening, and in the early morning the cold bites deeply, pushed by sharp winds. *Mwela*, literally "wind," begins in late April and lasts until mid-July. The hot season, *luzuba*, brings the dry season to a climax just before the rains. The heat increases, with daily temperatures above 100°F, and all life seems to suffer from the heat and dust.

The Bisa break their year into twelve periods which do not correspond with European months. These periods are described in terms of local activities or natural phenomena and reflect the close association between aspects of village life and the changing climate. Phenomena signaling the beginning of each of the traditional periods varies with individuals, and among the young of school age these traditional periods of time are supplanted by the abstract months and days of the European calendar. Since the rains are important to village life, it is appropriate to begin a discussion of the seasons with the activities and weather conditions just prior to the rains.

October and November

The first rains are expected in October, but October may pass without a drop of rain. The onset of the rains is met with a spurt of human activities. In the intense heat which characterizes the climax of the hot season, and spurred on by the changing signs in plant and animal life around them, the Valley Bisa begin clearing their garden plots preparatory to seeding and repairing their field huts for later occupancy.

Yet before planting seeds, villages around Nabwalya assemble to propitiate the spirits of their dead chiefs (*kupapatila mipashi ya mfumu*). In late October, headmen construct two spirit huts outside the chief's village, and the women of his village prepare a special beer (*bwalwa bwamipashi*) and flour from sorghum collected in the neighborhood. A small hole is dug in the soil under the roof of these huts for each of the chief's predecessors and into each is poured tokens of beer and flour. The chief solicits his ancestral spirits for a profitable agricultural year.

Leafing and flowering among the plants is gradual and almost imperceptible to one residing in the valley. Some trees flower as early as September with *Cordyla africana* and *Ostryoderris stuhlmannii* among the first. The white popcorn blossoms of the latter flake upon the ground as the new leaves begin to break on the twigs. These are soon followed in October by *Lonchocarpus capassa, Sclerocarya caffra, Adansonia digitata, Ficus sp.*, and *Markhamia obtusifolia*.

The initial showers are localized and capricious in distribution. Dark thunderclouds form in the east and drift westward pushed by high winds.

Rain is often seen falling in other areas. I found individuals uncanny in their ability to predict if rain would occur on a particular day, but was never able to determine the basis for their assertions other than, as some said, rains were expected with a new moon. At Nabwalya the first rains of 1966 fell on 22 October.

With the first showers, new life springs from the ground as if awaiting a signal. The open fields along the river become full of large, red, velvety mites conspicuous on the tawny sands. The locals refer to this species as "God's offspring" (*kana kakwa Leza*). Small yellowish millipeds emerge from the soil and mate. Back from the river as the mopane trees (*Colophospermum mopane*) leaf, the shrill of the cicadas (*vimunsha*) reaches deafening proportions. With the first rains, all active termitaria feature new additions of mud on their baked sides.

The rains in November and early December are preceded by strong winds. Such winds drive dust storms as they sweep across the cleared fields into the villages. The humid air and temperatures over 100°F make this time of the year enervating until some relief is brought by increases in frequency and intensity of the downpours.

December to April

The Valley Bisa now take advantage of the coolness which comes from the increasing number of overcast days. They work late in the mornings clearing, digging, planting, and finishing last minute tasks. Field huts are remudded and rethatched for occupancy by January. The weather in late November and December is still uncomfortably hot and humid especially if showers do not occur, for the air becomes heavy and muggy (*chitukumila*) making field work sweaty and difficult.

As the rains become more frequent, depressions away from the river fill with water and teem with aquatic and amphibian life. Suspended on the reeds and grasses over these ponds are white fluffy masses of frog eggs, and as one approaches the water's edge he finds the ponds rippling with scurrying amphibians and catfish. Game wanders farther from the river, and the large herds found close to the village during the dry season are no longer seen.

Around the village, insects of all kinds become a nuisance. Each night swarms of beetles, mosquitoes, flying termites, and other insects gather at our small kerosene light. Snakes and toads are now commonly found where least expected.

With the rains come many avian migrants. Pelicans, geese, and ducks occupy the banks of the flooding river and lagoons; queleas, weavers, and cuckoos make their appearance around the villages. In the evening, large flocks of cattle egrets fly at tree-top level to roost at Chinama lagoon, then grace the dawn on their early flights back to the hinterland and their favored buffalo herds. As runoff from rains elsewhere raises the water level in the Munyamadzi River, hippos return to their pools from their dry season recluse in the thickets of Chinama. Every morning the routes taken in their night's wanderings are seen in the gumbo of cleared fields.

Both crops and grasses respond quickly to the presence of the water. Light green grasses (*mwemvu*) sprout from beneath soil which seemed bare only a month before, and by January many are in seed. In late January and February, women journey into the mopane forest to collect seeds from the dense mats of *Echinochloa colonum* and *Panicum sociale* grasses which are ground into flour and consumed as porridge. As the vegetation increases in height and density, wide paths are cleared connecting villages and leading to areas frequently visited. For periods minor streams may flood and isolate villages. Everywhere the greasy clays make long journeys difficult. Throughout the first month or so of the rains, work in the fields involves weeding and thinning the growing sorghums. Midway through the rains, pumpkins, maize, and millet ripen.

The rains are labeled according to their frequency and duration. *Mvula ya mibundo* are the starting rains with several clear days intervening between showers. *Mvula ya miloche* are the long and heavy rains which follow. The most depressing are the light drizzles which last all day and into the night (*chivula ubuziku*). These rains disturb normal routines, and few venture outside their huts. Normally, the rains are expected to taper off in March or April. Then the infrequent and unpredictable rains, called *anula-nula*, keep people on guard at all times lest their drying flour or clothes be spoiled by sudden downpours.

Throughout April the grasses remain high and soaked with dew in the early morning. *Adansonia digitata, Sclerocarya caffra, Piliostigma thonningii,* and *Ficus sp.* come into fruit, signaling the beginning of a new season. Along the flood plain the winter thorn (*Acacia albida*) leafs. Almost imperceptibly a drying trend begins. Although the heavy cloud cover persists in April, the rains taper off. Clouds blanket the skies beginning before sunrise but these usually are broken by winds in late morning or early afternoon. The Valley Bisa refer to these blankets of clouds in the singular *mukumbi wa mpepo* ("cloud of coldness") whereas rain clouds are called *makumbi yàmfula* ("clouds of rain") in the plural form. With climatological changes such as these, the temperature begins to drop, heralding the beginning of the cold, dry season.

May and June

Slowly the lagoons and depressions away from the river begin to dry, and in 1967, most were dry by the end of May. As the volume of water decreases in each lagoon, catfish concentrate in their shallow pockets and are gathered in nets and baskets. Elephants open pockets of light, textured soil which are then used by other game for drinking and wallowing.

The end of the wet season heralds a busy time, for the ripe sorghums are attractive to many birds and mammals. My impressions of late April and May are of the bustling activities of children in fields beating tin cans, shouting, and brandishing slingshots to keep the numerous birds from alighting within the fields entrusted to their care. At night the adults take over the job of crop protection. Adults sleep lightly, remaining alert to the sounds of mammals intruding into their gardens. Their restlessness is suggested by the frequency with which we heard drumming, gunshots, and shouting in the evening and the frequency with which these raids were reported to us (see table 9). In early May, the Valley Bisa bend the sorghum stalks and lay them horizontally along the ground preparatory to reaping.

TABLE 9

RAIDS OR ATTEMPTED RAIDS BY LARGE MAMMALS ALONG THE MUNYAMADZI RIVER

Weekly Period			No. of Raids or Attempts[1]	Mammals Involved
1966	Nov.	6–12	2	elephant, buffalo
		13–19	1	elephant
	Dec.	4–10	5	elephant, buffalo
		11–17	11	elephant, buffalo, hippo
		18–24	8	hippo, ?
		25–31	1	hippo
1967	Jan.	1– 7	8	hippo
	Apr.	9–15	9	elephant, hippo
		16–22	10	elephant, 1 elephant wounded
		23–29	13	elephant, 4 elephants wounded in gardens
	Apr./May	30– 6	7	elephant, hippo, pig 1 elephant killed
	May	7–13	5	waterbuck, hippo, buffalo, elephant 1 elephant killed
		14–20	3	elephant, hippo
		21–27	7	hippo, elephant
	May/June	28– 3	1	buffalo—killed by lions in field
	June	4–10	1	elephant—wounded in field

1. Figures are the sum of my observations on disturbances within the fields and those reported to us. The two periods coincide with planting (Nov.–Jan.) and harvesting (April–June) of crops.

Men now gather poles, bark, and reeds for building the granaries and repairing their village huts. In 1967 the inhabitants at Nabwalya were content with a wealth of crops which included millet, sorghum, groundnuts, maize, pumpkins, and sweet potatoes.

The tall rank grass everywhere now harbors nymphal ticks and in short walks along the river, one becomes covered with them. One becomes impatient for the grass to dry so it can be burned, increasing visibility, and destroying pests whose haven is the tall grasses. The Valley Bisa seemed to be glad to have the tall, dense grasses burned, yet were relieved when most of the burning was completed, for grass fires pushed by steady winds become an inferno against which no village is safe. Burning began early in May with a few fires set in the grasses adjacent to fields as an adjunct method to keep mammals from the ripening crops during the night (see table 10). These early burns are of short duration, but in June and July, as the tall grasses along the river dry and become parched, the country becomes a tinder in which fires may burn for days. The smoke and soot rising from these fires produce the haze so characteristic of the dry season. This haze increases in density until it gradually obscures sight of the escarpment which, when the rains cleared the air, is discernible as a blue rim bordering the west.

TABLE 10

GRASS FIRES AROUND NABWALYA

Week		Time of Day		
		Morning	Afternoon	Evening
May	1– 6	...	...	1
	7–13	...	1	...
	14–20	...	...	...
	21–27	...	...	2
May/June	28– 3	1	2	2
	11–17	1	6	7
	18–24	...	2	1
June/July	25– 1	...	8	14
	2– 8	...	3	7
	9–15	...	1	...
	16–22	...	1	2
	23–29	...	2	4
Total		2	26	40

Note: Fire listed under time of day when first noticed.

With their harvests gathered and stored in village granaries, individuals generally look forward to a short reprieve from their labors. But in 1967, as they returned to reside in their villages, the Valley Bisa were beset by a plague of rodents (primarily *Tatera leucogaster, Praomys natalensis,* and *Aethomys chrysophilus*). People resorted to many techniques for killing these hordes, including a poison concocted from an unidentified grass, burning superfluous piles of straw and old huts in which rodents were hiding, and pots of water left overnight for rodents to drown in. As the rotting stink of decaying rodent carcasses enveloped their villages, the Bisa complained that the hyenas were no longer cleaning up their villages. During July, I clubbed to death more than four hundred rodents in the quarter-acre area surrounding our hut.

By June most of the deciduous trees are leafless but a few hardy thorn trees come into leaf or fruit. Gradually, the cloud cover lifts early in the morning exposing the valley floor to a hot sun.

July to October

The harshest season within the valley is also the time when the Munyamadzi Corridor is most accessible to outsiders. Beginning in the west at the escarpment and proceeding east to the Luangwa River, a group of workers clears the grass from a small track which is utilized by the vehicles of government officials and safari groups pursuing their various objectives within the corridor. The workmen fill in the deeper elephant impressions and grade the sharp banks of the streambeds.

In July the hot winds of the dry season begin with gusts in the afternoon and evening. There are few, if any, clouds in the morning; yet cloud cover builds in the late afternoon and evening smothering the valley floor with the heat accumulated during the day.

Due to the harshness of the environment at this time, the Valley Bisa lead a life of comparative leisure. The dismal climate, as both heat and humidity mount, precludes hard labor except early in the morning. Under the oppressive heat, many succumb to sicknesses. At this time, some take advantage of the absence of pressing duties and the ease with which they may catch a ride out of the valley to visit relatives on the plateau and in the towns.

With most of the vegetation burnt and pools in the hinterland dry, the river becomes the only dependable source of water for both man and mammal. The water level of the Munyamadzi River is at its lowest ebb and wide sandbars border its shallow channels. Game of all sizes frequent the margins of the river and make their trek to drink under cover of darkness. In this period of environmental leanness, mammals are frequently seen from village compounds and at night graze close to human dwellings. One of my fondest memories of Nabwalya was lying awake at night, listening to the grass being munched outside, and speculating as to the species of the visitor, or being awakened by the bellowing of buffalo or the thud of hooves and neighs of zebras as these herds passed the line of villages on their way to drink in the Munyamadzi. Hippos and smaller mammals frequently grazed the unburned grasses, purposely kept short by the school children, surrounding the school and its dormitories.

Almost any evening one could play the beam of a flashlight upon the eyes of nocturnal grazers.

The seasonal cycle of Valley Bisa activities may be summarized by a graph (figure 6) depicting the year-round tasks of resident adults (six males, eight females) of Mukupa village whose genealogical structure was given in Figure 4. From this graph it is possible to assess the relative amount of time allocated by villagers to various activities throughout the year. Most of the community's time is spent in agricultural endeavors and in the preparation and consumption of its products. Most socializing is accompanied by beer drinking and the amount of time so engaged is apparent in Figure 6. Social events included attendance at initiation ceremonies, funerals, and meetings.

No hunter was a fulltime resident of Mukupa, although two older men married there were hunters. One of these spent most of his time in another village where he was a headman; the other was away for most of the year on the Copperbelt. Two young men were inveterate guinea-fowl trappers and most of the time recorded for hunting and trapping from August to October is a reflection of their activities. Most of the animal protein for the village was derived from butchering and transporting kills made by hunters of neighboring villages. Inveterate hunters are few and in my opinion the relative time input suggested in this graph is representative of many villages throughout the corridor.

SUMMARY

I began Part One with an account of Valley Bisa history to illustrate the fickle role external circumstances have played in the plight of the inhabitants of the Luangwa Valley. The Bisa living there share a common background with other ethnic groups inhabiting the northern portions of Zambia, and their location along the mainstream of political and economic developments in central Africa during the past century is attested to by the visits of the Portuguese and other explorers. At this time Valley Bisa men were traders and hunters of ivory and were well known along trade routes throughout Central Africa. The establishment and consolidation of European political power and the dividing of Central Africa into spheres of influence in the first two decades of the present century switched the routes of commerce from east and west to north and south. As a result, the Luangwa Valley and its few inhabitants were isolated from the pervasive winds of change which swept across the plateau and to their southeast. Although attempts to reorganize and change Valley Bisa culture and social life began under the colonial regime and continue under the present government, their isolation in the valley and the piecemeal approach to their development has meant that change for the Valley Bisa has been uneven and slow.

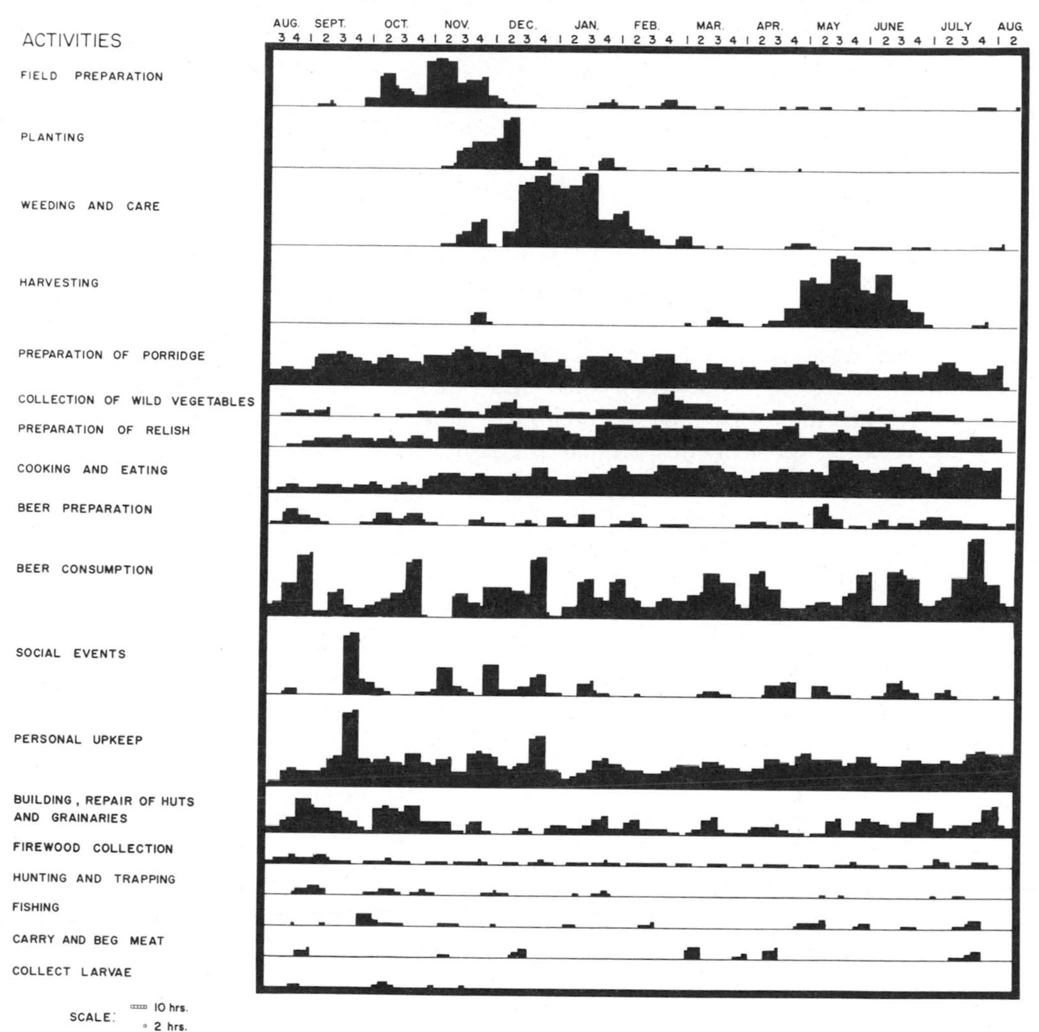

Figure 6. Histogram of time spent by adults in various activities in Mukupa village

The Munyamadzi Corridor remains sparsely populated with villages and settlements situated close to its major perennial streams. An unbalanced sex ratio is typical, with between 50 and 70 percent of the adult males away in urban centers. Therefore the male segment of the population consists mainly of children, young men returning home between interims in the urban centers, and older men. It is among this sex that hunters are recruited.

Descent groups, such as the matrilineage, stress group loyalty rather than individual independence, for fidelity to and identification with the group is the dominant value. Its cohesion is established through corporate rights over its members, land, and its products, political office and is reinforced by veneration of the group's expired members. Each corporate descent cluster competes with others for the goods of life and its male members compete among themselves for the few roles provided by the group. It is within the social and ideological context of village life that some individuals, as subsistence hunters, compete with their brothers and nephews, with differing skills and attributes, for leadership roles of these residential descent clusters.

Although the per capita consumption of wild meat for the Valley Bisa is greater than that recorded for other subsistence cultivators in Zambia, Valley Bisa residents depend primarily upon the products of shifting agriculture supplemented by the gathering of wild plants. The significance of hunting and its products in Valley Bisa life is attributable in part to the presence of the tsetse fly, which has discouraged their raising of domestic livestock, and in part to historic and present circumstances, which have encouraged their close association with abundant wildlife. In Part Two we examine changes in hunting traditions, sociological characteristics of those who hunt, and the ideological components of their hunting process.

Part Two

CULTURAL DIMENSIONS OF THE HUNTING PROCESS

V

Hunting in Prologue and Process

> [While competing with gun hunters] we have surpassed them, we hunters with spears.
>
> Bisa proverb

HUNTING IN PAST TIMES

ALTHOUGH the successful hunter still continues to command respect and esteem among the Valley Bisa, both the social organization and technological skills of hunting have changed during the last sixty to one hundred years. In the past, success and achievement in hunting were a major route to manhood, and a number of specialist hunters and organized guilds flourished. Until the middle of the last century when muzzleloading guns became available through trade with the Portuguese and Arabs, hunting weapons consisted mainly of spears, assorted traps, and bows with arrows, which often made collaboration and group efforts desirable. Today, hunting is largely an individual effort in which a person may choose to distinguish himself, but its social importance and legitimizing rituals have their roots in tradition. In this chapter we look at the forms hunting took in the past, its social organization, techniques, and the reasons for its subsequent change.

Elephant Hunters

Of the professional guilds, none surpassed the elephant hunters in status. These were the aristocrats of the hunting guilds. *Nkombalume*, a respectful term by which elephant hunters were addressed, were groups of skilled hunters whose magics and rituals gave them leadership roles and monopolies to exploit elephants. These guilds were closely associated with the chiefs, to whom belonged the valued products of the chase—ivory and tail hairs. Ivory was a major trade item in Central Africa, and its directional flow in the past from hunters to subordinate chief to paramount chief reflected alligiance and political strategies.

Most of my informants were of the opinion that both tusks and the tail were delivered to the chief, who then rewarded the hunters with gifts of beads, cloth, a slave, or possibly a gun. In some cases the right tusk, called *mwana ndelwa*, might be retained by the hunter, who was then free to sell it if he wished. The left tusk, *chimbo*, described as the one generally used for scraping off bark and digging, was always retained by the chief as a symbol of his domination over his territory. Today such a tusk is placed in the chief's spirit hut along with tokens of beer and sorghum flour. Miracle (1962) discusses the variability which he found among the neighboring Senga with reference to the ivory trade.

Prior to hunting elephants, guild members approached the chief and asked for his blessing, which if granted, was symbolized by the chief spitting softly on the hunters (*kupaza amate*). Councilors accompanied by two children (classificatory grandchildren of dead chiefs) took beads, sorghum flour, and sometimes beer for offering at the chief's spirit huts. If these offerings remained undisturbed through the night, and they perceived no adverse signs in dreams or omens, the hunt would proceed.

The night prior to his departure, each hunter poured flour at the head of his mat or in a gourd named after an ancestor and placed therein a string of white beads. He repeated a prayer for ancestral assistance, and provided this offering remained undisturbed and he dreamed favorably during the night, he would accompany the others.

Individual prescriptions for magics were varied and were solicited from many different sources. One charm carried by most elephant hunters was *chipeshi*. This magic, carried in a reed basket (*umusecke*), was believed to call elephants and to bring the hunters luck. Other types of magics were said to render hunters invisible to their quarry, make their spear thrusts successful, and to make game susceptible to their prowess. *Mfenzi* was of the former type, *chilembe* of the second, both of which Valley Bisa hunters employ today. Other prescriptions of elephant hunters included (1) *katumbi*, a protective magic against those who had committed adultery; (2) *kalonganzofu*, a sympathetic magic, included leaves and branches gathered by browsing elephants; and (3) *mwenje*, for protection against spirits of slain elephants.

An elephant hunting expedition might last two or three months, and it was expected that the wives and kin of the hunters remaining in the village were to restrict their behavior. For wives in particular, these restrictions were severe, for their husbands' safety and success afield were believed dependent upon the wives' maintaining behavior beyond reproach. Hunters afield could determine whether or not appropriate relations existed in their village by watching the behavior of their prey, for the sight of elephants copulating was a sign of adultery, and elephants lying down indicated mourning in the village. A current saying among the

Valley Bisa is that "elephants never tell lies" (*nzofu tebeba nangu chimo ubufi*). If any odd behavior was observed by the hunters, they returned to their temporary camps or to the village for divination into its cause. Hunting was undertaken again upon its resolution.

The existence of several elephant guilds suggests the significance of ivory in the traditional economy and its alignment with political authority and status. Each group was headed by a leader, who, by his knowledge of magics and rituals, protected those with him. Beliefs in magics and protective charms gave these hunters a virtual monopoly over rights to hunt elephants. Subscription to guilds was by initiation, proven skill, and the payment of fees.

The *Bakalongwe wa nzofu* hunted elephants with special spears (*kalongwe*) which were poisoned. These spears were roughly eight feet in length with a blade about a foot in length and three inches in width at its broadest point. When this group spotted elephants, the leader went directly into the herd and was the first to spear an elephant. Others followed and harried the wounded beast with dogs. When the elephant took a stand, hunters, each armed with a weighted spear, arranged themselves in two lines parallel to the route the wounded elephant was expected to follow while their leader approached it. When it charged between the two lines of hunters, they speared it until it died. This guild was undoubtedly the one Livingstone noted on the plateau (1874:167) and to which the valley chief, Kavimba, belonged (1874:163).

Bashimunina also pursued elephants with weighted poisoned spears, but used a different technique. Lacerda, a Portuguese explorer, provides a description of this spear (Burton 1873:271). These iron spears were "four palms long," one inch thick, and terminated in a flat, sharp head at one end. The other end was embedded in a heavy piece of wood and the spear's total weight was given as eight pounds. Experienced members of this guild climbed trees whose branches extended over elephant paths or at water holes while other members herded the elephants toward the tree. When an elephant passed underneath, the leader aimed and threw his heavy spear to pass between the shoulder blades of the elephant.

The *Bamutemakwangwa* hunted by concealing themselves in long grasses adjacent to elephant paths. When elephants were driven past, hunters took them by surprise from the rear and cut their tendons. Their weapons were axes whose blades were poisoned. This guild may have been restricted to the Luangwa Valley, for I have not found references to it in the literature.

When muzzleloading guns became available through the ivory trade with the Arabs and Portuguese, chiefs awarded them to hunters. Gun hunters, called *Bafundi*, also had their hierarchies, and their members took turns discharging their weapons at a beast until it died. The leader supplied the powder, shot, and in some cases, the guns. Elephants were also trapped in game pits whose construction is discussed later.

Youth who had proven their skill were initiated into the guilds. Gouldsbury and Sheane (1911:213) mention that killing an elephant, rhino, or two or three buffalo was generally accepted as evidence of hunting skill. Beyond this, however, payments were required which among the Bemba included sixteen yards of calico, a hoe, or a goat. Initiation ceremonies took place outside the village with guild members in attendance. Incisions were made in the initiate's right shoulder, right thumb, and above his right eye, with a magical concoction rubbed into these cuts. Additional incisions were added when the hunter killed subsequent elephants.

Elephant herds in the valley have been subjected to hunting pressure for a long time. Before the country was administered by the British South Africa Company, Portuguese traders (*Chikunda*) and their subordinates hunted in the Luangwa Valley. Some of them married local women and many Bisa joined them in their pursuits of elephants. The Valley Bisa today claim that their more powerful magics came from their association with the Chikunda. Early British administrators (Melland and Hughes) and hunters (Lyell and Letcher) noted the presence of "expert" elephant trackers in most villages in the valley. Baobab bark was used as wadding for muzzleloading guns, and Hughes (1933:242), who was stationed at Nabwalya Boma from 1901 to 1903, comments on the number of these trees which had their bark removed in square sections. He recalls once his trackers came upon a decayed elephant carcass. From its remains, his trackers retrieved a dozen "native-made copper bullets" which were later reshaped for use in their muzzleloaders.

Hippopotamus Hunters

Several explorers noted Valley Bisa seeking hippos in the Luangwa River. In 1798 Lacerda recorded their presence there, and in 1831 Gamitto encountered an intertribal group of Bisa, Senga, and Chewa hunters totaling some fifty individuals. These hunters were living in small leaf shelters on the edge of a deep pool inhabited by hippos.

Gamitto (1960:153) provides a description of the harpoon downfall utilized by these hunters. These traps (*chisumpi*) consisted of a barbed poisoned point embedded in wood and suspended by rope from a tree overhanging a hippo trail. The rope supporting the downfall was wrapped around a tree trunk or limb and tied to a thin stick lying athwart the trail. The harpoon was positioned to fall into the mammal's back; wounded hippos usually ran for the water where they died within twenty-four hours. The meat was cut into strips, dried in the sun, and used to barter provisions, slaves, cloth, and ivory. According to Gamitto, these same traps were used for elephants, but the recovery of these large beasts posed problems since they wandered considerable distances after being wounded.

In addition to the downfall, Bisa killed hippos with lances (*chibingu*). From riverbanks these hunters, called *Batinti*, probed with long poles into the deep pools to force submerged hippos to surface, whereupon they could be speared. Reportedly, these spearmen possessed magic to make hippos come into shallow water. Once it struck a hippo, the spear's shaft separated and would rise to the surface as a float indicating the wounded mammal's location underwater.

Hippos were taken by harpoon downfalls, lances, muzzleloaders, and pits, but organized drives from dugouts widely reported in other parts of Central Africa (Melland 1923; Mackenzie 1925; Junod 1962; Scudder 1962) apparently did not occur in the Luangwa Valley. Perhaps the reduced water level of the Luangwa during the dry season made the deployment of this technique unnecessary.

Although hippo ivory was not used, Gamitto (1960:153) reported that the cleaned skull was buried, "for they considered the brains a powerful poison." This and other observations suggest that hippo hunters were a flourishing guild and may have had initiation rites and special ceremonies. Today, with the decreasing importance of the hippo as a food species for the Valley Bisa, many details have been forgotten (see section on Game Abundance, Government Restrictions, and Selection of Game).

Lion Hunting

The Valley Bisa differentiate between three types of lions on the basis of observable behavior and circumstances. Ordinary lions, *nkalamo* or *nkalamo ya musidi*, are identified with the bush, sometimes metaphorically called the bush, *chonde* or *mpanga*. Spiritual lions, *mipashi ya chialo*, are said to be reincarnated chief's spirits in lion form. Generally these lions frighten and worry people but do not kill them. Lion familiars, *nkalamo ya kutuma*, are those sent by sorcerers to kill or maim people.

Lions are metaphorically "chiefs" of the bush and rule over all other animals, with the possible exception of adult elephants. In their chieftaincy over other animals, lions are brave, strong, and dangerous, all attributes which complement those ascribed the Ngona chieftaincy. In terms of prestige and its associated prohibitions, the killing of a lion is by implication similar to the slaying of a human being.

Lions are respected and are not prey or game in the general sense of those words. They are rarely hunted, and then only when they trouble people. In the last century, Gamitto (1960) noted the respect accorded lions at kills. In driving lions away from their kills, the Bisa knelt on the ground and clapped while approaching its slain prey. Similar behavior is traditional for a commoner greeting a chief.

In the past, if a lion killed a person, it was the chief's responsibility to mobilize warriors to destroy it. Such a menacing beast was called *chizwango*. Today the presence of the game guards and the scarcity of hunters which the chief can summon, make it unlikely that this ritual will be performed again. In 1966 a marauding lion was killed by game guards, and in 1967 a lion snared by a wire noose was killed by an individual with the chief's rifle. Individual rites of purification followed each of these killings but there was no ceremony involving numbers of hunters. Therefore this rite (*malaila abulanda*) belongs to the past.

Formerly, when a lion had killed a person, the chief instructed his councilors to summon warriors by beating on his war drum (*kamangu*). These men assembled at the chief's compound and were charged to kill the lion and any other game they happened upon in the bush. The chief prepared war medicine (*lamvia*) to protect them afield and to make their mission successful. One headman was designated as in charge of the group, and he was responsible for reporting to the chief every event and sign observed, including animals seen, wounded, and killed on their assignment. Then the group went to the spot where the lion was last seen. The warriors surrounded this area and prepared for the charge as the lion broke cover. Upon its death, the lion's carcass was hoisted on a pole and carried to the nearest village where it was skinned.

The lion's head and skin were carried to a village just outside the chief's compound. The chief then dispatched a councilor, carrying oil and red powder (*nkula*), to meet the hunters. The oil was smeared over the bodies of all participants and in the lion's mouth; the red powder was smeared in circles on the hunters' faces and chests. Then the assembled hunters danced and sang as they moved toward the chief's compound and their ceremonial entrance was similar to occasions when warriors returned from a campaign. Two of the songs associated with this procession were:

Nkalamo
Bamutula linso
Washala chipukula pongo.

[The lion
They have extracted an eye
It remains one-eyed.]

Mwamba mukulu
Nikapumpe
Chuni chiamutula linso.

[Mwamba, the great chief
Is the hawk
The bird that extracted its eye.]

When they entered the compound they found the chief seated on his throne in a red skirt. The hunters laid before the chief the lion's head and skin and all the other animals collected on the expedition. Then the leader gave his report indicating the animals killed and relating the contents, if any, in the lion's stomach. The initial killer of the lion was praised and new epithets added to his praise titles. When the people departed, the chief went to his spirit huts accompanied by his councilors for prayers (*mapepo yachialo*). All of the slain animals, with the exception of the lion skin, were buried beside the huts.

Ant Bear Hunters

Esoteric and elaborate rites were practiced by small bands of ant bear hunters, variously called *baimba muta, mupalu wampendwa*, and *mwimba nengo*. Small groups of from three to six men were led by one called *mupendwa*, who possessed and administered the magics thought necessary to make the ant bear vulnerable and to pacify its spirit.

Lyell (1913:210), who hunted in the Luangwa Valley at the turn of the century, saw three ant bears which had been killed by Africans. Ant bear hunters still exist in other parts of Zambia (Doke 1931; Stefaniszyn 1964b) and on the plateau, but in the Luangwa Valley traditions of their techniques have almost faded from memory.

Apparently, those who hunted ant bears were the most secretive of hunters. The ant bear's spirit was thought to be the most powerful and frightful, a reputation which reflects the potential dangers awaiting the hunter who pursued his prey underground. In answer to my questions as to why these hunters were so secretive, an elder who in his earlier years reportedly killed eight ant bears replied:

> It is just that our great ancestors told us this. The ant bear's spirit is fearful, and the hunter needs special medicines to kill it or the hunter or members of his lineage will die. When we are out in the bush following its spoor (*mu mulondo*) and find other hunters in the bush hunting elephant or buffalo, they must come and wish us well; otherwise, their pursuits will not succeed.

Usually members of these hunting groups lived in the same village and were related. Early in the morning of the hunt after the group left the village, its leader took branches from the *musolo* tree and tossed pieces behind their line of march toward the village and in the direction they were proceeding. *Musolo* has white bark and its color is associated with luck and good fortune.

When these hunters came upon the fresh three-toed track of the ant bear, they proceeded in line behind the leader, who began to chant:

> *Kanama liala*
> *Kalia kafutauka imicila, kaya*

Kaya kumalolwa
Kafutauka imicila kaya.

[The small mammal having claws
Moves its tail and goes
Goes away into the hole
Moves its tail and goes.]

This spell was said to make the ant bear vulnerable to the hunters. After locating its burrow, the *mumpendwa* ordered his subordinates to sit down around the hole while he gathered leaves of *kalamamafuka (Combretum sp.)* and *mutunga mbavala (Xeromphis obovata)*. Then the *mumpendwa* circled the entrance to the burrow, tying knots in grass stems (*chikochi*) at intervals around its hole. Leaves from both trees were placed on the knots while the chief hunter said:

Kalama mita
Umweni wanyingo
Nshifwenya waya nenama.

[Prescription used to placate ant bear's spirit
May my spirit strengthen itself to go
into the animal.]

Ant bear burrows harbor a number of other denizens (poisonous snakes, hyenas, warthogs, etc.) and the Ambo are said to use *ntesi* magic (from *kutesimuka*, "to slip") to enable them to glide by dangerous snakes (Stefaniszyn 1964b:71). This chant cleared the tunnel of undesirable or dangerous species and rendered the ant bear's claws "dead" (*viala yafwa*) or "cold" (*viala yatalala*).

After circling the burrow, the leader instructed his subordinates to use the name *chibinda* ("hunter") when referring to grass and trees instead of by their specific names and the word *ichanzo* when referring to spears, guns, or other weapons. Such references were said to fool the ant bear into thinking escape was impossible.

The leader stripped and went into the burrow while his companions followed the sound of his route from above ground. When the leader approached the ant bear, it pushed dirt toward the hunter and began digging. Its diggings were followed by the other hunters who located the point aboveground at which it stopped. Then these hunters cut a pole in which the axhead was embedded (calling it by its new name) and began digging. The leader withdrew from the burrow and waited until his subordinates approached the ant bear's new location from above. They then withdrew while their leader reentered the hole with a special spear. This spear contained a special magic, and its shaft was made from *mpaza (Julbernardia globiflora)*, a very hard wood. It was necessary for *mumpendwa* to awaken his prey slowly before killing it; then he speared it several times, saying, "*munanama*."

When the dead ant bear was taken from its burrow all ceased using the special terms assigned trees and weapons. The ant bear's tongue was knotted and severed before it was given to the leader. The leader took the head and *mutungwa mbavala* leaves and deposited them at another burrow or left it where an ant bear had scratched for food. When he deposited the head, he spat *mutungwa mbavala* leaves on the cranium, saying, "*we nama lala*" (you animal sleep).

Although my informant did not mention restricted sexual behavior on the part of the hunters' wives, one would expect this to be the case. For the Lambas, Doke (1931:338) mentions that the wives of these hunters could not close the door of their huts, otherwise the ant bear would shut its tunnel and bury their husbands. Doke (1931:103) also reports it as taboo to bring an ant bear's head into the village; rather it had to be severed and left in the bush.

Ant bear signs are common around Nabwalya, but the animal itself was rarely seen. Because of its nocturnal and secretive habits, black color, and three-toed foot, the ant bear is the focus of many malevolent associations. According to the Valley Bisa, it is a familiar of sorcerers and responsive to their spells. Its burrowing habits link it with the dead and the afterworld. Stefaniszyn (1964a:136) records two stories about ant bear hunters who in their wanderings in burrows glimpsed the world of the spirits and in this world reported that the only game were ant bears. Powerful magics are concocted from ant bear parts. The foreshoulders of these small animals reportedly never tire and farmers and fighters desire them to strengthen their own foreshoulders. The ant bear is knowledgeable about many kinds of magic from the numerous roots and herbs which it reputedly eats and any root left by it is valued for its powers.

The Game Test

Ritual hunts (*lutembo* or *kusowa libanda*) were an important method of divination for the Valley Bisa. If a person's survivors were suspicious of sorcery, they might request the aid of a hunter or another group, not members of the lineage, to divine the cause of death. In cases where an individual hunter was chosen, the lineage's white beads (*mupashi wezu*) were tied to his right arm and the sex of the mammal slain was given significance. If the hunter killed a female, the sorcerer was suspected to be a member of the deceased's matrilineage; if a male, then the sorcerer was sought among those outside this group. Suspects were given the *umwavi* ("poison") test as described below in an interview.

> Before the Europeans came, and once it was determined whether the sorcerer (*mulozi*) was in or out of the clan, some people went to the Luangwa to obtain poison (*umwavi*) from the *Bachikwa*. Upon their return, village elders soaked the poison in water and administered it to chickens belonging to sus-

> pects or to members of the whole village. The owners of the chicken(s) which died were said to be sorcerers. If these continually denied this accusation, the poison test was administered to them. An individual's innocence was proven if he vomited the poison; if not, the guilty person was taken to the chief in confirmation of his sorcery and his body thrown into a fire on Kapili Ndozi. An individual must confess his guilt; otherwise upon his death his spirit would haunt his matrikin. When the Europeans came they stopped this practice.

Beyond the above circumstance, the game test was employed in a number of situations, but the group had to decide in advance the significance of the sex of the animal slain. When Chief Chitala, who lived near the Muchinga escarpment, died in 1913, a dispute followed concerning his legitimate successor. Chitala's only nephew was captured with his mother by the Ngoni while still a baby and taken into slavery. A candidate claiming to be this nephew was supported by Chitala shortly before his death, although this individual was despised by other members of Chitala's lineage. Upon the chief's death, it was decided to make the decision of the candidate's legitimacy on the basis of a game test which resulted in the taking of a male duiker. This outcome strengthened public opposition to the heir's legitimacy, although he was appointed a chief by a commissioner at Mpika. In 1916 public criticism and pressures from other valley chiefs resulted in the formal dismissal of the chief and the appointment of a grandson in his place (Mpika District Notebook and Archival files).

Informants suggested the early 1930s as the period when this method of divination was employed for the last time. In 1967 a headman of a large village experiencing a number of deaths for which he was implicated suggested a ritual hunt to determine whether or not he was involved. His proposition was not accepted by his matrikin; subsequently his village split into two groups.

Other Types of Hunts

In the past, individuals and groups whose activities were not granted guild status also pursued game. Groups of men, accompanied by younger boys, left the village for several days and constructed temporary camps (*malala*) in the bush close to areas frequented by game. According to the Valley Bisa, game was not abundant around their villages in this century until the late 1950s, and as a consequence this tactic was used frequently until then. Even today when game in the village neighborhood becomes flighty, hunters will occasionally encamp in the bush for several days.

Small game such as warthogs and impala were caught by dogs. The hunters who used dogs (*chibinda wambwa*) used special magic to enhance the dog's sense of smell. In 1966–67 dogs were uncommon throughout the corridor and only two were found within the study area. These latter were not used for hunting purposes.

Formerly, group hunts for cane rats were common along the Munyamadzi River within the study area. Prior to 1956 the thick *matete* reeds and tall grasses were said to harbor many cane rats; these areas were encircled with fire and dogs were set inside the circle to catch and chase the rats. Since the middle 1950s this riverine strip has been cleared and farmed intensely. Along with the loss of their habitat, cane rats have been extirpated from the study area, although they are reported elsewhere in the corridor.

It should be noted that not all hunting in the past took place in groups; hunters did hunt and trap as individuals depending upon the type of game sought. When Livingstone (1874:160) shot a puku on the banks of the Mupamadzi, the noise of his gun attracted a hunter who consented for meat and pay to show him a ford across that flooded river.

A distinction should be made between an individual who hunts occasionally and the professional hunter. The professional hunter has been initiated into a cadre of adepts and through his initiation knows its magics and rituals. The killing of game is not of itself given special significance in Valley Bisa society unless the hunter wishes to be recognized for his prowess. Even today an individual may hunt and make a kill occasionally and there is no special ceremony commemorating his kill. Yet if one in his youth shows a knack toward hunting or if he meets with more than occasional success in killing larger game, he may feel the need for admission into the circle of professional hunters. His wish for initiation may stem from several sources. He may fear that his continued success will run athwart a professional's ambitions and the latter will use magic or his access to spiritual forces to arrest the uninitiated's success. Further, he may find his success or skill socially untenable without acquiring proper legitimization. Some believe that hunters are exposed to particular dangers in the bush and that they must ritually protect themselves against defilement. Formerly, renowned hunters were not buried in village graves. Rather, symbolizing their fierceness and courage, they were buried with their weapons along a game trail or some other specified site in the bush.

Professional hunters and nonprofessionals who occasionally hunt both exist today. But groups of highly organized guilds which specialized in taking game with particular techniques belong to the past.

DYNAMICS OF CHANGE

Having sketched the hierarchies of professionals, we may now examine the factors responsible for their demise. Change has involved mainly government and commerce, and neither its directions nor dimensions have been at the option of the local population. These factors are discussed under separate headings below, but to view each in isolation from the others is to minimize their effect. They are related as cause to consequence and all are a part of the greater matrix of change. In their effects on Valley Bisa society, these changes have been more than the sum of the parts.

Acquisition of Firearms

In keeping with other Central African groups, the Bisa adopted muzzleloading guns mainly for prestige, protection, and warfare. In tribal warfare the muzzleloader's noise was a deterrent and this novelty gave the weapons a value out of proportion to their effectiveness. Although less efficient for killing game than traditional techniques with poison, the impunity and success with which explorers and Arabs used their weapons may have hastened their adoption by Africans.

It was not determined when muzzleloaders were first acquired by inhabitants in the Luangwa Valley. The acquisition of these weapons did not result in the abandonment of traditional armaments, for today spears and axes are carried on hunts as auxiliary weapons to muzzleloaders and a variety of snares and bows and arrows arc used covertly. But the widespread use of firearms altered the methods of hunting and had implications for the Bisa economic and social systems. The hunting guilds with their hierarchies based upon a simpler technology lapsed into obsolescence. In 1866, Livingstone encountered several guilds of elephant hunters near the Luangwa River, but by the beginning of the twentieth century these guilds no longer functioned. Hunting became an individual pursuit and did not require the mutual assistance and cooperative efforts of former years. At the same time, reliance on these weapons edged the Valley Bisa into dependence upon outside traders for additional weapons and gunpowder.

The arms trade in Africa was linked to the development of a new type firearm and its supply in European arsenals. By 1878 all European powers had rearmed with breechloading weapons and this changeover made available for overseas markets a vast supply of obsolete percussion cap muzzleloaders. Many of these found their way into East and Central Africa where a large demand existed for them. Once past the coastal ports in East Africa, the bulk of the weapons were transported into the interior by Arabs who traded them for ivory and slaves. Beachey (1962) suggests 1,000,000 firearms, over 4,000,000 pounds of gunpowder, and millions of percussion caps and rounds of ammunition entered British and German East Africa between 1885 and 1902.

The wholesale acquisition of firearms in Central Africa alarmed many European explorers, but this trade was brought in check only after the defeat of the Arabs and the settling in of European administrations. When the British South Africa Company assumed control in the center of

Southern Africa, their agents collected, registered, and restricted the possession of all firearms. At the same time, the administrators took action to outlaw traditional methods of hunting which transgressed their Victorian values with reference to cruelty toward animals. Their attempts may have been successful if judged by Melland's (1938) remark that in his experiences in Central Africa, dating back to 1901, he had never come across a fresh-dug (game) pit, although older ones, of no danger to game, were abundant.

In the past, hunters' shrines (*chipanda*) were decorated with the skulls of mammals symbolizing an individual's prowess. These visible shrines were rapidly discontinued soon after European administrators arrived. Moubray (1912), who resided on the plateau between 1903 and 1908, mentions that "this practice has been put to an end" by the European occupation, although Turner (1967) in the 1950s was able to study hunter's shrines among the Ndembu.

After several decades of British administration, laws governing the ownership by Africans of muzzleloading guns were loosened, and men purchased these with the cash earned from their labors in the developing European centers. In 1934 Africans within Mpika District were listed as possessing 569 muzzleloading guns, 11 shotguns, and 15 rifles. Although I obtained no records of firearms in the corridor prior to 1953 (table 11), there has been a steady increase in the possession of muzzleloading guns by residents since that date. On the other hand, the ownership of modern rifles and shotguns has been rigidly controlled.

TABLE 11

REGISTERED FIREARMS IN MUNYAMADZI CORRIDOR

Year	Number and Types of Firearms	Source of Information
1953	176 muzzleloading guns	Tour report
1962	237 muzzleloading guns 7 shotguns 2 rifles	Game ranger formerly stationed at Mpika
1967	347 muzzleloading guns 7 shotguns 2 rifles	Local clerk's records

Changes in Bisa Economy and Social Life

According to Gamitto (1960), in the early nineteenth century most inhabitants of the Luangwa Valley were either merchants or cultivators. There were other professions besides the two which Gamitto mentions in which men could distinguish themselves, but there were not as many occupational options as exist for them today. Perhaps the greatest contrast between the modern and traditional economy is in the current dependence on cash income derived primarily from wages earned outside of the valley. Up to several generations ago, most sustenance and trade items were derived from the exploitation of local resources.

With the establishment of an administrative post by the government at Nabwalya in 1900, local men were pressed into government service as carriers, messengers, and laborers. All able-bodied males were assessed a head tax. In order to meet this new demand, most men had to find work. Labor recruitment for the Rand in South Africa and Rhodesian mines began in 1903. The District Report for 1909 lists 150 valley men away for work at Broken Hill, 250 at Fort Jameson, and 15 at Petauke.

In 1910 sleeping sickness was discovered in the valley including two cases of Europeans who were presumed to have contracted the disease between Fort Jameson and Mpika. All of Mpika District east of the Muchingas was declared a sleeping sickness area and officials were restricted from touring there except on urgent business. An attempt was made to restrict valley residents from going to Fort Jameson and elsewhere in search of employment. Despite these restrictions, residents continued to seek outside employment and many shifted their residence east of the Luangwa, which was outside Mpika District. In 1913, an official on tour reported seeing "practically no able bodied men" in the valley for many had fled into the bush (Tour Reports, Mpika District).

When the labor supply became critical during the years 1915–18, the administration reversed its policy against recruitment in sleeping sickness areas. In 1915, one hundred valley residents ("all that were seen") were engaged in defense work and in 1916, three hundred were sent north to Chinsali to carry war loads. In 1921, all restrictions on the recruitment of valley residents were lifted.

Since then the normal pattern has been for males to engage in urban employment during their youth and middle age and to return to reside in the valley during the later stages of their life. The diversity of their experiences and success in their respective jobs has led to economic differentiation among residents of the same villages and the emergence of new forms of power and social status. Some elder men now prefer to set up stores or become tailors rather than distribute their wares and cash among their matrikin as was the expected pattern. To minimize conflict with those who might demand gifts or money, it is often necessary for those with money to break from their matrikin and to set up smaller settlements where they can live surrounded by fewer relatives and acquaintances.

The occupations and economic activities of adult men over twenty years of age are varied (see table 12). Each individual surveyed was asked which occupation he was engaged in and, if several, with which he felt primarily identified. The possible choices were left open and only farmer, headman, and government employee were mentioned specifically. It should be understood that most of these occupations overlap, for I was mainly interested in how these individuals perceived themselves. For example, one man who identified himself as a lorry driver was also a village headman, farmer, and hunter. All individuals farmed, with the exception of the schoolteachers, and more individuals than those who identified themselves as hunters did hunt occasionally.

TABLE 12

ROLES OF ADULT MALES IN THE ENVIRONS OF NABWALYA

Occupation	Number
Farmer	34
Government employee	14
Headman	8
Storekeeper	4
Hunter	3
Tailor	2
Political party staff	2
Lorry driver	1
No occupation	1

Note: Total number of residents sampled was 69.

The most acute discontinuity between "traditional" values and "modern" ones, which is likely to have disruptive consequences for Valley Bisa social life in the future, occurs between those who were reared prior to 1945 and those born after that date. Those belonging to the latter group have been exposed in their youth to sustained contact with "outsiders"—government teachers and agents resident in the valley. Eventually they are confronted, at least in the classroom, with the fact that their own parents and older kin are considered inferior role models by these representatives of a larger society. Today the desire of youth to remain in the valley and follow traditional pursuits seems largely outweighed by their ambition to gain status and to seek positions in other spheres such as politics, education, or commerce. I did not assess how these young people plan to come to terms with their conflicting aspirations.

The implications of all this for traditional hunting patterns are clear. Close acquaintance with individuals who hunt has been an important factor in the transmission of traditional lore, as I will discuss later. In the past this association has existed, but I encountered no young people on the study area under twenty-five years of age who even showed a fancy for hunting in 1966/67.[1] However, it is safe to predict that as long as there are Bisa in the Luangwa Valley and abundant game, some of these will engage in hunting, although its configuration may differ radically from that of the past.

Decline in Traditional Authority and in Village Size

During the early phases of Bisa settlement in the Luangwa Valley, people lived in small scattered settlements which were abandoned, if circumstances warranted such a move. Such flexibility provided mobility in their pursuit of game or escape from war parties. Later, when the Ngoni and Bemba raided Bisa territory from the north, the Bisa initially abandoned their villages for refuge in the Muchinga escarpment. Here caves were kept stocked with provisions for such emergencies. Under pressures from these groups and the Arabs toward the end of the nineteenth century, patterns changed again. Large stockaded villages (*ilinga*) were built for protection and many smaller ones were subsequently abandoned. Each of these villages contained at least one hundred huts, but with the subjugation of the slavers late in the 1890s, stockaded villages broke up rapidly.

In 1906 the British South Africa Company instigated its policy of amalgamating all villages containing less than twenty huts, but this edict was upheld with difficulty after the outpost at Nabwalya was closed. In 1908 over one hundred adults were imprisoned at Mpika after they repeatedly refused to live in large villages. Such harsh measures met with short-term success, but to maintain their sanction, punishments were repeated frequently. Under indirect rule, the regulation of village movement and size was returned to the chiefs. Although they were expected to maintain the village size at a certain level, villages became progressively smaller in size.

The reappearance of small settlements in the valley seemed a response to new social, political, and economic influences, as Long (1968) has argued for the Lala, but the pace of change in the valley has been much slower. A Bisa headman seemed aware of the emergence of new standards of power and social status when he said:

> There is a big difference in size of villages now. The villages used to be big with many people living in them. Now these have split into many small villages. Long ago when we had quarrels, those quarreling were called together and the elder men gave them advice so that the dispute could be settled and all could live again in peace. Now when people quarrel with the headman, they just go to

1. In 1973, there were two young people under 25 years of age who were training to become hunters. These were students during my previous stay in 1966. Upon completing their studies, they were unable to find employment. I plan to publish elsewhere a profile of Valley Bisa hunters.

Plate 5. "Then Lubeles climbed on top of the elephant and hit its rib cage with the butt of the gun, saying 'You animal, we are with you.'"

Plate 6. "Tusk removal was a major task which required four hours of work by two to three men. First the meat had to be removed from the skull. Then the bone surrounding the tusks had to be very carefully axed away."

Plate 7. Overview of valley floor during the dry season. Picture taken from atop Ngala hill at the site of abandoned government boma. The Munyamadzi River runs through the center of the picture at the left. (September 1966)

Plate 8. Overview of valley floor during wet season from atop Ngala hill. Note the height of river level and tall sorghums along the river's edge. (15 April 1967)

the chief and ask permission to start a new village saying they cannot tolerate that headman anymore. . . .

It is not so much sorcery. The main causes are young people growing up. They speak unnecessary things to their elders. They want modern new things instead of the old customs. The old men say they must move on to a new village so they can hang on to their old way of life (*mibela*).

The decline in the traditional authority of the headman and chief has undoubtedly been a contributing factor in the deline of village size. British domination brought administrative duties to authorities in the previous social system, for both chief and headman were incorporated into a formal hierarchy at the district level under the commissioner. The chief received a stipend, but both he and the headman were expected to enforce new laws and the regulations governing taxes, the clearing of paths, the reporting of illness, and the construction of sanitary facilities. Whereas the headmen retained some of their traditional status and prestige, the chieftainship progressively came to represent outside influences. This association was clear in 1967, for when the government sponsored discussions about the removal of the Bisa from the valley and their resettlement elsewhere, the assembled headmen repeatedly accused the chief of compliance with the government's plans.

Under the colonial administration, the chief relinquished his rights over resources and the right to tribute from his people in the form of labor, goods, and game. Now few cases are tried in the chief's court and the chief has been barred from attending the local court administered by the government. His people pay taxes to the government, and license fees to hunt and operate stores. In addition, the chief is no longer the protector and defender of his subjects, since these functions have been absorbed by the Zambian police and army. These changes in orientation have shifted the focus for much of Bisa political and economic activity from the valley proper.

Game Abundance, Government Restrictions, and Selection of Game

Bisa hunters were repeatedly of the opinion that the numbers of larger game close to their villages were a recent phenomenon of the past decade. Some explained these changes in abundance by the proximity of the game reserves and the sanctuary offered there to game. For others the increasing enforcement of government restrictions on the use of their traps, snares, and poisoned arrows explained game increases near villages. The decrease in village size and their alignment along the rivers have brought the Valley Bisa into close contact and competition with game during the dry season.

Prior to 1960, there was little enforcement of game laws, but since then the Game Department has increased the numbers of its active patrols within the corridor and staffs its guard camps throughout the year. In 1967 the seven guard camps in the corridor were each manned with up to four guards. The presence and mobility of these units has increased the probability of hunters, especially groups, being apprehended as "poachers." Activities of the game guards have reduced the amounts of game meat reaching illicit markets outside the valley and the number of game law convictions at the local court (see table 5) testifies to the diligence of these guards. The violations include the killing of game without a license or area permit, trespass into game reserves, collection of meat from lion kills without first reporting to authorities, and failure to enter game killed on a license. Game guards were more effective in curtailing the hunting activities of outsiders and individuals just returning from the cities than residents, for these hunters have evolved their own tactics to avoid detection by the game guards. They hunted secretively close to their villages, as individuals rather than large groups, and kept abreast of guard movements through informants.

One suspects that changes in hunting technology and organization also entail shifts in the selection of game. The Valley Bisa no longer kill for consumption baboons, leopards, elephant shrews, monkeys, or hippos, and have become selective in their predations on other game. Perhaps the interrelatedness of these factors can be shown by a discussion of the reasons why the Valley Bisa refuse hippo meat today.

Of the mammals formerly hunted, the flesh of the hippopotamus is the most generally avoided today (see table 14 in Chapter 6). Other observations reinforce this evidence that the refusal of hippo meat is genuine. An individual confided that in 1963 he had helped his headman dislodge a hippo back into the Munyamadzi River. This hippo was mistaken for a buffalo during the night and was killed as it climbed the river bank into his garden. When a dead hippo washed up on a sandbank in the Munyamadzi during our stay at Nabwalya, its meat was not consumed by any residents. Instead, they sent for the Bemba schoolteachers and ridiculed them as they salvaged meat from its rotting carcass. Outsiders who eat hippo are the objects of social ridicule, as is illustrated by the following account of a schoolteacher:

> A report came to me that the male hippopotamus had been shot dead by the headman in his garden near his house store. I went there with my fellow teachers to see the animal and collect the meat. When we arrived at the headman's house, we saw the dead hippo just near the store some ten yards from the headman's sleeping room. We told the headman to let his village men cut well the meat so that we should have our share. The men and women who had collected there to see the hippo laughed at us when they heard that we wanted its meat very much, because many of the Bisa people do not eat hippo meat traditionally, and they believe that the person who had suffered from leprosy for a long time and was living a lonely life in the bush died and was

> buried but was later found floating with mats on the water of a certain river. And they went to the place where they had buried this person but didn't get or find any body in the grave. After some weeks they saw a young hippo swimming near the mat in which the dead body was rolled and the dead body was not there. So the Bisa people concluded to believe that the people who suffer from leprosy turn themselves into hippo after death and that whoever eat hippo's meat could suffer from the same horrible disease. We teachers had our share of its meat. We didn't pay attention to their laughter. We are eating the meat very well; and we like it very much. Chief Nabwalya too sent word that he should also be sent some meat, and certainly much of it was sent to him and he enjoyed it.

That more was at issue than fear of leprosy is suggested by the chief's observation that his people ate hippo during famines: "When there was famine we killed and ate hippo and there is no reason for not eating it now. The Europeans stopped the people from killing hippo and now the people aren't interested in killing and eating it anymore."

The following hypothesis may explain the refusal of hippo meat by the Valley Bisa. When they first settled in the Luangwa Valley, the Valley Bisa had few, if any, guns. With their bows and arrows, weighted spears, and pits many men cooperated in order to kill large and certain of the smaller mammals. Because of their amphibious habits and the limited number of wallows during the dry season, hippos were easy prey for these organized guilds whose depredations severely limited hippo numbers. When Europeans established their control over the territory, hippo populations were at low levels and undoubtedly some officials attempted to stop the hunting of hippo by Africans and other Europeans. But generally their efforts were not effective, or rather, the scarcity of hippo made hunting them unprofitable for the Bisa. Letcher (1911) and Gouldsbury and Sheane (1911), mention hippos as protected game in the middle Luangwa, and Lane-Poole's (1956) recollection of the valley in 1918 suggests that encountering any hippo on the Luangwa was worthy of mention. Attwell (1963) mentions a European hunter's difficulty in securing his allotment of twelve hippo in the 1930s. Although he hunted for several weeks, this hunter secured only four hippo. In 1939 the species was granted complete protection within the valley rivers north of the Beit Bridge (Attwell 1963).

Labor migrations instituted by Europeans drained the ranks of specialized guilds, and with the availability of muzzleloading guns, hunting in groups was no longer a necessity. The 1962 census of Nabwalya's chieftaincy showed 55 percent of the adult males absent and employed in urban centers. The percentage of males in the cities was probably higher in the past. I suggest that with the hippo population under some protection by the government and their numbers at low levels, it was unlikely for individual hunters to kill hippo. Instead, it was probably more profitable for them to pursue land mammals whose populations were increasing close to their villages. Consequently, several generations of Valley Bisa have not tasted hippo and it has become a prohibited food with informal restrictions against its consumption. Since many "traditional" values of the Valley Bisa are threatened, the refusal of hippo flesh often functions as a symbol of their unity against outside authority, for most government personnel in contact with them relish hippo meat. With this in mind, the following comment by a headman is relevant: "We have enough meat relish (*munani*) without having to eat hippo. We fear eating the meat because we might get leprosy. I know our ancestors ate it, but now we have plenty of meat without hippo and baboons."

Thus the Valley Bisa do not consume the flesh of hippo for many interrelated reasons, and probably they are not those reasons most likely expressed.

TRAPPERS AND TRAPS

The Valley Bisa possess a variety of traps, some of which are ingeniously adapted to the habits of their prey. Unlike hunting, anyone can set traps, for trapping (*kola*) is not considered an organized or specialized skill, nor one in which magic plays a major role. Although in the past they employed many traps around their villages and fields and in the bush along game trails, today due to government interference, traps are restricted mostly to the margins of fields or concealed around dry-season watering places. Certainly the frequency in use of the more visible kinds of traps and game pits has diminished, although the knowledge of a variety of techniques remains. Children set a number of traps for small birds and mammals in and around fields; and some of these with modifications may be used for larger game. My list of traps is suggestive rather than exhaustive for undoubtedly a wider variety was used in the past.

The use of the harpoon downfall (*chisumpi*), shown in Figure 7, was widespread in Central Africa (Lagercrantz 1934). This trap was deployed by the Valley Bisa against a variety of big game including elephants, hippopotami, and buffalo. According to a middle-aged man, these traps were in use around Nabwalya until the 1940s, and have been recorded in Kamwendo in more recent times.

The principle of the spring pole snare (*chitembo*), shown in Figure 8, is adapted for trapping a variety of game ranging from birds to buffalo. A bent sapling or branch provides the spring, while a string noose held in position over a hole by three smaller sticks becomes the trigger. When an approaching animal breaks the trigger twig, the sapling straightens and suspends the prey in the air by its leg or neck. Baobab fiber provides the string.

Figure 7. Harpoon downfall. Metal points embedded in a heavy log were suspended over active hippopotami paths

In the Luangwa Valley these snares are usually set in the late dry season around water holes. Bush fences around these water holes restrict access to a few openings in which snares are set. Magic is used by some to lure animals in the trap (*ulwito lia nama*). Prior to 1945, these snares were in regular use; if used at all now, they are well hidden.

The Valley Bisa use two kinds of game pits (*buzima*), one for smaller buck and another for elephant and hippo. These are shown in Figure 9. Generally these pits are dug along trails leading to water or around the margins of fields. Before digging a pit, the ground at the site is struck with a branch of *musolo*. Its white bark is a symbol of fortune and its leaves and fruits are reportedly relished by game.

For smaller game a rectangular pit is dug with the long axis in and parallel to the trail. A small pole is placed across each end, perpendicular to the long axis, then smaller ones are laid from the edge of the pit to the smaller pole and overlaid with grasses. The grass stalks are braided together at the ends and their length is adjusted so that their free ends meet in the middle of the open hole. The portions of the trap underlaid with

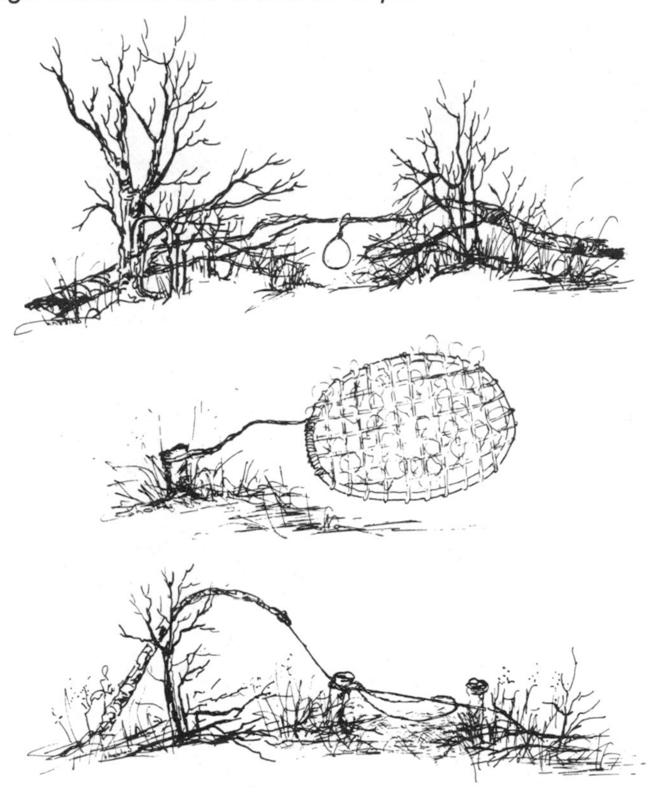

Figure 8. Noose snares and spring pole snare. Snare (above top) typically set for guinea fowl while snare (middle) here shown elevated at an angle was concealed in sand for small birds. The principle of the spring pole snare (below) was used for a variety of mammals.

sticks are covered with dirt while the rest of the pit is covered by grass and leaves.

Rectangular pits (*buzima bwa ntando*) are seven to eight feet deep. Some of these, while rectangular at the mouth, taper down to a rounded bottom. In the center of the bottom is placed a spear or sharp wooden spike (*kabonga*). Rectangular pits are used occasionally today especially around gardens plagued by game.

To my knowledge, the round game pit (*namunchimba*) is no longer used. Its primary use was for elephant and hippo whose paths are normally wide and free of litter. Pits were dug six to seven feet in diameter and nine to ten feet in depth. In the bottom were placed two or more poisoned spears in an upright position. Two long poles placed for support in the center were notched near the middle so they would break readily. Small sticks supported the canopy of grass which was smeared with mud to resemble the game trail.

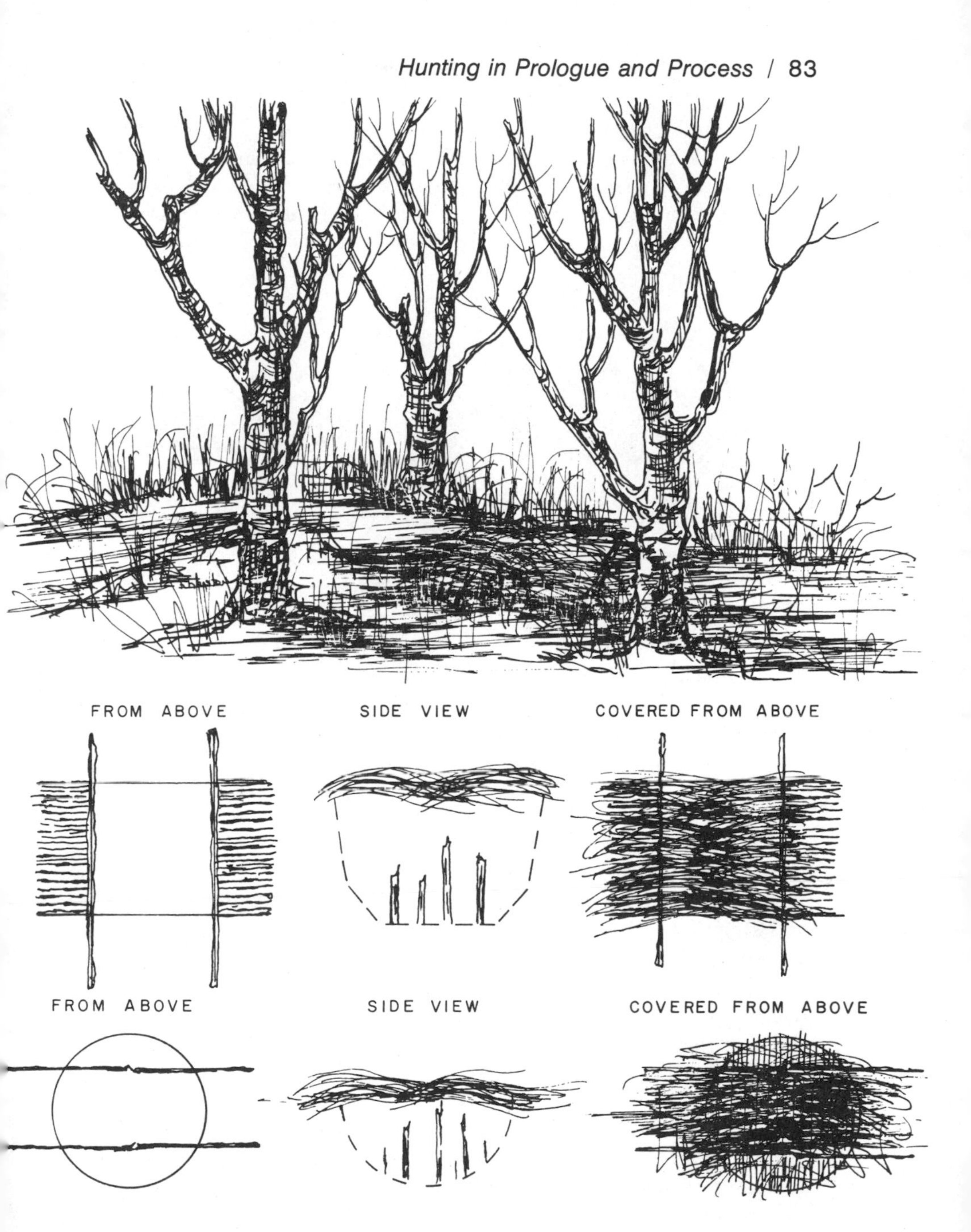

Figure 9. Game pits. Sketch shows pit hidden in landscape. Steps in construction of rectangular (center) and round game pits (below) are shown in two views.

Constriction traps (*muzeka chambala*), pictured in Figure 10, consist of a funnel constructed of small vines interlaced between supporting sticks. From a wide mouth, the funnel tapers to one end. These traps are placed along the trails of small mammals and used in conjunction with drives and dogs. Sometimes the entrance is modified with sharpened spikes facing inward so that an animal easily enters the trap but finds it impossible to back out.

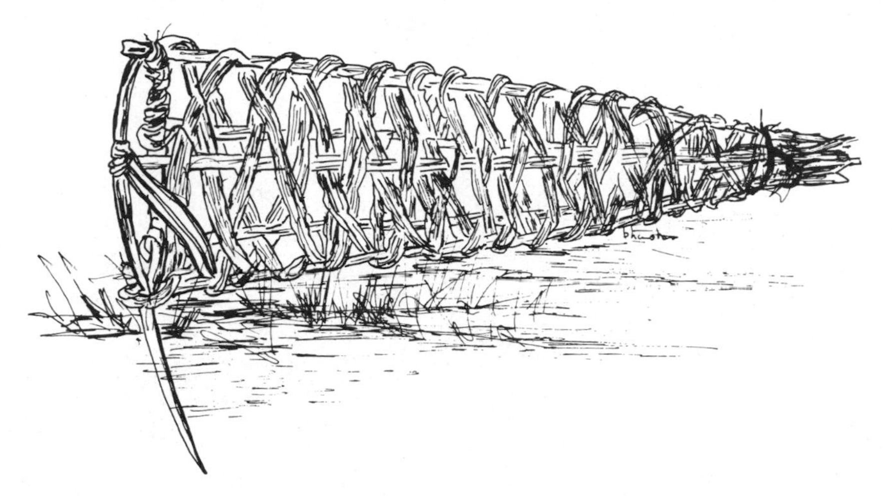

Figure 10. Constriction traps were effective for a number of medium-sized mammals.

Triangular basket traps (*ichumba*) are employed principally for monkeys and baboons and are set under large trees frequented by them. The trap is fashioned from poles joined together by bark lashings with the inside forming an open enclosure. The narrow end is secured to the ground with logs and rocks while the wider one is lifted above the ground and triggered with a stick lying horizontally above the trap and baited with sorghum. When the baboon or monkey pulled at the sorghum, the horizontal stick is released and the weighted basket falls and covers the animal.

Noose snares (*bukuka*), Figure 8, are commonly used today for guineafowl, francolins, and doves. A fence (*ombe*) of thorns and branches with small openings is constructed in an area frequented by these birds. Above the small openings, a noose (*idengo*) is suspended from a branch so that a bird attempting to go through the opening catches its neck in the noose and strangles itself. There are many variations of the noose snare. *Bukuka bwa kupompomela*, also called *chinzala*, is made of a round frame on which is tied a rough net of bark strips (see figure 8). To each of the knots of the net is attached a long black hair noosed at its free end. The frame is buried in sand and grain is scattered over its concealed position.

The noosed hairs then ensnare the feet, wings, or heads of birds feeding on the grain.

Chinanda is another type of noose snare used for many types of small birds. A cone of twigs is constructed and stood on end with its mouth on the ground. A small branch tied around with the cone three inches above the ground is suspended with nooses. Sorghum in the center of the cone attracts birds, which put their necks into the nooses and are strangled.

Boys are generally given free reign in their trapping activities and allowed to keep the birds which they snare. Most discriminating adults would not eat many of the common birds which frequent the environs of villages, but these are allowed boys. They are cautioned, however, against snaring the pied wagtail for if one of these is killed, it is considered a bad omen for the village.

VI

Programming a Hunter

> Seek ye, seek ye, (the spirits) of our land
> Those who killed without missing
> The spirits move in the evening.
>
> Bisa Song

BECOMING A HUNTER

SUBSISTENCE hunting involves commitment and training which relate to the social milieu within which an individual matures and lives. To ascertain the sociological factors responsible for an individual's choice of hunting as a career, I collected life histories of the main hunters within the study area and of four hunters living elsewhere in the corridor. The three factors predisposing these men to become hunters and the relationships which they considered important during the crucial stages of their training are discussed below.

Lineage Affiliation and Training

Hunting as a way of life involves the transference of skills from one generation to the next. An initial factor inclining an individual toward hunting is lineage affiliation and close contact with hunters during his youth. Usually a person does not become a hunter on his own initiative, but belongs to a lineage, the members of which are practiced in hunting traditions.

Hunters stressed that their ancestral spirits, through the medium of dreams, had initially summoned them to that specialty. In some cases, youths received their early training and instruction from their fathers if they were hunters. For most individuals, their mother's brother or maternal grandfather taught them basic skills.

The hunters' genealogy given in Figure 11 shows a preference of cross-cousin marriage between members of four lineages. In addition, the figure illustrates the decreasing number of persons identified as hunters in each generation. All deceased males in the B rank were identified by their descendants as hunters. Most males in the C rank, now over fifty-five years of age or deceased, were hunters, but only two males in the D

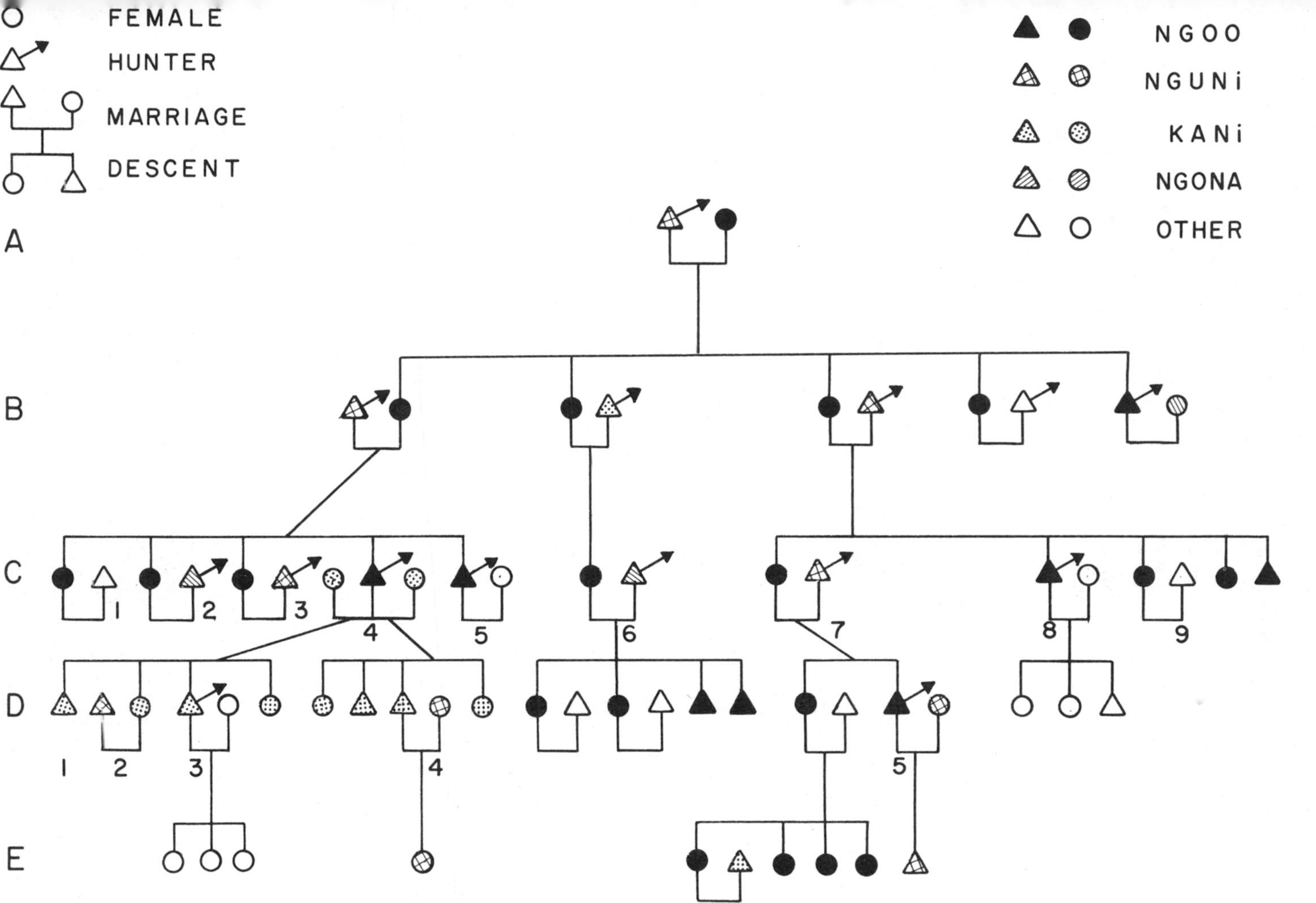

Figure 11. A hunter's genealogy illustrating the prevalence of cross-cousin marriage and decrease in professional hunting among male members

rank and none in the C rank considered themselves as such. C4 trained both D3 and D5 to hunt.

The ties of a young man with his matrilineage are largely of a legal nature. It is from them that he inherits his gun and among them that he distributes the larger share of his kills. Attachment between father and son is largely an emotional one in which the father, as an "outsider," is expected to aid his son in acquiring a skill. This is in keeping with the normative patterns of parents toward their offspring. The child's matrikin, particularly his maternal uncle, assumes responsibility for the child's nurture and development of that skill.

Young hunters usually begin by pursuing small birds and mammals with bows and arrows. Later they join adults on hunting trips and on these expeditions absorb information on animal signs, stalking, and techniques for killing mammals and the appropriate lineage rites over the carcasses of slain beasts.

Position in Matrilineal Descent Group

Another factor disposing an individual toward hunting is his position in his matrilineal descent group. An individual strategically placed for winning the support of his siblings and of succeeding to some position of influence and authority among his matrikin may prefer to remain in the valley among them rather than spend years away in urban employment. Of the twelve hunters for whom I have life histories, seven were village headmen, two were not. The remaining three were considered too young to succeed to this position.

The role of hunter is defined in terms of the rights and obligations of the individual toward others and of others toward him. An individual, by virture of circumstances, might be expected and prevailed upon to assume this role if no other lineage members are available. This role is implied in rituals which are held when the hunter first receives his weapon, upon his first kill, and in his solicitation of ancestral assistance before undertaking to hunt. The ritual establishing a youth as the hunter for his matrikin is described in the following passage taken from an interview:

> My maternal grandfather, a great hunter, visited me in a dream telling me to find a gun and begin hunting. When I told my maternal uncle about this dream, he advised me to go and purchase a gun in Serenje District. For this I used money earned while working in Wankie. When I returned, my uncle called all of our relatives together. Each elder in my lineage, there were three men and several women, put three white beads on a string and tied them around my gun. My maternal uncle as senior member of the lineage pronounced the following blessing: *Unwaice uyu akwate imfuti. Ayokwendo mutende muchonde. Ayokwipaya inama kulya palupwa.* [This youngster has the gun. May he go well in the bush. May he kill so we can eat.] Before dispersing we

put other white beads into a *nkombo* [special type of gourd given by his maternal uncle] and it was named for and dedicated to my late ancestor.

Although components of this ritual vary, the messages implied by the acts are similar. Through the idiom of an ancestral call, an individual establishes the validity of his professional choice. Then he must prove himself as a hunter in coping with real or imagined dangers in the natural world and the petty jealousies and rivalries of his kin in the social world, for when successful he must distribute the proceeds from his kill in accordance with their expectations. Unity among the kin group is represented through their assembly and corporate blessing. Yet the same ritual complex stresses that the hunter is not solely responsible for his demonstrated ability afield. It may be his ancestor whose spiritual help and protection is solicited, but in a wider sense this ancestor is shared by other members of his social group. Thus in the ritual idiom of the Valley Bisa, a hunter's success is dependent not as much upon his own accomplishments as upon the spiritual merit in his lineage.

Recognition of ancestral guidance and protection is symbolized in a rite in which a hunter asks for help prior to his departure from the village. Elements of these rites are described in the following passage from an interview relating to a hunter's protective spirit:

> If in a lineage there was a great hunter in the past, the hunter prior to leaving the village calls upon his name (*ishina lia mutoto*). The hunter takes a special gourd (*nkombo*) and places therein sorghum flour and water. If the dead ancestor has a surviving young grandson or granddaughter (*bazikulu*) these items are placed in the gourd by this relative. Also in the gourd are placed a few white beads. Then the hunter holds the gourd and, after mentioning the ancestor's name, says "*Muntangilela muchonde*" [Go before me in the bush].
>
> If an animal is killed on that day, the heart is taken and cut down the middle. Blood is smeared on the outside of the gourd. In the process the hunter says "*Tuamupake inama, inshiku yonse okuipaya. Mwilafulwa muyo ukuntangilila penape.*" [We give you meat every time a kill is made. Do not become disappointed with me. Guide me always.].

When a hunter kills his initial animal, there may be further ceremonies (*vizimba viamutwe wanama*):

> In the past, a hunter would cut off the head of the slain animal. The head was cooked outside of the house without salt. The hunter invited his fellow hunters, who brought their guns, and other matrikin. Beer was brewed especially for the occasion. Drums would beat and those present danced and sang songs about hunting. They consumed meat from the head. Early the next morning the young hunter took a piece of the nose of the animal, a piece of magic which he used to secure the animal and buried these in a path used by those same animals. After this, the hunter could sleep with his wife if he wished. He could not have intercourse with her before the ceremony was completed.

Such ceremonies and rituals punctuate stages in the development of a young hunter's career. They define the young hunter's role as it relates to other professionals, his matrikin, and his ancestors. From adepts, a youth seeks knowledge, techniques, magic, and eventual acceptance. From his matrikin he solicits understanding, status, and recognition. The primary arena for his role is among his close matrikin, and his adroitness in his relations among them in large measure determines his eventual success or failure. Although the ceremonies, rituals, and lore differ in minor detail among lineages, these differences emphasize the importance of internalizing one's own traditions.

The implications for a young man who accepts the role as hunter is suggested by the circumstances of Lubeles, a middle-aged hunter who had been consistently helpful in assisting me and to whom I felt indebted. Knowing of his desire for local employment, I made arrangements for him to work in the South Luangwa Game Reserve. His work there would not allow him to hunt, a consideration which troubled him. Shortly before I left he confided that his ancestral spirits would trouble him if he accepted this employment because he would not be allowed to kill game. He pleaded that I intercede with his future employer that he be permitted to kill occasionally to appease his spirits.

Although game is scarce and many of the traditional hunting techniques of the Gwembe Tonga are prohibited by the government, Scudder (1962) records that hunters still, for fear of angering their predecessors' spirits, pour occasional libations and perform token acts of the traditional rituals.

Nature of an Individual's Urban Experience and Personality

Another element, actually a complex of interrelated factors, predisposing an individual toward hunting is the nature of his urban experience and personality. With the exception of those who were teenagers in 1967 and who had obtained up to five years of schooling, most Valley Bisa males are illiterate. As good jobs carrying status in the cities have become difficult for illiterate migrants to acquire, most adults resign themselves to accepting employment, when and where it can be found, either underground in the mines, as domestic servants for Europeans, or as menial laborers for more skilled workers.

Previous generations of men were able to combine migrant labor with traditional skills. Money derived from time spent at jobs in the cities was exchanged for gifts and cloth for their dependents back in the valley and time between jobs or vacations was spent in the valley farming and hunting. This was the pattern for many of the older men on the study area. But those in the age group between the elders and young boys with education are the ones who face the most difficulties in bridging the gap between urban and valley life.

Of the hunters on the study area, two younger men spent more time hunting than did the rest. Both had worked in towns on occasion but both harbored a dislike for the regimentation and impositions of city life. It was said of both that they felt more at home in the bush than in the village, which may have reflected their age and stage in life rather than dislike of people. One of these individuals, moreover, harbored a distrust of Europeans and was said to refuse the advice of his kin, for which he had been given the nickname of *mupaza* ("long headed one"). During the days when Zambia (then Northern Rhodesia) was federated with Nyasaland and Rhodesia, this individual refused to pay his levies. Instead, these were paid by his maternal uncle. Several times he evaded police, sent from Mpika to reprimand him, by fleeing into the bush and subsisting there for several days until the police left.

Within recent years a possible factor predisposing individuals toward remaining in the valley has been their disenchantment with the rigorous routine and imposition of city work. Both of the two young men mentioned had close association with hunters in their youth, and had appropriate training and background as hunters; consequently, their disillusionment with the city led them to return to the valley.

These three factors were important for those interviewed in their choice to become hunters. If these are the major factors then we should expect that deficiency with respect to one or more of them (especially inadequate training or improper genealogical ranking) would bar an individual from becoming a recognized hunter. The abbreviated life history of Mbozo and the comments of one who attempted to hunt lends substance to this assertion.

> When I was born the people said my mother had slept with someone else and that was how I was conceived. The people wanted to kill my mother and me. We were taken to a diviner who said that my mother had not slept with someone besides her husband and there was no case. As my father was dead, we returned home where I was reared by my mother and grandfather.
>
> My mother and grandfather were responsible for giving me counsel and advice as to how to live. They told me to be kind to all people or else I would die. . . . A stepfather cared for me until I married. When I married, my mother told me that I should work very hard digging sorghum and that I should not be a "restless" person. When my first son was born, I was told not to meet any woman privately in the bush lest my child die, but that I should remain faithful to my wife and child. This is what I learned from my stepfather and when my child matured I gave him the same advice.
>
> I started hunting with a bow and arrows which my maternal grandfather left me when he died. The spirits of my grandfather came to me and forced me into the bush and I started killing animals. When I went to another hunter and asked for medicines, I was given *mubambangoma*, *kamulebe*, and *motamfumu*. I collected the medicines and put them in a *chikombe* pot and washed my bow.

Apparently Mbozo was successful in pursuing game with bow and arrows, for he told me that with these weapons he killed buffalo, zebra, waterbuck, impala, and warthog. He went to Luanshya and after a few years returned with a muzzleloading gun which he had purchased from wages received for working in the mines. He hunted for a year before he left for work again.

After working in Salisbury, Kitwe, Wankie, and again in Luanshya, he returned. For a while he enjoyed success at hunting, but when his luck abruptly changed he had questions. When Mbozo visited a diviner concerning this misfortune he learned another hunter had prepared a special magic to keep him from killing game. Shortly thereafter Mbozo was charged by a wounded buffalo and barely escaped with his life. This experience convinced him of the seriousness of that hunter's intentions and he subsequently abandoned hunting, for he was convinced that should he continue, the other hunter's magic would eventually kill him.

As long as game is numerous and guns are easily accessible for most males, there will be those who will try their luck at hunting. The comments of one who did so and his reasons for quitting are illuminating.

> Question: Were you ever a hunter?
>
> Answer: I bought a muzzleloading gun but am afraid it will burst in my hands. I gave it to my elder brother (a headman). I tried to shoot a buffalo once with another hunter, but it got away. I am not from a hunting lineage so even the possession of a good gun will not turn me into a successful hunter.
>
> Question: How do you regard hunters who are successful?
>
> Answer: Some people are born brave (*ubukali*). When they get guns their bravery helps them. Some people say it is the spirits and powerful magics which help them but I don't believe that for it is their bravery instead. I was born not very brave.

INFORMATION INPUT

The ideology of a group is an important component of social life, for it defines dangers and develops attitudes and sentiments among group members. The traditional world view of the Valley Bisa is heavily personal and human-oriented. Elements of nature are generally considered well-disposed toward man, although not actively benevolent. In this section I describe the cognitive patterns through which the Valley Bisa perceive mammals and their pursuit.

Classification of Mammals

For mammals and their groupings the Valley Bisa employ many of the same terms by which they differentiate among humans. *Mutundu* is the common word for tribe; it is also employed in reference to a natural species. For example, elephant, buffalo, impala, and warthog all belong to different *mitundu*. *Lupwa*, meaning family or matrilineal descent group in references to humans, may also imply a group of mammals with offspring. I heard the Bisa refer to a herd of cow and calf elephants as *zilibumba*. A village headman uses *ibumba* in reference to his sorority group of female dependents. *Mulongo* may be used interchangeably with reference to small groups of people and animals, whereas *kasanje* is restricted to animals only.

All cultural systems possess rules or codes which permit the classification of large numbers of things in a relatively simple fashion. The Valley Bisa refer to all edible game as *nama* and distinguish between species (see table 13). Mammals are classified according to size, sex, age, color, and individual peculiarities. The multiplicity of terms and linguistic usuages relating to a game species may serve as an index of its significance. Largeness is a characteristic stressed and it is synonymous with "maleness" if the species shows obvious secondary sexual characteristics. In species where the sexes are similar, the specific name modified by an adjective relates its sex. Additional terms may be employed to distinguish age in most species: *kana* refers to a young mammal, *chilumelume* to most, if not all, young males, and *mukote* to a very old mammal.

In addition mammals are classified by relative size. *Nama ikulu* refers to large mammals such as elephant, buffalo, rhino, eland, zebra, lion, hippo, and giraffe. Most antelopes are called *nama mpele*. Smaller mammals such as the bushbaby (*changa*), bush squirrel (*kazidiye*), and rats and mice (*bakoswe*) are collectively called *tunama tunini*.

The elephant, because of its size, is figuratively called the "mother of all animals." An elder whom I pressed for a reason why magic was not used to keep elephants from raiding fields rationalized as follows:

> Magic (*muti*) can't stop elephants. The elephant is wonderfully made. Its body is a mixture of all animals. The muscles in its neck (indicating with his hand the area on his skull behind the ears) are made of the same substances as impala, zebra, and all other animals. All *vibanda* are in the elephant. People used to call the elephant *zimwe-zimwe*—the most powerful and biggest of all mammals.
>
> The elephant is like a python (*luzato*), the "mother" of all snakes. The python when it bears young, bears them alive. It produces cobra, python, and all other snakes. The poison of all snakes is in the python. If one is bitten by a python and lives, he will be protected from all other snakes. The elephant is the biggest in the whole country. It is all-powerful. You cannot make magic against it.

Mammals are also differentiated depending on whether or not their skin is useful (*nama ya masako* or *nama yambula masako*) and as to whether the species has hooves (*vibondo*) or claws (*viala*). But for the Valley Bisa, the primary categories are those of color. As with many other Central African groups, their scheme is based upon a triad of red, black, and white. *Nama ziasweta*, literally "red animals," includes the tawny or

TABLE 13

DIFFERENTIATION WITHIN SPECIES CATEGORIES AMONG THE LARGER MAMMALS RECORDED FOR THE VALLEY BISA

Bisa Name Species	Categories	English Equivalent
nzofu		Elephant
	nkungulu	Large bull elephant
	nyinanzofu	Cow elephant
	chibuluma	Young elephant (without tusks)
	chipembe	Elephant with one tusk
	sante	Elephant with four tusks
	nyungwa	Elephant without tusks
	tondo	Elephant without tusks (cf. *tondo*—elephant shrew)
chipembele		Rhinoceros
	bukodi	Large rhinoceros
mvubu		Hippo
	chipandwe	Bull hippo
ndyabuluba, nkalikiti		Giraffe
mboo		Buffalo
	kakuli	Large, solitary bull
	nyinangombe	Cow buffalo
	mukuni (ibumba)	Herd of buffalo
nzefu		Eland
	bulundwe	Bull eland
	bulundwe nguno	Solitary male
	cinsombonsombo	Juvenile eland
mpulupulu		Kudu
	magobede	Male kudu
	nyinampulupulu	Female kudu
chuzwe		Waterbuck
	chipangala	Male waterbuck
mpala		Impala
	kakonje	Male impala
	namavwamba	Female impala
chikwiba (chisongo)		Bushbuck
nsebula		Puku
	kapempe	Male puku
nyumbu		Wildebeest
	munpangwe	Male wildebeest
nkonzi		Lichtenstein's hartebeest
	chinkovanya	Large hartebeest
	nkonkotela	"Twisted horns"
mpelembe		Roan antelope
kashilye		Sable antelope
	iloko	Male sable
mpombo		Common duiker
	nsha	Used in proverbs
katidi		Sharpe's grysbok
cibushimabwe		Klipspringer
mfwi		Reed buck

TABLE 13 con't

Differentiation Within Species Categories among the Larger Mammals Recorded for the Valley Bisa

Bisa Name Species	Categories	English Equivalent
chimbwete		Zebra
	chingalika, munkoloto	(Word onomonopoetic for the way it runs)
munjili		Warthog
	chembelume	Male warthog
	itunta	Young warthog of either sex
ngulube		Bushpig
	chilondo	Adult male bushpig
kolwe		Baboon
	tumbidi	Male baboon
chibuli		Honey badger
	nzenga	Male honey badger
nkalamo		Lion
	mundu	Male lion, hunter
	nyinankalamo	Lioness
	mukutu	Nickname
ngoo (mbwili)		Leopard
	lunda	Large leopard
chimbwi		Hyena
	chindingo	Large hyena
mumbulu		Hunting dog
	kamutu	Adult hunting dog
cizumpa		Cheetah
nkalamo lubwabwa		Caracal
mumbwe		Jackal
ngwena		Crocodile
	ngandu	Large male crocodile
	ipungwe	Small crocodile

Note: No hierarchical ranking is suggested by the order in which names are listed.

khaki mammals such as impala, lion, puku, roan antelope, and hartebeest. In this group belongs the hippo (*zwetulukila*, or "red-like"). The configuration and placement of these colors is important; the roan antelope, for instance, belongs in this category because it is *wabuta kanwa* ("white about the mouth"). Black mammals, *nama ziafita*, form another group which includes the buffalo, rhino, elephant, jackal, antbear, warthog, and waterbuck.

Occasionally white or albinistic mammals are encountered. Such mammals are considered *mipashi*—protective "presences" which guard the herds with which they run. Other "mythical" animals, variously described as red or white or combinations of these colors, associate with and protect large herds of buffalo.

All other mammals which have two or more distinct colors on their pelage are grouped as *vizemba.* Included in this category are zebra, leopard, wild cat, bushbuck, kudu, eland, wild dog, cape polecat, and giraffe. Most of those in this class are considered nonedible, yet those which are palatable (eland, kudu, bushbuck, and zebra) may be prohibited to individuals.

Chizwango (*chipondo*) refers abstractly to any wild animal capable of harming or killing human beings. Normally elephant, hippo, buffalo, lion, leopard, venomous snakes, and crocodile are referred to as *chizwango*, although the term may be extended to include an individual hyena, wild dog, rhino, or other wild beast which has killed a human being. *Chizwango* also refers to a person who accidently or purposely kills another human. Dangerous mammals are never addressed or spoken about by their specific names should they be encountered in the bush. Otherwise, their spirits might think they are being summoned and attack rather than flee. All large mammals have nicknames which are used in casual conversation, such as *munyepe* for elephant, *chigwele* for hippo, and *pundangala* for lion.

Since not everyone is knowledgeable about classification, my list was compiled from information gained from hunters. In East Africa, Whiteley (1966) mentions that the variability he recorded in classifying schemes of fish was related to the range of experience and uses of these vertebrates by his respondents. Saleability and size were important categories for merchants ashore, but for fishermen, criteria of behavior or bait selection were the basic categories.

Attributes of Mammals

Each group has its own leader or guide (*ntungulushi* or *chilongozi*). This individual usually has the largest body size and hoofprint and is most often seen in front leading the rest.

> The *ntungulushi* has to lead its group where there is good grazing. Where it goes, others must follow. These *ntungulushi* are very difficult for us to kill, and if one happens to kill such a leader when a herd is raiding crops, it will be a long time before that herd will come back to raid those crops again. This is because there hasn't come another leader to replace their dead one.

Implicit in this and other comments is that such large, powerful leaders possess magic. Some older mammals were said to possess more powerful magic (*bwanga*) than hunters and for this reason are able to escape predation. In particular, eland lends a protective presence to other species with which it associates. Large herds of buffalo have their own protectors, as illustrated in a response to my question about why a large buffalo, which had been wounded, escaped.

> There is a little animal in the form of a spirit which protects the biggest buffalo. It is called *kakoba*. To know that there is this little animal about there will be many animals, black and white grazing together, buffalo and other animals. This "satanic" animal is going around protecting his herd and any hunter will shoot his gun in vain.
>
> Question: What color is this small guard and what are its other characteristics?
>
> Answer: It is white. It is rarely seen. It walks on the buffalo and protects them. The *kakoba* is like a priest (*shimapepo*) among all the animals. It won't be found in small groups of animals, only among many. The hunter will not kill an animal where *kakoba* is because it is like an evil spirit (*chiwa*). If a hunter happens to shoot at an animal which *kakoba* is protecting his bullet will go elsewhere.

Elephants and warthogs, which frequently dig in the ground for roots, are said to be looking for magical substances to protect themselves from predators. Like their human counterparts, lions and other large carnivores are believed to possess powerful hunting magics (*muti wabufundi*).

> The lion is the best of all in searching for magics to help it catch animals. We suspect it to have hunting magics because when it catches an animal it first opens the abdomen and picks out the *kafiza* [one of the several parts of an ungulate's stomach—said to have "pages" like a book]. The qualities of this magic are known only to the lion. Then it digs a hole and buries the *kafiza* before it comes back to feed on the carcass. I have seen this behavior many times, also the hole and its contents.

Mammals also have their protective spirits (*mipashi*) but these spirits are not normally as powerful as those of humans. Like humans, mammals hold certain areas sacred where they worship and solicit assistance from their ancestors.

Of more concern to hunters is the belief that all mammals have evil shades (*vibanda*) capable of afflicting hunters and their relatives should the proper death rituals not be performed. Such *vibanda* are described in the following manner: "Some have very nasty *vibanda*. There are many people who have short tempers. Some game have such tempers also. They have bad hearts and are easily made wild. When you shoot one of these dangerous mammals, elephant, lion, or eland, you must get the ritual substances from an experienced hunter who has killed such a mammal previously." Mammalian shades are ranked, with those of eland, lion, wild dog, and elephant being the most dangerous. The consequences for not placating the spirits of these mammals is sickness or death to the hunter or someone in his lineage. The *vibanda* of other game may enter the hunter's gun and render it impure (*kuikate mfuti*). These consequences are expected to follow should a hunter deviate from traditional patterns of rituals and behavior.

Live mammals show an uncanny awareness of human customs. This thought is apparent in the following account of a tragedy:

> In 1961 Chikunda, a game guard, was called to Kalinka Village to kill a bull elephant which had been persistently raiding village granaries. The elephant was surprised and shot within the confines of the village but only feigned dead. At that time it was customary for villagers to present chickens and sorghum to game guards when they had killed a marauding elephant. So when these presents were given, the elephant recognized his tormentor, charged the hunter, knocked him to the ground, mangled his leg and punctured his abdomen with a tusk. Chikunda took a full year in the hospital to recover.

Most mammalian attributes are similar to those ascribed to humans, and in this sense the Valley Bisa are not so different from other preliterate societies. Both mammal and human spirits are believed to interact continuously with the human community and take an interested view in the moral decisions and acts of its members. Yet this is not to say that there are no critical distinctions made between the two. As one informant stressed: "Mammals do not have houses as people do. Also game animals are not selective in their matings. They have intercourse with any other of their species whereas people select man and wife together. Game does not do this; they may have intercourse with their own mothers. Mammals do not have shame. These are some of the ways in which we differ from them."

Ascribing anthropomorphic characteristics to game from a functional standpoint reinforced traditional patterns of social organization and control. The conviction that important game species were infested with malign spirits subjugated young hunters to adepts, and adepts to the chiefs on whose land these species were slain. To avoid mystical alienation, each group had its part in the prescribed rituals. Beliefs attributing haunting shades to lesser species suggested that hunters follow traditional norms in the distribution of meat.

The beliefs about mammals presented above are based upon traditional premises and these patterns have been given substance for some hunters at least by their own experiences. But the degree to which beliefs were expressly held varies among individuals. With recent changes in social organization and weaponry for a few individuals there have been concomitant changes in their cosmology, for I recorded some interpretations at variance with those expressed above. An apparent break with previous traditions was in reference to the nature of mammalian shades, for those who had hunted with Europeans or who had had access to modern breechloading weapons often dismissed the importance of these spirits. One individual claimed that mammals had no spiritual essence, only life (*muoyo*).

Some hunters told me that the spirits of slain game, if properly placated, would influence and send other members of their species to the hunter. But when I asked another about this belief, he replied: "No! If a hunter has magic, his magic will attract (*kuite nama*) animals. It is not another animal's spirit which sends them." However, with few exceptions, the patterns of beliefs described seemed functional in the minds and behavior of most hunters.

Prohibitions on Meats

From the standpoint of cultural adaptation, the most important use of animals is for food. All cultures are selective regarding the palatability of various species and have differing ideas about what people should eat. The Valley Bisa do not indiscriminantly consume all types of game meat, and some individuals regularly abstain from eating one or more types. In addition, there are other meats which they normally will not touch, but with the exception of the hippo, most Valley Bisa consume one or more of the animals listed in Table 14. Most food prohibitions are imposed on the individual by an African diviner who makes the cure of the patient conditional upon the avoidance of certain foods. A few individuals institute their own prohibitions because of a sinister association with a particular species. For example, an elderly woman refused buffalo meat because her father was killed by one.

Striped mammals (*vizemba*) are a group of mammals prohibited in many parts of Central Africa. Among this group zebra, bushbuck, kudu,

TABLE 14

FOOD PROHIBITIONS AMONG ADULT VALLEY BISA

	Males	% Sample	Females	% Sample
Mammal				
Hippo	56	90	91	100
Baboon[1]	27	44	34	37
Zebra[2]	11	18	19	21
Bushbuck[2]	6	10	4	4
Eland[2]	2	3	3	3
Elephant	2	3	1	1
Warthog	2	3	. . .	. . .
Other large mammals	3	5	5	6
Fowl				
Chicken	1	2	6	7
Fish				
Kaponta (catfish)[2]	5	8	13	14
Mbubu[2]	2	3	3	3
Other fish	1	2	2	2

Note: The total of respondants for 12 villages was 62 males and 91 females.
1. Probably should show much higher percentage of refusal.
2. *Vizemba:* animals with two or more prominent colors on body.

and eland are edible. In her discussion of food taboos among the Bemba, Richards (1939) writes that pregnant women avoid bushbuck flesh; otherwise their children become spotted like the bushbuck. For the same group, Moore (1940) records that whereas many people ate bushbuck, they did so at the risk of acquiring rashes or blemishes on their skin. The Kaonde refuse bushbuck meat "for the fear of rash" (Melland 1923), and the Konde believe the flesh of eland and bushbuck will cause leprosy in some people (Mackenzie 1925).

This class of mammals is also among those meats prohibited to chiefs. Among the Ambo, who reside in the Luangwa Valley south of the Valley Bisa, chiefs are prohibited the flesh of zebra, bushbuck, and rhinoceros (Stefaniszyn 1964a). Kazembe, the paramount chief among the Lunda on the Luapula in Zambia, was prohibited eland meat (Cunnison 1959).

A reigning chief among the Valley Bisa has his own food prohibitions which may not apply to all members of his lineage. The present chief does not eat zebra, for, as he explained, "The first Bisa chief was buried in the skin of a zebra. Thus, the zebra has remained a part of our kin's traditions. Since the death and burial of this first chief, other chiefs have refused to eat it." If zebra is the only meat currently refused by the chief, surely there have been other prohibitions in the past. Bisa chiefs on the plateau reputedly refuse bushbuck and kudu in addition to zebra. Although kudu is not consistently mentioned in the literature, this species is not as widespread in its distribution as the others and is neither plentiful nor conspicuous where it occurs.

But the question still remains, why is the flesh of mammals in the *vizemba* class consistently prohibited? Attempting to find a clue for this avoidance, I solicited comments from many individuals but they never satisfied my curiosity. The following was a typical response:

> Kudu, zebra, bushbuck, and eland were made like this by God (*Leza*). . . . Some people fear leprosy and don't eat animals with spots and stripes. God created such animals as evidence (*buboni*) and warning not to eat game of this type. . . . Sometimes many people eat animals with white stripes on them. If a person gets leprosy, we say that the meat is to blame. Others can eat such meat and never suffer.

Douglas (1966) suggests that the concept of pollution is an unconscious reaction against the inconsistencies of cherished principles and categories. That which is either ambiguous or contradictory from the standpoint of a society's classificatory theories is inclined to be labeled unclean, dirty, or dangerous. Things which fall between categories or combine several components may also share these same labels. According to the Valley Bisa, the pelage of those mammals in the *vizemba* category combines at least two colors, and their white stripes or spots are prominent. Both the ambiguous classification of these mammals and the meanings of basic color patterns in other contexts may be the basis leading to the flesh of these mammals being labeled as dangerous.

The Valley Bisa say that the fear of leprosy legitimizes individual abstentions from the flesh of striped mammals. For them, leprosy is a dread disease, appearing capriciously, and according to district reports, rather common in the Valley until recently. The initial stages of the disease they say appear as spots, blemishes, or open sores; advanced stages of the disease are recognized by everyone, and leprous individuals are isolated from their kinsmen. These are built huts in the bush and are prohibited from eating with other villagers. By nature a gregarious and social people, social isolation and rejection is for them undoubtedly the most feared aspect of contracting this disease. Upon their death, lepers are not buried in the ground like others, but wrapped in their sleeping mats and placed in a tree and left to rot. Stefaniszyn (1964a) suggests the prohibition against burying lepers rests on magical grounds. The body must be willfully rejected; otherwise the disease might reappear among other members of the leper's matrilineage.

Other studies of African societies show the significance ascribed to colors. Lienhardt (1961) shows the interdependence of perception of a color and its shades in nature and in cattle among the Dinka of the Sudan, and suggests that this relationship is a deliberate attempt to link cattle with features of both their natural and social environments. Needham (1967), deciphering the significance of a Nyoro legend, shows the complexity of symbolism and meaning attributed to the legend of a hunter's kill of a curious animal, a part of which resembled a colobus monkey (black and white), and another part a lion (red).

The flesh of other game refused by individuals was prohibited them by African doctors after they had experienced prolonged sickness or vomiting. Those who showed signs of epilepsy or madness (*bulwele buanjili njili*) refused warthog. The name of this sickness is similar to the vernacular name for warthog (*munjili*). According to hunters, warthogs sometimes are found mad and unconscious, and while in this condition may be killed easily with an ax or a pole.

In addition to the pied wagtail, several birds and small animals are considered nonedible by adults. Rats and mice inhabiting villages and their immediate surroundings are not edible, although the cane rat and elephant shrew are eaten. But there is ambivalence about the palatability of both species, and some people will eat neither. Wild pig, likewise associated with abandoned village sites, is also refused by some adults. The fork-tailed drongo (*muntyengu*), black kite (*pungwa*), racquet-tailed roller (*chole*), and others frequenting villages or fields are not consumed by discriminating adults, although they may be killed and eaten by children.

These restrictions probably assume meaning provided we order these species according to their "social distance" from human habitation and spheres of influence (Leach 1964). Thus, consumption of birds and mammals showing close affinities for areas of human habitation, either past or present, is prohibited or restricted by adults.

Omens

Although a natural occurrence, an omen is an event or observation which is rarely observed or expected. According to hunters, omens are sent them by their guardian shade; therefore by being sensitive to and correctly interpreting these signs, hunters believe they can foresee potential and prospective dangers. Good or bad connotations of the various omens are usually associated with the name, color, or other attribute of the mammal, bird, or insect.

Good omens are collectively called *mipashi* (*mupashi*, singular). For a hunter to encounter a troop of banded mongooses (*munzulu*) suggests that he should soon make a kill or come upon a carcass killed by a lion. In this case the name associates it with good fortune (cf. *azulula nzila bwino apelika izjuko*—"it makes the path straight and gives fortune"). Most birds whose plumage combines black, red, and white are good omens. These include the ground hornbill (*mungomba*), helmet shrikes (*bulwendolwendo*), bateleur eagle (*chipungu*), and maribou stork (*mukanga*). Of these, the ground hornbill, by virtue of its size and comparative rarity, is considered extremely auspicious, although if the birds remain hidden and only their mournful cry is heard they are said to forecast a tragedy. Hawks are favorable signs especially if observed clutching their prey.

Observation afield of *lucebu*, a small black and white beetle, is a good sign (*kuchebula*, "to beacon"). Likewise, encountering a band of soldier ants (*minyau*) returning from a foray laden with food suggests the hunter will be equally successful. *Bwenda longwe*, described as small, black gregarious insects, occur in the wet season. If these are encountered actively swarming it is a good sign. The verb *kulonga* means "to pack, or to fill." The monitor lizards (*mbulu*) are generally considered auspicious, but if one is found dead and uneaten, its connotation is bad.

Bad omens, *chibanda*, *mupamba*, or *mwiko*, are less numerous. Upon sighting one of these afield, the hunter should return immediately to his village. *Lukote*, the small reddish marsh mongoose, is a bad sign, for its name is associated with the verb *kukota*, "to become old quickly" (i.e., the hunter becomes tired and old, thus losing his power for killing). For a hunter to see a cobra (*kafi*) or another large black snake (*lubobo*) is likewise bad. The cobra, a deadly snake, will stand its ground and attack rather than flee. To encounter a quaking praying mantis (*manzombwe*) means that one will soon experience death among kin. The trembling posture of this mantis connotes death. Black chameleons also forecast a death. Louries or turacos with red primary feathers or black and white birds flying from east to west are considered bad omens. The spirits of the dead go west.

In my notes I recorded the hunting trips on which omens were called to my attention. Their frequency is presented in Table 15. Note the relative scarcity of bad omens. Good omens were frequently associated with subsequent success.

TABLE 15

RELATIONSHIP BETWEEN SIGHTINGS OF OMENS AND OUTCOME OF HUNTS

Type of Omen	Outcome	Number
Good omen	Kill	11
	Wound	3
	Failure	6
Bad omen	Failure	1
Total		21

My impression was that hunters generally looked upon omens ambivalently unless they were experiencing a period of fruitless hunting. During such times, hunters often pointed to encouraging signs after leaving the village as if orienting their psychology toward success. My observations tend to support the idea suggested by Moore (1965) that if a hunter permits his search pattern to be determined by the sightings of omens, this may serve as a crude heuristic device for randomizing his routes. In situations where both the hunted and hunters act and react according to the other's activities and behaviors, and past experience provides potential for future reactions, there may be a marked advantage in avoiding a firm pattern on the part of the hunter. Unconscious regularities in the hunter's behavior provide a foundation for evasive actions on the part of game and Moore suggests that in time a successful hunter may become victimized by his habits if game becomes sensitized to his patterns. Since the distribution of species which serve as omens and game are independent events, the hunter introduces irregularity into his search pattern if he occasionally permits his route to be determined by events other than his past experience.

Besides serving as harbingers of fortune or disaster, some species communicate information to hunters by their sounds and behavior. For example, some game are said to communicate by their behavior whether or not the wives and kin of hunters remain faithful back in the village. But apparently this idea had currency when groups of men spent several weeks away from their villages. I witnessed copulations by zebra, buffalo, and elephant and none of those whom I was with gave any indication that they suspected misbehavior on the part of their wives.

A hunter's dreams the night before undertaking a hunt also serve as signs. The most frequent apparitions in the dream of hunters are their matrilineal ancestors and these are thought portentous of success. Likewise, dreaming of antelopes, or of killing a buffalo is a good sign. But to dream of elephants, hyenas, or lions is inauspicious.

Since for the Valley Bisa nothing happens by chance, misfortunes with animals are thought to reflect social tension between classes of relatives. In the following account, one brother-in-law is suspected of using unnatural means to achieve respectability among his in-laws.

> Mwape and Lemek married sisters. Mwape worked in town, became financially well-established and was able to furnish his in-laws with clothes and other things. Lemek remained an ordinary villager (*kamuzi*) and was consequently ignored by his in-laws. In town Mwape acquired a 7.3 mm rifle and was returning to his natal village laden with gifts for his kin and in-laws. Some say that he planned eventually to kill an elephant and had made inquiries about the medicines to placate its spirit.
>
> Outside the chief's village he was set upon unexpectedly by an elephant and killed. Locally the tragedy was explained by asserting that Lemek's jealousy had led him to cast a spell (*chisomo*) with sorcerer's magic and begged the elephant spirits to kill his brother-in-law. As a resident exclaimed, Mwape had both the weapon and ammunitions to kill an elephant; how else could one explain the circumstances?

On the other hand, attacks by wild animals sometimes foretell future tragedies as the following account illustrates:

> In 1960 Chando was hunting buffalo with his nephew Katwishi. Chando wounded a bull which escaped into tall grass. While Chando recharged his muzzle-loading gun, Katwishi climbed a tree and watched the movements of the wounded beast in the grass, and from this perch directed his uncle toward where it lay. Before he could fire again, the buffalo tossed Chando on its horns and carried him some distance. Its horns penetrated and mangled his eye and leg. When Chando was eventually thrown to the ground, he sat up, took off his belt and stared at the buffalo. When it left, Katwishi returned to the village for help. Chando was carried across the Luangwa River to Mwanya dispensary where he spent three months recovering.
>
> Chando explained his misfortune by saying it was a *mwiko* [bad omen]—a sign that something was wrong. Later that month he received a letter announcing the death of his older brother in town.

Empirical Knowledge of Ecological Relationships

Some Valley Bisa show a remarkable sophistication of empirically derived knowledge about components of their environment. Consider the following sequence of questions and answers:

Question: What is the best type of soil for farming?

Answer: We recommend black soil for farming. On other soils sorghum may grow but not to any great height and will not produce good yields. When rain falls on good soil, it can retain water and when the sun shines on it, the soil becomes hot (*kubangama*), the crops grow well and the water is released from the soil. In sand, water goes down deeper so when the sun shines the soil drys rapidly and the plant dies.

Question: Why does one see the same type of trees (*Combretum sp.*) growing here in riverine savanna and on the hills? These here are very large but those on the hills are small.

Answer: The kinds of *kalama* trees found here are different species (*mitundu*) from those on the hills at Ngala. On the hills, *kalama* trees are very small and poor and grow there only by the help of God. On the hills there is no humus (*muvundo*). Here along the river it is very fertile (*mwafuka*).

Question: What makes soil fertile?

Answer: When vegetation grows, matures, and the leaves dry and fall to the ground, they are not carried from the area and this decaying matter stays on top of the soil. Their decay makes the soil fertile. On the hills all of this is washed away by the rains.

By comparison with the Valley Bisa, the Bisa and Bemba living on the plateau do not reside in a fertile country; as a consequence, they must continuously clear land each year and augment its fertility with ashes of branches and leaves from pollarded trees. The Valley Bisa realize that the fertility of their land is derived primarily from the deposition in the valley of eroded soil elements from the plateau; and if now they reside in the valley rather than on the plateau this is a fortunate circumstance due largely to the benevolence and foresight of their ancestors.

Hunters seem to know the food preferences of most game. While collecting plants, I compiled for each plant a list of mammals for which it was a major food source. Although I did not judge the accuracy of this information, its existence implies a degree of precision in hunters' observations. Some of the esoteric portions employed in rituals to pacify the spirits of slain game are reported as the preferred food of these species.

Hunters generally seek large, fat animals (*kayambo*), although in times of hunger probably any susceptible one may be killed. When lush forage is available, bulls accumulate fat in noticeable portions along the back and hindquarters, while internally, fat is deposited around the intestines and kidneys. Bisa awareness of vegetative cycles may explain why some game species are hunted at certain times and rejected at others. In November 1966, when I offered to kill a hartebeest which had wandered within range, a hunter refused, claiming hartebeests at that time had no fat (*koikoi* or *waonda*). In May of the following year the same individual went with me specifically to hunt hartebeests for at that time they were supposedly fat.

Although hunters were generally knowledgeable in their interpretations of animal behavior as it relates to game being pursued, some interpretations of animal behavior are colored by anthropomorphic motivations.

> Question: Why do some animals, like impala, typically form two types of herds—one of bachelors and the other with one male watching over many females?
>
> Answer: During the night they mix together. At dawn the males depart because they fear that if they stay with the females they won't pay proper attention to the dangers from lions and hunters. One male may stay with the females to sexually satisfy himself.
>
> Question: Why do animals prefer only certain types of grass for food?
>
> Answer: It is just like people. Europeans eat and like certain things that we Africans don't. Impala eat the flowers of the sausage tree which ripen along the river, and at certain seasons one can find many impala under these trees. Most of the time, however, they are found in mopane woodland. As there are some people who don't drink our beer [an obvious slam at me!] there are many people who do drink it. There are some animals interested in eating certain grasses which others do not eat.

Grysbok and impala typically deposit piles of dung at intervals. According to hunters, these piles are deposited in play (as by impala) or are individual defecation sites (grysbok). It is difficult to assess another culture's understanding of the function of animal behavior in the abstract, and for the Valley Bisa, objective interpretations, I suspect, have limited utility. Some observations seem entirely erroneous. For example, some say elephants are carnivorous and claim to have witnessed them consuming fish and cane rats.

External and internal parasites are visible entities on most slain game. Each type has a specific or generic name, *munyololo* (roundworms), *vizimu* (flatworms), and *nkupankupa* (ticks), but the role of parasites in the transmission of disease is not recognized. One individual asserted internal parasites functioned to ". . . protect the particular animal. When *vizimu* start moving and wiggling inside the animal, the worms know a predator or hunter is about. The animal becomes nervous and consequently leaves the area although it may not have sensed any danger. These [parasites] also aid people, for when one is in the bush and his stomach begins to shake he knows danger is imminent."

Magic as an Adjunct to Skill

Magic is an important social adjunct to hunting skills, for all individuals who take their profession seriously possess one or more kinds. In joshing with their fellow professionals, hunters claim wonders for their individual prescriptions, since the possession of these are one way of accounting for the differential success among hunters of the same or different ranks. Further, belief in the efficacy of their potions has an important psychological dimension, for with these hunters seem competent when facing dangerous game with their often unreliable muzzleloaders.

Magical lore plays an important role in the ranking of hunters and in the exercise of social control by elders. Generally hunters do not obtain magic until they have demonstrated their skill through one or more kills. Then simple magics, such as *chilembe*, or game attractors (*ulwito lia nama*), may be acquired from one's father or matrikin who are professionals. A more powerful magic, *mfenzi*, normally acquired later in one's life, may be solicited from those outside the hunter's primary kin; and for revealing his secret potions this individual expects compensation.

That magic serves an important function in social control and is a logical extension of ancestor veneration did not escape the attention of Bisa elders. Their awareness of this function is clearly revealed in the following excerpts from interviews:

> All men need magic for hunting because they can not kill game without going to get potions from the old and big hunters (*bakalamba*).

> When the hunter goes into the bush to hunt, finds animals, and shoots at one of them he finds it doesn't die. The hunter returns to the village and sleeps. In the morning he goes into the bush and finds game and shoots at them but no, nothing. When he returns he says, "I have failed twice." Then he decides to go to the diviner. The diviner says "the one who wants to eat is one of your ancestors who has died, that is why the animals go away. Brew beer in his memory and give it to him so that you can kill." When the hunter brews beer and gives it he goes into the bush, and is quite able then to kill. . . . Because those already dead are the people who cause misfortunes on the living ones. Ancestors play a great part in the efficacy of medicine. If they don't help, then the potion, though strong, will be weak.

Magical prescriptions are varied and individualized. I distinguish between legitimate and illegitimate magics for this typology highlights the distinction between the sorcerer and the hunter, a distinction which the Valley Bisa themselves make. Legitimate magics are bona fide potions which hunters may in time acquire. On the other hand, illegitimate magics are those ascribed by some men to their competitors with the obvious implications that they are sorcerers or at least are employing their techniques.

Legitimate Magics

Most hunters claim to have some magics, for the possession of these is tantamount to claiming competence in their profession. Here I discuss three types: *chilembe*—to prevent game from escaping; *ulwito lia nama*—to call game; and *mfenzi*—to hide the hunter from dangerous game. The possession of these various types also ranks hunters with those who have acquired *mfenzi* at the apex. In addition, some hunters possess individualized potions to make them see animals (*nkuma yanama*), to protect their kills from hyenas (*muti wavimbwi*), and to protect them should they stay overnight in the bush (*musileko*). A partial list of *vishimba* which I recorded in use by Bisa hunters is summarized in Table 16. These activating particles (*vishimba*) are mixed with other personalized items to make the full magic. Prohibitions are prescribed for each hunter.

TABLE 16

PARTIAL LIST OF BISA VISHIMBA (ACTIVATING PARTICLES) AND THEIR USE IN HUNTING MAGICS

Bisa Name	English or Latin Name	Use and Symbolism
lunteunteu	Small seeds of plants carried by wind	*lwito lianama*—call mammals to hunter
muanjano	Unidentified shrub	*lwito lianama*—mammal caller—name of tree means "to turn back"
musolo	*Pseudolachnostylis maprouneifolia*	*muti we lwito*—mammal caller—considered "lucky tree" *kusolola*—to drive away misfortune
munga wa buta	*Acacia sieberana*	*lwito lianama*—mammal caller—tree considered a *lubuto*, gives hunter good fortune
chilembe, *Mwanzabamba*	*Euphorbia decidua*	*chilembe*—to kill mammal immediately, causes massive blood clots (cf. *bulembe*—arrow poison)
chimpakasa	*Lonchocarpus capassa*	*isambo*—ritual washing—*muti we shuko* (good luck charm)—probably related to onomatopoeic *pakasa pakasa*, the sound of fleeing animal (to chase one's problems away)
kambaza	nightjar	*mfenzi*—renders hunter invisible to his prey
ikubi	vulture	To help hunter find game, keep hunter's heart from fluttering when stalking game
kapume	African goshawk	mainly for trappers of birds and for fishing
manzombwe	large praying mantis	*chilembe*—causes hunter's quarry to shiver and die when wounded; also a fighter's medicine

TABLE 16 con't

PARTIAL LIST OF BISA VISHIMBA (ACTIVATING PARTICLES) AND THEIR UUSE IN HUNTING MAGICS

Bisa Name	English or Latin Name	Use and Symbolism
lukungwe	cobra (head only)	*chilembe*—to kill mammal immediately as does cobra
kaponta (slime from)	species of *Clarias*? mudfish	*mfenzi*—enables hunter to slip away from wounded and dangerous animal when it charges
luvunyemba	chameleon	*chilembe*—mammal becomes black quickly (dies)
musunsungila	*Crocidura hirta*	*chilembe*—shrew said to follow a straight path
mununga, fyekefyeke	small unidentified shrew which smells	*chilembe*—shrew often found dead in paths
mulopa wankalamo	lion's blood	reputedly used only by chief
nkaka	Pangolin	probably used by trapper—*kukaka*, to tie up, to secure

Chilembe. A magic in use by most gun hunters is *chilembe*. This enables the hunter's bullet to cause massive internal bleeding and clotting in his quarry, thus preventing its escape. The action of *chilembe* was described to me by the following analogy:

> It works the same as electricity on the Copperbelt. When you have the magic in your blood, your blood is strengthened. When you take aim with a gun and fire this force leaves your arm, goes into the gun and out with the bullet. When the bullet hits the animal its blood becomes affected by that force and it clots here, here, here (pointing to his chest) so that its blood can no longer flow freely and is clotted in pieces. The animal cannot move and soon dies.

This magic may have assumed its importance when hunters switched to muzzleloading guns, for previously their arrows and spears were poisoned with *bulembe*, an effective concoction which caused the death of prey through the coagulation of its blood. With muzzleloading weapons, however, the fate of wounded game became far less certain, and one hit in a vital area might survive indefinitely. Note the etymological similarity between *bulembe* and *chilembe*. *Chilembe* is also the term for large clots of blood found in the pleural and thoracic cavities of slain animals. *Euphorbia decidua*, the plant from which is obtained the most powerful *chishimba* is called *chilembe* or *mwanzabamba*.

There are several types of *chilembe*. *Chilembe chikulu* (the most powerful) uses the *Euphorbia* tuber mentioned above, and is possessed by the chief and others who have procured it from him. The power of its sap is said to stem from its whiteness and the tingling sensation produced when mixed with the blood in one's veins. *Vishimba* of lesser value (*chilembe chiachepa*) are generally of less ominous sorts.

One individual said he mixed *luze* (sugar cane) with other ingredients to make his kills taste sweet and palatable. Components of a more sinister nature are the heads of cobra and chameleon. Both of these suggest rapid death (blackness) and have overtones of illegitimate magic.

Ulwito lia nama. Another prescription which many hunters possess is one which lures game. These recipes are generally inherited within lineages. Although a few hunters possess potions to lure specific species such as warthogs, the two prescriptions below are for calling up any species.

> Find two trees in the bush whose trunks are twisted together so when the wind blows, the trunks scrape together and make a noise. This noise sounds like someone calling, and the animals will turn around to face the direction from which it comes. From one of these trees take a piece of bark from the region where it rubs with the other branches.
>
> Then take a root from the *kamulebe* bush (*Ximenia americana*). The fruits of this bush are relished by game; they seem to run to it.
>
> Take any rubbish being blown in a whirlwind (*kankungwe*). Such whirlwinds can blow things over long distances, even from Malawi to Chitaba.
>
> Finally pick a seed from *lunteunteu* [small seeds which when dry are dispersed by the wind]. One of these seeds can be carried from far away to here. Likewise game will run as far away as the Mupamadzi River to meet the hunter.
>
> Burn all of these ingredients and grind them together. Place them in a small container and mix with oil. Smear some of this mixture on your face, arms and on your gun. Mention the names of each expired hunter in your lineage and say "*Tangileni pantanzi mwebale kulye nama*" [Go before me, you who used to eat meat]. Then you should kill an animal very soon.

A second prescription for *ulwito* is to

> take the roots of *munga wa buta* (*Acacia kirkii*). This tree is considered a *lubuto* because of its whiteness and brings the hunter good fortune. Mix these roots with the bark of a tree where a person has hanged himself (*chiti ichiakulikilako umuntu*). A person who has hanged himself is considered "mixed up." The next animal which is hunted will also become mixed up for instead of fleeing from the hunter in the normal pattern, it will instead come toward him. Place both of these substances into a container of water. Before going into the bush, the hunter washes both his face and gun in this mixture.

Stefaniszyn (1964b) records the use of a decoy flute, or duiker pipe, in use among the Ambo. Although such a whistle is used for duiker on the plateau I did not record its presence among the Valley Bisa.

Mfenzi. Today whether a hunter acquires magic stronger than the two described above seems to depend on circumstances. In contrast to *chilembe* and *ulwito lia nama*, *mfenzi* usually is acquired from those outside primary kin. As one young hunter who was in the process of obtaining it explained: "I will not ask either the lineages of my father or mother for this magic. I might not give them sufficient meat and they might give me in return weak magic. They feel a mixture of love and jealousy toward me. Instead I will ask another hunter who is unrelated to me. He will demand money and in return he will give me a good strong prescription."

Several elder hunters claimed they did not possess *mfenzi* and gave as their reason that they had never had a close call with game or felt the need to acquire protection other than that already provided by their ancestral spirits. Three others who had been wounded or charged by large game each possessed it. The hunter from whom I purchased the following prescription had paid a white hen for the recipe after he was severely wounded by a buffalo.

> Take the slime from *kaponta* (*Clarius sp.*, a catfish). Pull the fish through your hands until they are covered with slime. When you try and catch one of these fish it slips away and all you are left with is slime on your hands. Similarly the wild beast, if it intends to harm you, will miss and slip past the place where you are standing.
>
> Next take a charcoal from a tree stump in the bush. The stump will be black since it will have been repeatedly burned. The place where the hunter stands in the bush will be seen by the animal as black, for the hunter will have this substance in his body.
>
> Then take a feather or bone from the nightjar's head (*kambaza*). One can get very close to this camouflaged bird, can almost step on it, before it flies away. Likewise you will be able to approach very close to an animal and it will be unable to detect your presence.
>
> Grind all of these ingredients together into a fine powder like snuff. Then make two cuts on your forehead and two cuts on the back of your neck. Put the remaining potion in a piece of cloth, fold and sew the cloth into a rope. This cloth is worn either around the stock of the gun or on your upper left arm.
>
> If you meet an elephant it will pass right by because it can't see you. Other people may see the elephant coming and ask if you are still alive. You will say "*iyoo, epo ndi*" [I am here].

Ntezi is a variant of *mfenzi*; at least, hunters at Nabwalya said it served the same purpose. I recorded only one prescription and this came from an elderly man whose village was located adjacent to the Luangwa River.

> Take a portion of *nyezi* [electric catfish]. It is used because when it is touched one gets shocked and one feels "cold" and "coldness" even while approaching it. When a person is approached by a dangerous animal it will feel "cold" and shy away from the spot occupied by the hunter. It will not be attracted by the "hotness" of the hunter.
>
> Mix *nyezi* with the roots of *mwanya* [unidentified]. These roots are full of water and very slippery (*kutelela*). The hunter is able to slip away from a dangerous beast.
>
> These two substances are mixed together with water and the hunter washes all his body. If he overlooks one part of his body, when the hunter confronts danger, that unwashed portion will become vulnerable.

Hunters did not put blind faith in their magics, for when pressed for details of their hunting exploits, they showed a pragmatic orientation toward the assurances offered by their magics. Although armed with a rifle and known to possess *mfenzi*, one hunter fled his field when charged by a bull elephant rather than stand his ground.

Illegitimate Magic

The inversion of the socially accepted use of charms constitutes illegitimate magic. The Valley Bisa say such magics are employed by sorcerers to gain status or achievements to which they legally have no right. In common with other societies possessing a low productive technology, the Valley Bisa show little differentiation in wealth. Both wealth and status are concentrated in the hands of lineage elders who achieve their standing often by simple seniority and are secured in these positions by magics and strong ritual sanctions. Few, if any means, are open for ambitious men to achieve economic, ritual, or political power by their own efforts.

As a body of cultural theory accounting for many misfortunes, beliefs in sorcery leave open the definition of exactly who the sorcerer is, although hypothetical stereotypes suggest their typical actions and attributes. All professionals and important men have magics or potions, but the possession of these does not mean a man is necessarily a practicing sorcerer. Circumstances or his behavior determine whether or not he is a suspect. One of the issues perennially at stake in a society believing in sorcery is the identification, elimination, or rehabilitation of sorcerers, for each misfortune or social disruption is fresh evidence supporting their activities.

Kulowa is the Bisa term meaning "to bewitch" or "to cast a spell." Hunters jokingly use the same term in reference to the power of their potions over game (*kulowe nama*). Among humans, the Valley Bisa say the desire to bewitch another stems from a feeling of envy (*muvimbila*) or from a feeling of being held back by another person from attaining one's ambitions (*buvuba*). They say these feelings are aroused by watching another enjoy life, provide good food and clothes for his wife and children, demonstrate an expertise which another lacks, or have a number of children who survive and show respect. The sorcerer brings sickness, misfortunes, and death to those for whom he feels envy or resentment. The victim may have unintentionally refused him food or the sorcerer may resent his worldly success. Sorcery is combatted by additional sorcery and those not initially involved may become so, for those to whom life has been good often feel that they must take steps to protect themselves against the unsuccessful or unfortunate. Occasional attempts are made to control these vicious activities by inviting sorcery detectors, who administer purgatives which cause sorcerers to confess their activities. Upon their confession and surrender of charms, suspects are released, but their testimony lends credence to sorcery's prevalence.

At present the common way of dealing with a kinsman suspected of sorcery is to move away or to force him to move. The Valley Bisa assert that sorcery is usually not practiced over long distances, for to be effective the sorcerer must maintain close contact with his victim. This may be one reason why *mfenzi*, a potion which hides the hunter afield, is similar by reputation to those magics used by sorcerers. Another way to gain protection from sorcerers is by purchasing magic from a well-known doctor.

Direct accusations of sorcery are rare, for little is gained by openly informing a person that he is a suspect. Therefore, gossip and backbiting are the main avenues by which word of and evidence against suspects travel. I was privy to unsolicited details on the activities of some with whom I hunted.

> The reason why you are unsuccessful is because you go [hunting] with bad people. Bulaya in his early days was a sorcerer and even today many people suspect him of bewitching and killing others. When he was younger he used two shots for game and retained the third for a human being. Today his gun bursts after the third shot [Bulaya had recently repaired one of his two muzzleloaders]. Neither of his sisters produced surviving children and we suspect their fetuses are part of his magic.

Accusations leveled at hunters relate to the kinds of activating particles they are suspected of using for their magics. Some hunters are said to have acquired their power by incestuous acts. Magic so acquired is called *chisoni* ("shame, confusion"). A fetus conceived through incestuous intercourse is aborted and then used in magic. In such a manner the hunter acquires control of the child's spirit which calls game for him. But such magic robs the hunter's sister of future progeny and his kills are reputedly lean and supposedly taste like dirt. In some cases the hunter himself is unable to produce offspring.

I have not delved deeply into this aspect of cosmology, for the operation of sorcery in Bisa society could itself be the subject of lengthy research. Here I have only intended to present one of the dangers within the social environment of hunters. For should a young person be unduly haughty in his accomplishments, or deviate from traditional patterns of rituals, he may find himself the scapegoat for others' misfortunes.

VII

Drama of the Hunt

> Hunters are killed by their prey as the farmer eventually succumbs to his labors.
>
> Bisa proverb

THE HUNTING PROCESS

HUNTING is an active process, a comprehensive and integrative behavioral system. Laughlin (1968) defines hunting as a series of five behavioral complexes consisting of (1) the programming of children to become hunters; (2) the collection and scanning of information on game; (3) the pursuit and stalking of game; (4) the immobilization and slaughter of game; and finally, (5) its recovery or retrieval. The ideology and the main sociological variables found in the life histories of hunters were discussed in the previous chapter. In this chapter we examine subsequent elements in the hunting process as exhibited among the Valley Bisa.

Scanning

As an activity preparatory to the hunt, scanning (*kulolesha*) encompasses the gathering of information on when, what, and where to hunt. The assessment of this information reflects the hunter's knowledge of animal behavior, its daily and seasonal movements, and his commitment to those in his community who depend upon him for meat. Hunting, for the Valley Bisa, is not usually a spontaneous activity and not undertaken solely for sport or pleasure. It is serious business and the hunter prepares himself for the bush.

A hunter's ancestors are believed to play an important role in his protection and success. If a person plans a hunt, he repeats the names of his ancestors before retiring, asks for their guidance and assistance, and may place a small offering of flour in a gourd or at the head of his mat. In addition, there are unstated codes of conduct to which a hunter ascribes to gain the aid of his spirits. He should not start quarrels or curse anyone, for such disruptive actions may lead to the withdrawal of ancestral aid. Furthermore, prior to the hunt, he must abstain from having sexual intercourse. I was told: "We don't have intercourse before a hunt because when we are hunting we are helped by the spirits of dead hunters. These spirits are 'neutral' and have no sexual intercourse. When we have sexual intercourse before a hunt, we get out of tune with the spirits who will help us in the bush."

Prohibition on sexual intercourse before a hunt becomes meaningful if we understand what is implicit in "getting out of tune" with the spirits: the pattern expressed is the distinction between village and bush, or the two disparate worlds within which the hunter operates. People live in villages; game and spirits inhabit the bush. The bush is metaphorically "cold" (*kutalala*) as are spirits, and they are dangerous to anything not in a similar state. A village involved in quarrels and social strife is "hot" (*kubangama*) as is a person who has engaged in sexual intercourse. Therefore, the hunter tries to conform to the nature of the bush as expressed in the following paradigm which contrasts its symbolic attributes with those of the village:

village	bush
human sphere	spirit sphere
dependent	independent
sex	neuter
strife	quiet
"hot"	"cold"

If other persons join the hunter, each should protect himself against the infidelity or quarrels of the others. Such was the function of the ritual washings practiced by the guilds of elephant hunters, for were this rite not performed, the "hotness" of any errant individual would be apparent to dangerous spirits and sorcerers able to discriminate the hunter's position in an otherwise "cool" environment. For the same reason, hunters generally seek to avoid other persons in the bush whether these be women gathering grasses or other men collecting poles or fishing.

Many factors influence an individual to undertake hunting. In discussing with me why they decided to hunt on particular days, hunters often said they either dreamed about an important ancestor or "forcefully dreamed" about animals or previous hunts. According to one informant:

> The force (behind the dreaming) is brought by animals which have been killed some time ago. While asleep it may seem as though you were hunting in the bush. It will be just a vision, but it will seem very real even like you have killed game in real life. When you wake up, you can know that today you can go out hunting and kill an animal. After getting your gun and going out into the bush, during the course of the day one should kill an animal.

The term used for "forced dreaming" was *kulotesha* from the verb *kulota*, "to dream." *Kulotesha* is an extension of the verb to dream and means "to continue dreaming one thing for a long time." This informant suggested that for him dreaming was caused by the spirits of game previously slain which he had directed through his rituals into the herding of other animals. Others expressed the opinion that ancestral spirits caused these dreams which indicated they were satisfied with relations among their surviving kin.

An individual may take up hunting because his kin beg him for meat or for different relish dishes. The Valley Bisa make a distinction between meat and vegetable relishes and have a term, *bukasha*, to describe a long sequence of relish dishes without meat. Individuals also hunt because they lack other pressing responsibilities and because they like wandering in the bush.

Usually hunting commences early in the morning. For the Valley Bisa the normal manner of hunting is a brisk walk with pauses at intervals to listen and to scan portions of the bush. Hunters sometimes used the morning flight direction of cattle egrets or oxpeckers to orient themselves in the direction of game. I was repeatedly impressed by their sensitivity to sounds and sights in locating game. They were able to discern the groans (*kukamba*) of foraging buffalo or the excited grunts (*kuwowela*) of impala at play and to determine the direction these sounds came from.

Detecting buffalo at a distance is important for planning subsequent stalk strategy; surprise and unexpected encounters are important for success with impala and warthogs. When either of these latter species are encountered in open country or in mopane woodland it is rare for a hunter to approach sufficiently close for a shot. But by traversing thickets and scrub mopane, it is possible to come upon these species suddenly and unexpectedly. When this happens, a hunter freezes, for if he has not been detected by the game, he has a chance to withdraw to prepare his weapon for firing, for they never leave the village with their weapons fully functional. It is only after spotting game that they fill the firing nipple with powder and place the firing cap. Even if the hunter's movements in dense bush are noticed by game, his freezing action is often sufficient to hold game temporarily, for there seems to be a definite limit of time in which animals can concentrate on a stationary object without further stimulus. In the end the game may move away slowly, or show by the movement of its head, ears, or by the resumption of its previous activity that it is beginning to allay its suspicions.

Although I describe the normal hunt pattern as a brisk walk, the hunters depart from this routine occasionally. When they reach Malanda hot springs, they sometimes wait in cover to scan the open areas for game. Another area is Chinama, where heavy thickets surround the lagoons. Here near one of the dry season waterholes a hunter constructed a hide or blind (*muzaza wakulindishamo inama*). Since most game are quick to pick up moving objects while their ability to discriminate stationary objects is poor, it is surprising that the Valley Bisa do not use these strategies more often.

Stalking

The sequence of stalking (*kubensha*) begins for impala and warthog when an individual or group has been sighted and tested, but for buffalo and elephant the hunter may commit himself to an individual or herd before it is seen. Herds of buffalo leave copious signs that are evaluated as to freshness and direction of movement. Hunters claim the ability to determine its hour of deposition and the condition of the buffalo by examining the consistency and color of its droppings.

Although hunters do not go out of their way to avoid visual perception by most game, whenever possible they take precautions to prevent the detection of their scent. If conditions allow, they test the direction of the wind both before and during a stalk. During the dry season the direction of the wind is assessed by dislodging dust from the ground by a quick rub of the foot and noting its direction of movement. To test the wind during the wet season the hunters carry a small sack of sorghum flour tied to the stock of their gun, which, when flicked, the fine powder spilled from the bag indicating the direction of the wind. Others employ wildcat fur which is plucked from the skin and the direction of the wind is determined as the fur floats to the ground.

Hunters read many situational variables in deciding whether or not to stalk. The time of day indicates the game's subsequent movements or activities, for many species rest or doze during the middle of the day and if unaware of the hunter's presence may be stalked less cautiously than at other times. The composition of a group in terms of the sexes, ages, or species represented is also studied. The association of wary species, impala, or eland, with an unwary group of buffalo or waterbuck may preclude a stalk. In addition a species' behavior is analyzed to assess its wariness. Hunters are rarely able to get within range of impala once the hunter is noticed, but for buffalo, sight of the hunter does not necessarily spook the herd. But on occasion even the lack of sufficient cover may preclude a stalk of buffalo. In May a hunter and I watched for over an hour the casual movements of a buffalo herd in the open of an abandoned field. When they eventually bedded in an open glade, we left and returned to the village. In this case, the openness of the habitat, referred to as *kuaswetisha* (redness) or *kuabuta* (whiteness), may not have been the only reason for the hunter's decision against a stalk. Earlier we salvaged a foreshoulder of a buffalo killed by a lion.

Once a hunter commits himself to a stalk, his attention focuses upon getting as close as possible to his prey. During a stalk the hunter moves rapidly toward the prey when it is facing away or has its head down in feeding. Freezing follows his forward movement when the prey looks in his direction. The time invested in stalking varies according to prey, and the average time listed for this phase of hunting behavior in Table 17 is only suggestive. Each observation represents a different composite of situational factors and their evaluation by an individual.

TABLE 17

STALKING TIME OF BISA HUNTERS FOR DIFFERENT PREY

Species	Observations	Range (Minutes)	Mean
Elephant	3	4–40	21
Buffalo	24	9–60	31
Zebra	3	3–10	7
Impala	8	2–15	7
Warthog	12	2–15	8
Waterbuck	6	2–25	11
Puku	2	7–10	. . .

The typical stalking strategy described below is taken from my field notes for 12 December 1966.

The morning was heavily overcast when Chizola and I left the village at 8:30. We walked through the flooded bottomland of Ngala and the adjacent mopane woodland without seeing game. Beyond in the riverine savanna we spotted two warthogs and a small group of four impala. There was no hesitancy in Chizola's forward pace for it was obvious both groups had noticed us. We saw two elephants along the edge of Kawele thicket. We circled to the west of Ndozi hill and gained the foothills. At 9:05 Chizola paused and indicated the direction from which he had heard the sounds of buffalo. To me these sounds were scarcely audible when he indicated their occurrence a second time. We proceeded toward the sounds and at 9:16 saw three buffalo, two adults and one subadault, feeding on a hillock. From the noise he knew the herd was dispersed and feeding; therefore we slipped past these initial three and moved toward a group of eight adult males. At 9:20 Chizola left me and moved on his haunches for cover behind a small shrub. This small shrub was seventeen paces from a large bull which was feeding with its head in the grass. Gaining the cover of the shrub, Chizola removed a small piece of leather from between the nipple and the hammer of his gun, cocked his weapon, and placed the firing cap on the nipple from its previous position embedded in wax on the trigger guard. With his gun readied, Chizola paused until the large bull turned broadside. At 9:25 the animal was briefly obliterated from view by a cloud of smoke from the charge of black powder. Chizola stood and with his finger kept track of the wounded bull until it was lost among the swirl of stampeding buffalo. He returned to my station, recharged his weapon and we set off in the direction the buffalo had fled. Although we saw the same herd on two occasions, they remained unapproachable and we were unable to stalk them again.

Killing

The Valley Bisa rarely kill (*kuipaya*) game outright for frequently they cripple it initially and it must be pursued farther. At this time their spooring skill is tested. Elephants and buffalo may survive repeated assaults by hunters with muzzleloading guns.

When seriously wounded, buffalo frequently leave the herd, seek dense cover, and remain there for some time. In dense bush, hunters rarely pursue wounded buffalo immediately; instead they locate its position and wait for the wound to hemorrhage and debilitate the animal's functioning. Many mammals are lost or linger several days before expiring as indicated by excerpts from my field notes:

> 20 September. In the early evening, Chibinda wounded a buffalo in a herd moving towards the river. Unable to track it at night he returned to his village. The next morning he found the carcass had been consumed by hyenas.
>
> 28 October. In the early morning Chibinda wounded a buffalo and followed it until its spoor led into a thicket. He returned to the village and that afternoon entered the thicket and wounded the buffalo a second time. The buffalo escaped. The next morning, members of another village chased a lion from a buffalo carcass and claimed the meat.
>
> 2 December. I heard a shot at 5:30 A.M. near Mupete lagoon. At 7:45 A.M. I encountered Chibinda returning to his village and inquired as to his success. He replied he had wounded a lone buffalo and it had escaped. That same afternoon at 5:00 P.M. I heard another shot. When Chibinda returned to his village towards dusk he told me he had again fired at the same buffalo but his shot this time had been high.
>
> 20 December. In the middle of the afternoon Lubeles encountered a large herd of buffalo resting on Muchingo ridge. Undetected he crept up on a pregnant female which was dozing. When he fired, the startled herd stampeded towards him. Lubeles escaped by climbing a tree as the herd swirled around under him. Convinced he had inflicted a fatal wound, he sent his maternal uncle to check the site the next day. His uncle found nothing.
>
> 9 June. While watching a subadult elephant bathe in Mupete lagoon, Lubeles, my father, and I became conscious of movements in the tall grass behind us. We ascertained its location when a group of oxpeckers dropped into the grass, but we were still unable to identify it. We entered the tall grass along a game trail. When we were within seventy-five feet of it and still unable to see it, Lubeles scaled a tree some six paces from the trail. Lubeles was signaling us that it was a buffalo when it charged and halted near the base of the tree. Its charge and subsequent halt enabled us to kill the buffalo eleven paces from where we stood. This buffalo, an adult female, had been wounded twice before with muzzleloaders. The wounds on its neck and left foreshoulder were gangrenous.
>
> 26 June. Chando wounded a buffalo near his village at 7:55 A.M. It retreated into dense grass. When he returned to his village, he informed villagers to avoid the area in which the buffalo was hiding. That afternoon he found the buffalo wary and was unable to approach it for a second shot. The next morning I saw vultures swarming near Chando's village and presumed the buffalo had died.

8 July. Chibinda wounded a buffalo which entered his field at night. The next morning he followed and killed it with a second shot.

Once wounded, smaller game may be chased in the direction of the village. By Western values this practice appears cruel, but from the standpoint of the Valley Bisa it reduces the distance over which its carcass must be carried to the village. I observed this once.

After hunting unsuccessfully all morning Chizola and I were returning to his village when at 10:22 A.M. we surprised a female warthog in Kawele thicket. His shot entered the warthog's hip, crippling both back legs. Since it was still capable of movement on its forelegs, Chizola prevented me from killing it with my shotgun. Instead he picked branches and tossed them at the warthog which fled from us in the direction of the village. After struggling some one thousand yards the warthog fell exhausted and could be herded no farther. Chizola suggested that I kill it with guineafowl shot rather than waste buckshot.

Hunters say pregnant females are more difficult to kill than males, for according to them the fetus must die before its mother. Also, fat mammals supposedly die quicker than skinny ones.

In approaching downed game, hunters advance toward the carcass along the trail used by the game rather than approaching from the rear as it is common among Europeans. From the front direction they claim it is easier to tell by examining the animal's eyes whether or not it has expired.

If the prey slain is an eland or elephant, the hunter ritually treats the carcass according to the traditions of his lineage, provided, of course, he has previously killed these before and knows their appropriate prescription. It seemed to me that these rituals were directed toward animal spirits as appeasement ceremonies and were similar in form to their ancestral rites. When I broached this to an elder, he replied: "No, one does not appease (*kusekela*) the spirits of animals like one does one's ancestral spirits. One only tries to neutralize (*kusisintila*) the animal's spirit so it won't follow the hunter and cause trouble. In this way, one shuts (*kuisalila*) the spirit in the carcass."

Other species of game such as buffalo and rhino may also be ritually treated each time they are killed but this depends upon lineage traditions and the experience of the individual hunter. An older hunter whom I watched make a kill did not perform a ritual over a buffalo. When I asked him why he had not performed the ritual, he replied: "Being an experienced hunter, I do not always use *muti* [magic] on dead animals. I may do something to the meat when I return to the village. Also I take the bark from *kamulebe* [*Ximenia americana*] bush, soak it in water, and cleanse myself and my gun."

Once the ritual is performed, the hunters tie a knot in the mammal's tail. Hunters claim this behavior prevents those who are to consume its meat from contracting diarrhea or other stomach ailments, but this behavior also may be related to the hunter's wish to "tie up" (*kukaka*) this ailment, or possibly it is a survival of a previous pattern designating ownership of a carcass. A slain animal may be claimed by another party if it shows no sign of ownership.

> Timothi killed a buffalo near another village. Apparently he did not cover the carcass or tie a knot in its tail but immediately left for the village into which he had married. When he returned to the carcass with his in-laws that afternoon, he found the carcass already butchered. When he learned the adjacent village was enjoying fresh meat, Timothi asked them from whom they had obtained permission to cut the meat. They replied that they had found the buffalo dead and assumed it had no owner. They delivered the meat to Timothi's village and there was no case.

Before leaving the kill site, hunters generally cover (*kuvimbile nama*) the carcass with thorny branches or grass. This action camouflages the site from aerial scavengers and makes the kill site difficult to detect by other persons who might have heard the shot and be moving toward the kill.

If a kill is made toward evening and the distance to the village is far, the hunter may apply hyena magic (*muti wavimbwi*) to prevent hyenas from locating the carcass. I saw this magic applied once. This hunter took two shreds of mopane bark and with his eyes closed tied a strip to a foreleg and to the opposite back leg; then covered the carcass with branches from a thorn tree. When we returned the next morning, the carcass was intact.

Retrieval and Consumption

Once game is slain, the hunter's attention shifts to his knowledge of gross anatomy and to the distribution of the meat. Meat is a perishable, yet precious commodity, and its distribution by the hunter represents a social strategy which may be used to his immediate advantage or at some future date.

My field notes for 21 December 1966 describe the butcher of a male buffalo.

> Chizola surprised a small band of buffalo near Ndozi hill. His shot, audible from the village at 7:30 A.M., entered the thoracic cavity and heart of a large bull. The wounded animal ran some fifteen hundred yards before dying at the edge of Kawele thicket. Chizola found the carcass, covered it with branches, and returned to the village at 8:30 A.M.
>
> At 11:15 A.M., accompanied by seven men, six women, and three boys we left for the kill site. Upon our arrival at the carcass, Chizola removed the branches and instructed a small child to tie a knot in its tail. Then he plucked a blade of *luiba* grass [*Digitaria milanjiana*] and placed it in the animal's nose.
>
> The buffalo was an adult male, although not old if judged by the wear on its teeth and the spread of its horn bosses. However it was fat and this condition became the main topic of conversation by the assembled group. They poked

along the flank and the back exclaiming excitedly "*kayambo.*" *Kayambo* refers to the peritonium which in healthy animals is lined with fat deposits and serves as a synonym for a fat animal.

When the men began to butcher the carcass, the women took a position some distance away. Young boys collected branches and leaves and placed these alongside the carcass.

Initially the men removed the skin in chunks which they placed alongside so when the meat was removed it would not touch the sandy soil. Then the foreshoulders were disarticulated and placed on skin. The stomach was punctured, and it with the other internal organs were placed on leaves. Two men removed the plant tissue from inside the stomach and large intestine by an incision along its margin. The liver and heart were cooked and distributed.

Next the back legs were disarticulated. The sternum was cut from the ribs and the rib cage from the backbone. Each of these portions was cut into portable sizes. The meat from the limbs was removed from the heavy bones and cut into strips approximately one inch thick, facilitating both its carriage back to the village around a pole and its subsequent curing over a small fire. Chizola spent some thirty minutes removing the tongue from the head. This he split down its center.

After all the meat was cut, Chizola distributed it among those present, sorting the meat into fifteen piles and designating a person to each pile. The men cut poles and wrapped their assigned meat around either end, then balanced the pole on their shoulders for portage to their respective villages. The women, each of whom had brought large white bowls, filled them with meat and placed them atop their heads. We left the kill site at 4:20 P.M. Left behind were the head, small intestine, spleen, kidneys, skin, and many of the bones. These soft portions were rapidly consumed by the many vultures and maribou storks which had gathered around the site prior to our departure.

The pattern of distribution of meat varies with the size of the carcass and according to the commitments of the hunter. One hunter distributed the meat from an impala to the following people:

hind limb—village headman, his maternal uncle
foreshoulder—wife of nephew in another village
foreshoulder—his mother
neck—maternal niece
one side rib cage—classificatory niece
saddle and girdle—wife of maternal nephew
one side rib cage—wife of classificatory nephew
chest, intestines, hind leg, head—retained by hunter

For larger game it is often difficult for hunters to be discrete in their determinations of whom the meat should be given to. The word of such a kill travels quickly, and the hunter may find by force of circumstances or through persistent begging by those more distantly related or unrelated that he distributes meat to more people than he anticipated. But with a larger carcass the hunter also has a wider choice of whom he can give meat to.

A young man accompanied by an older headman and the latter's son and brother-in-law, initially wounded a buffalo but to kill it, borrowed the headman's gun. Consequently he gave most of the meat to the headman. The killer retained only a foreshoulder, the liver, and the heart. The headman claimed both back legs, chest, stomach, and intestines. The killer distributed the other portions as follows: rib cage to the headman's brother-in-law; one-half of the foreshoulder to the killer's niece who was also the headman's sister-in-law; backbone to the killer's sister; and the neck to a friend.

Young hunters are expected to give a sizable portion of their kill to those from whom they borrow weapons. No one "owns" a gun in a restrictive sense; these remain normally in the custody of the headman or elder and are symbolic of his senior status. Junior kinsmen may request their use and their requests are rarely, if ever, denied. Through their custody of weapons, elders, whose social responsibilities usually preclude their spending much time pursuing game, are assured meat for their dependents.

Portions of kills, such as the heart, head, and intestines, are reserved for hunters and are thought to maintain their mystical powers of huntsmanship. The tongue and heart of dead prey are often mutilated. Some chew the tip of the tongue claiming that this causes prey which they will stalk in the future to continue feeding rather than notice them. Others cut the bottom of the heart and throw it away saying that their heart will thereby remain strong and without flutters while stalking. The spleen (*lamba*) is consistently left in the bush although some informants suggest that it could be consumed by an old barren woman. As explained by one hunter, the spleen is located on the side and if consumed, future prey would pass out of range. *Kulamba*, a verb, means "to shun," "to avoid," or "to pass nearby." If a pregnant female is killed, hunters avoid contact with the fetus, for hunters shun things which are considered weak (*tekakozele*).

Hunters claim expended bullets found within carcasses. Before their reuse, these slugs are purified by fire, since this prevents the previous hunter's misfortune from being transferred to its new possessor and his weapon.

Nonhunters may wish portions of carcasses for potions and these the hunter may yield for favors. Adult males fearing impotency often desire the tail of warthogs. Warthogs, while running, hold their tails rigidly erect, a characteristic which some men seek to enable them to have prolonged sexual intercourse.

Meat is used by hunters to reinforce sentiment among their kinsmen, for meat is the most prized relish of all. But the possession of meat by a successful hunter is paradoxical, for its distribution often brings him social strife in the form of jealousy, expressed hatred, envy, and quarrels over amounts given. Among the Gwembe Tonga, those who have meat also have to cope with jealousy (T. Scudder, personal communication, 24 March 1970). In some cases, where illness is involved, the diviner prohibits the meat in question henceforth to the accusing consumer. Jealousy and envy of hunters by nonhunters and the lack of respect shown them is a common theme in Valley Bisa songs as shown below in literal translation.

Chibinda mwantana inama, nao muntepaya alatola. Nkalowa nama. [Hunter, you begrudge us meat. Don't you think those of us who are not now hunters will some day be blessed with the power of killing game?]

Bakazi banji chibula kuwamya. Kamone chibabula. [My wife, don't worry about this lack of appreciation (literally, swallow and be kind). You shall be brought another animal.]

Tuatobela nenu, mwebapalu banama / Kubapa chiliyaze pano / Eo, mwatina nama. [We eat together with you important hunters. / (The hunters) Let's tell them a big story / And they will forever fear animals.]

The model of reciprocal social systems described by Gouldner (1960) suggests that stability depends on reciprocity of exchanges between members such that over a period there is a balance between sharing and receiving of goods and services. If over a period of time an imbalance develops, this condition builds pressures leading toward social disintegration unless within the system there are compensatory mechanisms. For example, in communities where hunting activities are the prerogatives of men, it is usual to find a few individuals who are more productive than the rest and their success leads to an inherent imbalance in reciprocity. In such situations, Dowling (1968) suggests the compensatory mechanism is to bestow esteem on exceptional hunters who by virtue of their productivity become influential men.

In simple societies the kinds of competition between individuals vying for status and leadership are social in nature, and the goods one possesses and distributes serve as social capital. Social gains accrue to individuals as a result of sharing, but one can give too much or too little or even distribute his goods and services inappropriately. Real social manipulators are sensitive to the expectations and needs of others and manage their exchanges judiciously.

In the distribution of meat, a hunter's obligations are primarily to his matrilineal relatives, and through his wife, to her relatives if he happens to be a resident in her village. A hunter should appear generous and distribute meat as widely as appropriate. Relatives expect meat in amount and kind to be of the same proportion as their claims of kinship and to refuse them meat is tantamount to denying their kinship. Esteem and status accrue to individuals who appear to sublimate their own gain by sharing with others. On the other hand, the accumulation of goods or their inappropriate distribution prompts feelings of envy and distrust in others which reduces the respect which one might otherwise enjoy.

Coping with Failure (kubambaluka)

The Bisa word *izuko* is often translated as chance, luck, or good fortune, and its opposite *izamo* as bad luck or misfortune. But our idea of chance is foreign to the Bisa way of interpreting events. For them, luck is conceived as a function of the individual, rarely as a matter of fortuity.

As animists, the Valley Bisa believe nature is pervaded by forces personified as various spirits which make things happen and which show concern with the different spheres of their existence. Of these, the spirits of their ancestors are the most approachable and therefore those with which they are most concerned. Ancestral spirits are concerned with the rules of the living, the ways that individuals behave and act in relation to others and other things, especially in activities relating to production such as agriculture, hunting, fishing, and so on. In approaching each of these activities, in addition to life crisis events such as birth, puberty, and death, individuals should be mindful of a multitude of rules, the infringement of which brings misfortune. Even unintentional violation of these rules is thought to bring angry reprisals by spirits, although their wrath is more severe if the infringement was intentional. Therefore the things a person does or does not do are thought to determine his success or failure in everyday life and are regarded as indicators of a person's standing with the spirits. Hunters do not expect to kill every time they go into the bush. But after many unsuccessful trips, they usually resort to a ritual bath (*isambo*). The following is an example:

> The morning before a hunt, take the leaves of *chimpakasa* [*Lonchocarpus capassa*] and place them in a pot of water. Take the pot to a refuse pit and wash your arms. The arms are what hold the gun. Chimpakasa is considered to be a good luck charm (*muti we izuko*). [Connotations of luck asssociated with the name of this tree are probably related to the verb, *kupakasha*, to say good-bye.]

If he continues his failing streak, the hunter consults a diviner, for there may be any one of a number of social reasons for his unsuccessfulness.

> There are many reasons, but [lack of success for long periods] is mainly caused by one's relatives. These relatives may not be satisfied with the hunter's distribution of meat. So the hunter must go to the *bamulota* [dream diviner] and confess to him what he thinks is the problem. Then the *bamulota* dreams and the next morning identifies for the hunter the source of his problems. If it is caused by relatives, the hunter must go to them and discuss the situation. If they agree that it is they who are causing the hunter's lack of success and ask him to continue to kill game for them, then the hunter can resume killing game.

> Question: Can you explain to me how these relatives affect the success of the hunter?
>
> Answer: It is because the spirits of that lineage are causing that to happen. When one's living relatives become hardhearted (*bululu*) and are offended, they refer it to the ancestors. It is the spirits of ancestors which then affect the hunter's success.

Normative ideas of conduct play their part in regulating the degree of success achieved by hunters, for quarrels within the village are thought to affect adversely the hunter's success. Contact with a gun by pregnant or menstruating women may cause it to malfunction. Hunters should be selective about those with whom they hunt. Before learning these rules, I asked four men to a hunt. Although we saw plenty of game, we were unsuccessful. Upon our return to the village, one of them volunteered the information that our failure on that day stemmed from one of the men having a "bad heart." When I asked him what that meant, he exclaimed:

> Say, four of us make plans to go hunting and we make arrangements for a certain day. All of us are married, but one forgets and has intercourse with his wife. That person instead of confessing this and remaining in the village decides to come along. We see many animals and may even shoot one and see much blood, but the animal escapes. A true person would admit that he had done this thing and confess to having a bad heart.
>
> Or suppose that we were very good friends or at least you think I am your friend. But when I get with other people I talk about you. I don't really trust you and I say unkind things about you. We go hunting. You may shoot an animal but it will charge and wound or even kill one or both of us. My bad heart has thus affected your hunting.

The Valley Bisa in their hunts with muzzleloading guns often encounter problems which cannot be resolved through the application of skill and knowledge. In May 1967 after a long and arduous stalk of a buffalo herd, a hunter and I abandoned our attempt after we found the powder missing from the nipple of his gun. At other times, wounded animals escape despite repeated shots. When all skill and knowledge have not brought success, the multitude of rules governing social relationships serve as a plausible explanation for a person's failure. With so many rules there is always someone unconsciously or not breaking them, and these situations serve as an explanation when things go wrong.

A RITE OF PASSAGE FOR ELDER HUNTERS

Hunting by professionals is more than a subsistence technique. It is a chosen route to manhood involving commitments and goals. It is a social strategy by which hunters compete with other males for positions of leadership among their matrikin. Generosity is considered a necessary qualification for prestige and leadership, as is knowledge of rituals and tradition. We examine in this section the interrelationship of individual and social variables involved in the pursuit and kill of an elephant by a young hunter. We begin by examining the life histories of the two major participants in the social drama.

It was during the latter part of my stay in the Luangwa Valley that I became impressed by the elaborate rituals which surrounded the killing of some game. Yet in collecting information on these various rites, it became evident that important elements of behavior were missing; symbols in themselves are of relatively little use without a description of how they are used. Therefore it was necessary to witness the killing of an eland, elephant, or lion to describe the meaning and sequence of the rites. When the game department granted me a permit to kill an elephant, my objective was for a hunter to kill it while I observed his action and the attendant rituals. I chose Lubeles, for he had been an acquaintance for some time and I knew his background. I accompanied him afield and after he initially wounded the elephant, I helped him kill it. As a consequence, I was taken through the rites.

My association with Lubeles was more intimate than with Chando, his father. Lubeles and I were comparable in age, both of us stood on the verge of a change in status, and shared an enthusiasm for hunting. As a consequence, details of his life history are more complete than for Chando.

Life History of Chando, Adept

Chando's father (B1 on figure 12) married a woman of the Ngoo lineage who resided in Bope village along the Luangwa River. After living for awhile in Bope village, Chando's father and mother resettled in Chibale village where Chando was born about 1903. His father initially taught Chando to hunt game. In 1921, Chando enlisted as a labor recruit. He spent five years as a cook at Ndola and upon his return to the valley he married a woman in Thomas village. In 1927 he left the valley for two years as a worker at Changa Mine and in 1929 spent one year as a cook at Wankie, Southern Rhodesia.

Upon his subsequent return to the valley in 1930, some problems developed with his in-laws, for he divorced his wife in Thomas village. I was unable to gather details for Chando told me only he felt "insecure" in her village and wished at that time to join his lineage in Chibale village. After he came to live in that village he married a woman, Elizabeth (C2) in Chibulu, a nearby village and shortly thereafter went to look for work again on the Copperbelt.

Beginning in 1931 Chando and Elizabeth spent some eighteen years in Luanshya with intermittent returns to the valley. In Luanshya, Chando found initial employment as a policeman, and while in that capacity learned to drive a lorry. Then he found employment as a driver for a

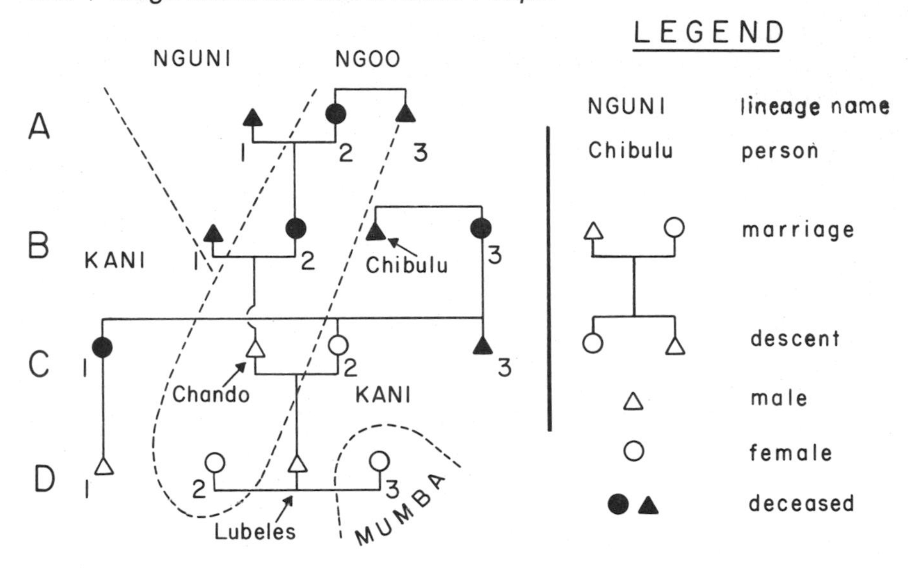

Figure 12. Skeleton genealogy of adept and initiate in elephant rite of passage

commercial firm. Three sons and a daughter were born to Elizabeth in Luanshya.

Upon returning to the valley in 1949, Chando at first settled in his wife's village of Chibulu. From the city he brought a muzzleloading gun which he had purchased. His son Lubeles was then a young boy. Chando taught both Lubeles and a maternal nephew to hunt with his muzzleloading gun. When Chando shifted the residence of his wife to Chibale village, Lubeles remained in Chibulu. In Chibale village Chando was senior in rank among the Ngoo kinsmen residing there. At about this time, Chando also married a clan sister of his wife but she remained in her own village.

Between the time of his return to the valley and the establishment of his own village Chando gained a reputation as a hunter. He often took his nephew and son on hunting trips of several days and during this period was reputed to have made two kills a day with his muzzleloader. From his maternal uncle (*bayama*) he had obtained *chilembe* medicine to strengthen his efficiency in killing game; its principal ingredient was the quaking mantis. With his success came accusations that he was not fairly distributing his kills among all the people in Chibale village. Chibale village contained some thirty-nine huts at this time and not all of its residents were closely related to Chando. Within a large village it is possible to imagine the difficulty a hunter faces in seeing that his kills are judiciously apportioned according to everyone's expectations. Indeed under such circumstances it is understandable that the choices Chando had to make regarding the distribution of small game would antagonize many within the village. That disputes were common was reflected in statements solicited from two of Chando's sons who recalled that living in Chibale village at this time was difficult. Some villagers, they said, respected their father and reciprocated his gifts of game with goods and invitations to beer parties. Others remained antagonistic and were suspected of using sorcery against him. One son told me his father usually left his share of meat in the bush for a day or so before bringing it into the village. In this way he was able to say diplomatically that he possessed no meat in his house. Then after the clamor for fresh meat had subsided, the meat was moved into his house at night.

Given this background of strain, Chando decided to establish his own village and the death of the headman of Chibale village provided the occasion. Chando contacted his classificatory grandfather to prepare *chishipa* medicine with which to purify and protect the prospective site of his village. For his first village Chando chose a locality near a previously abandoned village site and the new headman of Chibale acquiesced to his clearing garden sites among its abandoned hut mounds.

Chando was joined in the new village by a nephew Mupanda and his wife; Elizabeth, Chando's first wife, and their married daughters; Chando's sister Christina and her husband and married daughter; a younger brother Samwele and his wife; Timothi, an unmarried nephew; two married women of another lineage whose husbands were then on the Copperbelt; and an elderly woman unrelated to the headman.

Although Chando continued to hunt, he found his new position as headman demanded that he spend more time in and around the village. He made several trips outside the valley or across the Luangwa to find parttime work in order to buy clothes for his sisters and their children. In his absences, Mupanda a nephew, took charge of village affairs.

Between 1951 and 1966 Chando moved his village twice, once north of the Munyamadzi River and then in 1963 to a location near Chibale village. Time and space had healed some of the bitterness between residents of the two villages. The lineages of both villages had a tradition of marriage and mutual help (*bunungwe*). Chibale married Chando's sister and it was in Chibale that Timothi married a cross-cousin. Prior to the *vizimba* ceremony for his son, Chando had killed two elephants and perhaps to reinforce his bravery afield in his declining years had purchased a prescription for *mfenzi*, for in 1960 he had had a nearly fatal encounter with a buffalo.

During 1966–67 Timothi was not a resident of Chando's village but was a frequent visitor there. Although gaining in stature as a hunter, Timothi possessed no gun. Consequently, he borrowed either his uncle's or

Chibale's. If he borrowed Chando's gun and made a kill with it, he was expected to give his uncle a hind leg, brisket, and if a large buffalo, additional portions.

In 1962 Lubeles married a cross-cousin (D2), then a divorcee, in his father's village. He was expected to divide his time between Chibulu and Chando. Should he make a kill while resident in Chibulu he was expected to provide some meat for his wife in Chando. Although Chando was often away from his village and only infrequently hunted, by these arrangements he was able to keep his village supplied with meat.

Life History of Lubeles, Initiate

Lubeles was the third of four children born to Chando and Elizabeth in Luanshya around 1933. Although born in town, Lubeles spent most of his formative years in the valley, for soon after his birth, Elizabeth returned to Chibulu and it was in this village that Lubeles was reared.

When he was six years old, a maternal uncle made Lubeles a bow and arrows. With these Lubeles practiced stalking birds around the village. Later in his early teens, his father provided him a larger bow and showed him how to kill impala. His technique for killing impala was to advance as close as possible to the herd, then to shoot his arrows above the herd so the arrow came down within the group. Lubeles recalled killing six impala in this manner. As he was unmarried at the time of his first kill, he had no one to prepare beer or porridge for his *vizimba* ceremony. Therefore on this occasion, his guests consumed only meat.

Before leaving for town in 1950, Lubeles married a classificatory cross-cousin. That year he found employment as a guard on an underground train in Luanshya and remained there for two years. When he returned to Chibulu in 1953, his maternal uncle (C3) had died and his older nephew, Packsoni (D1), had returned from South Africa to assume the headmanship of Chibulu. Packsoni purchased a muzzleloading gun at a government auction in Lundazi but since he was not much of a hunter, Lubeles was the one who used the weapon most.

Packsoni provided Lubeles with a prescription for *chilembe* magic. The roots and bark were ground and prepared by his wife who then cut two slits on his right wrist. His father taught him how to hunt buffalo with a muzzleloader. Now that he was married, when Lubeles killed his first buffalo he arranged a large feast. His wife prepared both beer and porridge in addition to the meat for the occasion.

When his first wife died, Lubeles married another woman (D3). Until his return to the Copperbelt, he alternated his residence between Chibulu and that of his new in-laws. Marriage to another woman in a village closer to Chibulu ended in a divorce after a short period.

In 1957 Lubeles returned to the Copperbelt and worked underground as a rock crusher. After a short leave he returned to the Copperbelt and worked as a concentrator. He soon became restless in city employment and returned to the valley in 1960 to resume his hunting and farming activities. After spending a few months in his wife's village, he paid the traditional sum of five shillings to his in-laws and brought his wife to live in Chibulu. Lubeles continued to hunt and in a normal year claimed to kill three or four buffalo in addition to other game. In 1962 he married a cross-cousin (D2) in his father's village. This additional commitment doubled the demands on Lubeles' time and energies.

When Luangwa Safari Ltd. recruited laborers in the valley, Lubeles gained employment as a gun bearer. This role suited him for he often commented on the power, prestige, and accuracy of weapons used by safari clients. Their generosity also impressed him for they often paid him bonuses for locating large trophies. Once he had been rewarded a twenty pound (sterling) bonus for locating a large bull elephant for an American.

I met Lubeles soon after he returned to Chibulu from his safari work and went hunting with him several times before he asked me to pay him for his services as a hunter. I had anticipated this request and told him that I was in no capacity to pay him for hunting, but I was willing to give him an equitable share from each kill I made and would give him occasional work for which I could pay. I fully expected Lubeles to withdraw and refuse to aid me further. When he returned in a few days and said he was willing to help me I was somewhat surprised. I mention this incident for it was not monetary benefit that made Lubeles a close associate.

In many ways Lubeles was a traditionalist. His credentials as a hunter were impressive. Both his father's and mother's lineages were those of distinguished hunters and in his youth he, under their guidance, had become skilled in the pursuit of game. His competency was reflected in the large numbers of game which he had already killed and this success was mirrored in the esteem in which he was held by others. At the same time he had no formal education or any prerequisites for securing a skilled job; he felt foreign among the machinery and impersonal aspects of the modern city. This side of his personality gradually revealed itself as I became acquainted with him over the months. Lubeles saw in me an ally that would work to his advantage on the local scene.

Lubeles was assistant headman in Chibulu's village and, after Packsoni, he was in line to succeed to that position. At this time, he felt alienated from the city and wished to remain among his kin, gain local employment if possible, and supply his dependents with meat. Despite witnessing European and African hunters kill elephant, lion, and eland, he had never killed one of these himself. When I inquired if he would be willing to kill an elephant on my license, his response was immediately affirmative.

Lubeles had attended the *vizimba* ritual when Chando killed his first elephant in the 1950s. Similar rituals had been performed by him when he killed his first buffalo and he had been present at the same rites of other hunters. So he was aware of the significance of the rites.

At the time of the hunt Lubeles possessed a weak *chilembe* magic, but he was desirous of obtaining *mfenzi* magic to hide him from dangerous game. He approached me once about giving him the prescription for *mfenzi*, which he knew I had obtained from the chief. Fearing that such action on my part would be condemned by those who had confided in me and might lead to others withholding information, I refused.

Lubeles was confident that his muzzleloading gun would kill elephants. Since my time remaining for study was growing short, we discussed another possibility. The chief had a .375 Magnum rifle the same caliber as the one in my possession, and Lubeles had on occasion used this rifle so he was familiar with it. Knowing that the chief was being summoned to an important meeting on the plateau, Lubeles asked that I request to borrow the chief's rifle while he was away. To this request, the chief generously acquiesced.

THE RITES

Beliefs and values of a society are often expressed through the symbols employed in their rites. But what is a symbol and how is it used? Beattie (1964) suggests that symbols, first of all, provide information not only about the society but are considered appropriate for the uses in which they appear. Because of their appropriateness, it is important to discover the nature of the association between a symbol and its referent and for this a researcher uses insights provided by knowledgeable participants in that society. Secondly, symbols usually stand for and suggest an abstract notion. They provide a vehicle by which a people express profound ideas about themselves and their world. Finally, symbols are for the most part expressive and dramatic, that which is symbolized is thought sufficiently worthwhile by its members to be portrayed. Since rituals are dramatic and must be acted out, comprehending them is similar to understanding a play or a work of art, for there is structure in rituals just as there is in language.

In the previous chapter I noted the Valley Bisa refer metaphorically to elephants as "the mother of all mammals," a figurative reference to more than just their massive size. Implicit in this association is that any hunter who kills one of these large beasts possesses stronger magic than those who confine their pursuits to smaller quarry.

The hunt begins. When we begin hunting for an elephant, Lubeles is a resident of Chibulu village where he resides with his second wife (D3). On the fifth day of the hunt, however, he shifts his residence to Chando's village, where he is married to a cross-cousin (D2). Married males refer to the residence of their first wife, or if she is dead that of the second wife, as *inanda ikulu* ("great house") and that of subsequent wives as *inanda inono* ("small house").

For eight days of hunting, Lubeles and I are unable to secure an elephant. But on 24 July 1967, as we are walking eastward toward Mupete Lagoon, he tells me that he is confident we are going to be successful. Early the previous evening, as he and his father Chando and mother were sitting around a fire, Chando invoked the ancestral spirits with the following words:

> *Mwe fibanda (mipashi) bwezu. Ntangeleni patanzi. Tuapapata. Namwe BaChibulu, tuapapata. Ntangeleni pantanzi. Pabe lubuto.*
>
> "You our ancestors, go before us we pray. And you BaChibulu, (Lubeles' mother's mother's brother, a great hunter in the past) we pray go before us. Let there be light (luck)."

With these words Chando invoked both Ngoo and Kani ancestors to aid Lubeles the next day. It was a special type of appeal since normally it is the hunter alone who requests the aid of his matrilineal ancestors.

Interpretation. A hunter's ancestors are believed to play an important role in his success and safety. The timing for the above blessing is significant. It is believed that in the early evening ancestral spirits come from the surrounding bush to the edge of the village and at this time are particularly open to supplications by their descendants. For Chando both A1 and A3 are revered ancestors. Chando describes A1 as *nkalamo yanama* ("lion among animals"), a title reserved for great hunters. For Lubeles, Chibulu, his maternal grandfather is the spirit he venerates. Chibulu was an excellent hunter and a village headman who was placed as a *capitao* ("leader") over the local inhabitants by the Europeans when they operated a post at Nabwalya from 1901–1908. Lubeles told me: "He was famous for his bravery. He was called to make peace when quarrels and disputes broke out. He helped when lions were troubling the people. When Kanelli (Nabwalya) post was set up, the Europeans asked him to be their hunter. He was very brave. He was killed by an elephant."

Others whom I asked about Chibulu told me that his status and position with the Europeans at this time made some feel jealous and envious. Consequently they cast a spell (*bwanga*) and caused him to be killed.

Killing a Male Elephant. Lubeles and I see only one elephant during the day. We creep to within twenty-five yards and just as it is beginning to "feel" our presence Lubeles shoots, aiming at the heart. I fire as it speeds away, hitting it in the head. Lubeles runs after the elephant, finds it standing, and shoots twice more, exhausting his supply of ammunition. He says the elephant fell with each shot, only to rise and walk farther after each round. When I catch up with Lubeles, the elephant is standing in an opening about fifty yards away with its back toward us. Since there is no cover, I try to shoot it in the backbone but twice only hit it near the spine. It spins around and falls with the second shot but attempts to rise, whereupon I shoot it in the head. The elephant does not move again. Lubeles approaches to within forty yards and throws some dirt at the carcass and shouts. When it fails to move, we know the elephant is dead and we leave for the village.

Interpretation. While returning to the village, Lubeles exclaims that this elephant has been very difficult to kill. He confides that the first mammal of most species is difficult to kill because one must depend entirely upon ancestral help. After the *vizimba* ceremony and the spirit of the mammal is returned to the bush, then the *chibanda* of that slain one is expected to call others for the hunter. His next elephant, Lubeles confides, should be easier to kill.

The carcasses of large game are not approached by a hunter unless he has the appropriate prescriptions for fear that the slain mammal's shade will enter his head causing him trouble, or worse, return with the hunter to the village. As Chando explained: "It is because we are afraid of the *chibanda* that it will come out and cause us to go mad (*kupenena*). If the animal's spirit is not placated, a hunter may wake up in the night screaming and shouting and will say that the *chibanda* has come and he will feel very sick and perspire." As to how the spirit affects the health of children, Lubeles offered this explanation: "The children may just die of suspicion (*mutunganya*) because their father has the fact that he has not properly placated the animal's spirit on his mind and it worries him. So the children become afraid of what their father has failed to do, are not happy, sicken, and die."

Returning to the village. We do not find Chando in his village; instead we find him with another headman sitting under a tree making a mat. Lubeles asks permission for us to enter the circle and we sit down. After we are settled, Chando begins the conversation by saying that early that morning he has heard an elephant scream several times and is wondering why—were we following it? Lubeles, with his head bowed, says that we heard that elephant also and had gone toward the area from which it came but had not seen it. Perhaps it had sensed our intention. Chando says that he later heard seven shots and he describes the interval between them. Only then does Lubeles say that he needs to talk privately to his father. Chando fetches his hat and excuses himself from the other headman saying that he now has other work. While walking back to Chando's village, Lubeles tells him that we have killed a very large elephant near

Mupete Lagoon. Chando inquires if we have gone close to the dead mammal, and we assure him to the contrary. Lubeles wants Chando to prepare the *vizimba* rites since this elephant has been very difficult to kill. Chando agrees and then tells us about its prescription. He then inquires about the elephant's screaming and wonders if that is the reason why it took us so many shots to kill it. We tell him that another elephant was the one which he heard screaming. This being our first elephant we did not want it to get away; as a consequence, we tried to immobilize it by fracturing its vertebrae. Chando laughs and points under his arm and between his eye and ear as being *chipingu chia nama*—the areas where "life" is found in an elephant. When we return to Chando's village, we are greeted with *mwabombani bankambalume*, a respectful greeting reserved for the return of successful hunters. After discussing plans for returning to the carcass that afternoon, I leave Chando and Lubeles.

Interpretation. Hunting matters are reserved for discussion among hunters. In conversation it is the elder person who leads and the younger who follows with appropriate comments. A screaming elephant is said to be under the influence of a malicious spirit and is feared for this reason.

Collection of magics. When I return in the afternoon, Chando has collected *mwanya* (unidentified) roots. These he has tied in leaves from another tree and placed them in his shirt pocket. In the bush, Chando pauses at a *musebe* (*Sclerocarya caffra*) tree and shows his son where to remove sections of the bark (plate 3). Initially he takes the inner bark from the side where the afternoon sun is shining. Then he goes to the far side of the tree (in the shade) and cuts another section of inner bark. He puts these sections in his shirt pocket and we continue toward the elephant. As we approach a small anthill about fifty yards from the carcass, Chando tells us not to go farther but to wait while he prepares the prescription.

Interpretation. Mwanya root is used because it is white and very slippery, for as Chando stated, "when the *chibanda* of the elephant wants to enter a hunter, it will find that hunter is like a very slippery *mwanya* root and will be unable to enter and possess him." *Musebe* inner bark is used because elephants frequently debark this tree. Again as Chando put it, "the *chibanda* of an elephant when it wishes to enter and bother a man will instead enter a *musebe* tree for that is what it likes."

The color white as a symbol has connotations of purity, harmony, health, and life, and is used frequently in remembrance rites. The inner bark of *musebe* is red and redness likewise has many values with which it is associated. In hunter's rites red is associated with the blood of game and the mystical powers of huntsmanship. The color red figures prominently in rites used to purify the slayer of dangerous game such as a lion or animals which have killed a person. A frequently used synonym for meat is *buswete* ("red thing").

Musebe bark is taken from opposite sides of the same tree. Inner bark is taken from the east side because it is here that morning light first strikes the tree. West is the direction of spirits. Inner bark is taken from both sides of the same tree—east and west. Another dichotomy stressed is light/dark for light is able to penetrate and neutralize (*kusidika*) darkness.

This symbolism may be expressed by the following paradigm:

chibanda	*mupashi*
west	east
mammalian shade	human shade
darkness	lightness
evil possession	avoidance of possession
evil	good
red	white
musebe bark	*mwanya* root

Doctoring the kill. Chando takes the *mwanya* roots, large, white, slimy, and about the size of medium carrots, and flattens them with the tip of his ax. Some is given to Lubeles along with pieces of *musebe* bark taken from both sides of the tree. Lubeles puts these in his mouth and chews. Then Chando presents the same preparation to me. In my mouth the *musebe* bark tastes resinous; the *mwanya* root soon becomes a gelatinous, fibrous mass. Chando retains portions of the prescription. Then Chando tells me to hold onto Lubeles' belt, and we are instructed to close our eyes. Lubeles holds the .375 rifle with which he has shot the elephant. Chando then with his eyes open leads us in a circuitous route to the carcass. We go first to the trunk, where we all stoop to the ground. Chando then lifts the trunk, takes each of our hands, places them on the trunk and says, "*uyu nama* (*chibanda*) *ni apa*—the animal is here." We are instructed to spit in the trunk (plate 4). Then we stand and go around to the anus. Holding the tail to guide us to the anus we each spit in this orifice. Then we open our eyes. Lubeles runs the gun through the elephant's back legs along the belly and between the front legs. Then he climbs atop the elephant and hits its rib cage with the butt of the gun saying, "*We nama tuli nenu*—you animal, we are with you" (plate 5). I am ordered to do the same. Chando then goes around to the tail and ties a knot in one of its hairs. It was only after this phase of the ritual is concluded that they permit me to take pictures of them reinacting its various phases with Lubeles holding his muzzleloading gun rather than the .375 Magnum, for any deviation from the traditional ritual procedure might be taken as a breach of tradition or as lack of respect.

We remove the elephant's tail and trunk and take these back to Chando's village. While walking back to the village both Chando and Lubeles are concerned over how the meat is to be distributed the next day. They know that since the elephant has been killed close to several villages that many people will gather and expect meat, and it is evident that both of them want most of the meat to wind up in their villages. They suggest that before the carcass is butchered I make a speech in which I claim to have killed the elephant alone and that I want the meat distributed to those who have been helpful in my study. People from other villages may get meat only if they helped carry meat back to Chando's village. I agree, hoping that this might spare fights like those which had inevitably broken out over the elephant carcasses which the game guards previously had killed.

Interpretation. A novice hunter must be led by one more experienced. His eyes are closed, believed to affect the *chibanda* with a similar disability, for the *chibanda* is said not to see the approaching hunter as if it were in the black of night. The *chibanda* is thought to reside in the head as Chando explained "breathing, reasoning, and eating are all done with the head." The trunk and anus are the two orifices through which the *chibanda* escapes to "catch" unprotected humans, but is innocuous to a hunter charged with the appropriate magics. Why is the gun passed between the elephant's hind legs and moved toward the head? Chando said, "The *chibanda* might try and follow the hunter. It would look in the gun and see that the gun, not the hunter, has killed it. The legs make the animal move. The gun then passes near the heart of the animal and the part of the animal which touches the ground first." The slogan used when Lubeles climbed on the carcass does not give much insight into the meaning of this action. Other lineage slogans emphasize, "You animal, it is not I who has killed you. It is God. Don't follow me."

Butchering the elephant. As expected, many people were gathered near the carcass when we arrived from Chando's village at 8:20 A.M. on 25 July. They had chased four lions from the carcass when they arrived. The lions had disemboweled the elephant and had eaten portions of the stomach, letting out the cavity juices and leaving parts scattered.

The cutting of the meat proceeds without conflict. The top of the carcass is skinned, and the meat cut in large chunks. These are put in piles on sections of skin or on branches. As the head is skinned, the sections of meat are placed in a separate pile. Meat from the temporals and around the ears, *nama shabwanga* (*munofu*), is kept separate for the *vizimba* ceremony. This meat is carried to the village by Chando's wife and daughter. Another pile of meat is set aside for the chief.

After the men have removed the meat from most of the carcass, several widows beg knives and continue to cut small pieces of flesh remaining on the skeleton. Some men ridicule them, but they continue to glean small portions of meat. When the butchering ceases, meat is distributed to all present. The distribution of meat goes smoothly, although it is always a source of contention.

Interpretation. The elephant is one of the larger mammals identified with the chieftaincy. Tribute is no longer given to chiefs, but since I had borrowed the chief's rifle for Lubeles to use, Lubeles suggested it appropriate to send meat in return. He designated four women to carry meat to one of the chief's wives.

Widows and older women, who have no relatives who are hunters, are the constant beggars around good hunters. Cutting meat is not considered women's work; they normally sit in the background watching. Their work is to help carry the meat. The three women cutting meat were not sure of obtaining any and were notorious beggars. Though they were ridiculed, apparently they felt that under the circumstances this was the only way in which they could secure meat for themselves and their small dependents.

Removing the tusks. Removal of the tusks requires four hours of work by two to three men. First the meat has to be removed from the skull (plate 6). While the meat is being taken from the skull, Chando leaves temporarily to collect leaves for treating the tusks. For this he requires leaves from one of the following trees: *musimbite* (*Combretum imberbe*), *musambamfwa*, or *musolo* (*Pseudolachnostylis maprouneifolia*). The bone surrounding the tusks is carefully axed away, and the tusks, with the pulp tissue inside, are taken away by two men. Women and young men turn their heads in the opposite direction while each tusk is carried away. The leaves which Chando has gathered are chewed and then spit on the pulp tissue before it is taken out of the tusk, and also into the pulp chamber. The two carriers build a fire and warm the outside of the tusk. Then the tusk is tapped until the pulp falls out. The pulp tissue is burned. No person is permitted to witness this action except older men who protect themselves by chewing leaves. While the nerve pulps are burning, a young man approaches the fire to obtain a light for his cigarette. Chando rebukes him strongly.

After the meat is distributed, the crowd disperses. Lubeles takes some elephant dung and returns to the spot where he first wounded the elephant. He flattens the dung on the ground with his shoe and leaves the scene.

Interpretation. The leaves of the three trees mentioned are described as strong trees (*chiti chakosa*) and capable of neutralizing the weakness inherent in the pulp (*nteta*). The pulp, white in color, when taken out of the tusk resembles a limp penis, and if doctoring is not performed it is said the hunter, or any males present will not have sufficient strength for an erection (*mwanalume kuti tabuleya wakosa iyoo*). I was told that if women see the pulp, they would become incapable of producing offspring. In some areas, men removing the pulp tissue wear an apron of "strong leaves" around their waist. To be without descendants is social death, and for the Valley Bisa, to be unable to procreate is the ultimate curse. Formerly, sterile adults were not buried in the ground as were others who had produced living offspring. The nerve pulp may be used in ominous magic, for, according to one informant: "It is used by sorcerers. If a person goes to where an elephant has been killed and takes the nerve pulp, that person can be accused of being a sorcerer. Therefore, the nerve pulp is burned so it will be destroyed."

In many songs sung by Bisa huntsmen over beer, it is the successful hunter's opposite who is derided and jeered. A continuously unproductive hunter is a *fomba*, but this designation has additional connotations—a society "dropout," a sterile man, a person unsuccessful in all professions and roles who resorts to sorcery, a person dependent upon the productivity of others, etc. Some attributes of *fomba* are implied in the following songs:

Fomba, ukutekuleya
Wangkalola ee wakola.

[Fomba, you must go now
You have already scraped together more meat
than your share.]

Munyante chibola
Munyante chibola
Munyante chibola
Atabuka

[Step on the impotent man (his penis). . . .
He (it) doesn't rise.]

Mwine mulya tukomupoka
Manga tutina kuli chibola
Musolo wimba namaseba
We mwana wa ngombe tukoya*

[You owner of that house, we shall take our daughter back
Witchcraft we fear from impotent men.
The honey guide sings its denunciation
You "child of an uncareful mother"* we go.]

(**Ngombe* means cow, woman, or navel, but undoubtedly this expresses the belief that if during birth, blood falls on a child's genitals, it becomes impotent.)

The symbolic motif expressed in reference to the pulp tissue is the following paradigm:

hunter	*fomba*
producer	nonproducer
legitimate magic	illegitimate magic

strength	weakness
descendants	sterile, impotent
dependents	no dependents
pride	shame

Kusidika chibanda ("to neutralize the haunting spirit") is what Lubeles called his action of going back to the place where he first wounded the elephant (*bulambo*) and pressing his foot over its dung. This is, he says, so that the mammal's shade will not follow him. If the elephant had run far from this place, Lubeles told me, he would not have performed this action. When an elephant is resting peacefully or feeding it is said to be under the influence of a "good spirit" (*chibanda chisuma*). Once wounded or enraged it becomes under the influence of a bad spirit. Lubeles told me that both good and bad spirits have to be placated.

Rites of reincorporation, 30 July. Several days before this date Chando calls Lubeles and asks him where he wishes to hold the concluding rites of the ceremony. He inquires whether Lubeles wishes it to be held within Chibulu or within his own village. Lubeles replies that since he was a resident in his father's village when he killed the elephant, the concluding rites should be performed there. Then Chando tells his son that he has to be away and that Lubeles prepare for the ceremony himself.

Lubeles is instructed to take bark from the east side of a *musangu* tree (*Acacia albida*). Next he should collect *malenje*, an unidentified plant which grows within streams. He is to divide the *musangu* bark into two pieces and to tie *malenje* roots around each piece. These are to be placed in the elephant's internal auricular canals. The meat and cartilage saved from the head is to be cooked unsalted in a special container.

Lubeles spends the afternoon preparing for the ceremony that follows in the evening. This preparation includes buying beer and collecting the roots and preparing the three poles that are to support the pot in which the head meat is to be cooked.

When I arrive at Chando's village about 6:00 P.M., some women are cooking porridge on an adjacent fire. The tin can for cooking the meat is placed on another log fire and is elevated and supported on the sides by three poles. Lubeles makes sure that I have come with the chief's rifle and ammunition. Women sit on the east side of the fire while the men assemble on the west. A space for dancing is left vacant between groups of men and women. I notice that there are few men in attendance and of these only one old man, a cripple, is a resident of Chando's village. The others are all from Chibulu.

The men lead the singing by beginning a chant and then by leading the women in a response, during which they alternately sing and clap. Then Lubeles and a few others, either women or men, go into the center around the fire and dance. Usually the men enact hunting scenes while dancing. There is the hunter holding the rifle, walking in one direction and pointing with the rifle, straining his neck and shading his eyes looking for game, pointing in one direction, kneeling and creeping up on prey, shooting the rifle, running out of the circle and collecting a child and bringing him back as a dead animal, and finally dancing around and leaping over the child's body. Sometimes the gun is placed on the ground and the hunter dances around and over it. A woman holds the gun on one occasion and is teased by the men about "her gun." Intervals between dances and songs are spent drinking beer. During several of the dances, children are dragged into the circle by adults and told to mimic adult movements. Lubeles and a cousin enact one scene simulating the stalk of the elephant. The meat prepared for the spirits is stirred at intervals, and care is taken that there is plenty of water in the pot.

Translation of some songs provides insights into the world of the Valley Bisa hunter:

Bamuya nenama, silabamona
Kansi konkemo

This is a song of intercession to the hunter's ancestors. The hunter requests their aid in being able to find mammals and to pursue them successfully.

Mfuti yanji nimawezela
Yenda ne kawele

A song of happiness upon the success of the hunter. He and his gun have been successful in securing game. There will be noise of happiness from the people who return with him to the bush to carry the dead beast back to the village.

Musekela kubamba
Yafwa kale yatwanula amenso

A song in which the hunter expresses disappointment in those to whom he gives meat. These recipients seem fond of him only when he has killed game (their eyes light up with happiness upon seeing the dead mammal).

Balya baleya
Nibamunjili nakuba bambona

A song of misfortune. The hunter has been hunting for some time. He sees prey but as he begins to stalk, they see him and run away. Warthog is mentioned in the above song, but the name of any mammal may be substituted.

About 9:00 P.M. I leave with the party returning to Chibulu's village. The following morning, Lubeles tells me that after we left, all remaining members of Chando's village ate porridge and the meat which had been cooked. Then the pot containing the cooked meat was emptied outside the village and cold water placed therein. Everyone washed his hands in this water after eating, and it was poured in front of the hunter's hut. When everyone retired to his hut, Lubeles took some cold water and washed himself and his wife. The medicated meat from the head (*nama shabwanga*), some porridge, and the stirring stick were saved for the remaining rite the next morning.

Interpretation. The *vizimba* ceremony is held as the sun sets, for this portion of the rite shows appreciation to the ancestral spirits who have helped the hunter secure game. It is a display of harmony among clansmen. Richards (1939:339) mentions that during Bemba fishing rites, a priest exhorts the people to express their grievances for the rite to become efficacious. Although no catharsis was mentioned by those with whom I talked, I suspect that the communal consumption of food and the ritual washing symbolizes the cleansing of adverse relationships.

Chando was absent from the *vizimba* ceremony, and the absence of a key figure in the previous rituals may be effective in symbolizing a change from previous relationships. By his absence, Chando enabled Lubeles to preempt the role of village headman and provider.

To prepare the meat from the elephant's head, two strips of bark are taken from the east side of the *musangu* tree (*Acacia albida*), where the rising sun (*kuntulo kasuba*) first strikes the tree. *Vibanda*, or evil shades, are associated with the west side. Both *malenje* and the *musangu* tree were said to be relished by elephants. These portions are placed in the elephant's external auricular orifices to prevent, I was told, the next elephant from being aware of the hunter's approach. No salt is used, for it is used only for purifying ceremonies and is described as hot (*kubangama*). Ancestral shades are said to be cold (*kutalala*); one cannot purify the purified.

All implements used for cooking the head meat are brought into the village from the bush and to the bush they are returned; otherwise the village might become contaminated. These rites concluded an initiation begun on 17 July when Lubeles withdrew from sexual contact with his wives. This final ceremony reestablishes him as a full participating member of society.

Returning nama shabwanga to the bush, 31 July. Early the next morning Lubeles and I locate a fresh elephant trail in the nearby bush. Lubeles carries both the stirring stick and the head meat which was prepared and cooked the previous evening. This meat is surrounded by porridge (*nsima*). When we find an elephant path, Lubeles digs a shallow hole and places the meat and porridge therein. Next he covers it with dirt, places his foot atop, and while throwing away the stirring stick says, "*We nama shala apa*—you animal stay here."

Interpretation. The *nama shabwanga* is buried in a place where it can influence other elephants to succumb to the hunter. Thus when a hunter dreams continuously (*kulotesha*) about elephants, it is considered a good omen (*mupashi*). After the conclusion of the rite, the hunter knows the full ritual procedures and can "doctor" any subsequent elephant he or someone else kills.

An additional rite. Several days prior to my leaving Nabwalya on 8 August 1967, Chando approaches me. He confides that should the elephant's spirit plague me, there was an additional rite about which I should know. He tells me to collect *mwanya* roots and a slab of bark (*mukwa*) from a *musebe* tree. Gelatin should be squeezed from the roots and smeared with water on the smooth side of the bark slab. Then I should proceed to a river pool where the current is swift and the depth of the pool is over my head. Before wading into the pool, I should place and hold on top of my head the slab where the *mwanya* roots have been smeared. When the water of the pool reaches my neck, I should quickly sink into the pool. Once immersed, the *musebe* slab should float away with the current. In like manner the *chibanda* troubling me will be carried away forever. I express to him my appreciation for his continuing concern for my welfare.

THE ROLE OF RITUAL

As in all rituals, the acts and materials described above are symbolic and expressive; their real meanings, however, may remain obscure to the observer who confines his scrutiny to the elephant. Clues to understanding these rites are to be found in the nature of Valley Bisa society and their perception of the world, for if we wish to know what part these rites play within that cultural system, we must integrate our knowledge of their world in terms of rank and role, ancestor worship, headmanship, magic, and the interplay of these in their interpretation of success and fortune. The slaughter of an important and prestigious mammal by a maturing huntsman provides the opportunity for elders to reinforce by ritual the matrix of beliefs and values, the building blocks of Valley Bisa society. Ritual provides a means of expressing in sensory form and within an idiom comprehensible by a given society its own concepts, attitudes, and values.

Radcliffe-Brown (1948) suggests that one of the functions of ritual is to express and reinforce certain "sentiments" and social values upon which the proper functioning of society depends. In *The Andaman Islanders,* he argues that a society cannot endure unless a sufficient number of people in the society hold and act upon basic values. He suggests that it is the function of ritual within a society to keep values and "social sentiments" central in the minds of its members. Studies of ritual since those of

Radcliffe-Brown have demonstrated that ritual may also symbolize values and notions other than social cohesion and solidarity (Turner 1957; Middleton and Winter 1963; Gluckman 1965). Forde (1964:261) suggests that rites may reflect "values and hazards attached to material resources and techniques, the incidence of disease and other risks to health and life." In previous chapters I suggested the environmental harshness with which the Valley Bisa must contend. Illness and death from diseases are common, and the infant mortality rate is high. Famine and accidents with wild game are not uncommon. Due to their technology, the margin of security which they can maintain is not much above "subsistence." Methods of storage and preservation of food are few and unreliable. Under such circumstances it is natural and understandable that the Valley Bisa would attempt to control misfortune and fortune by resorting to magic and appeals to their ancestral spirits. Such was the theoretical theme of Malinowski (1948). My mention of these hazards was mainly to suggest that given the circularity and closed belief systems of many groups, frequent occurrence of disasters only reinforces their implicit premises and does not challenge them.

Beliefs and rituals among such societies contain strong moral elements which refer to the social relations between members of society. Radcliffe-Brown (1948) also perceived this function in his studies of the Andaman Islanders. The moral universe of a "simple" society is closely tied to their community of relations. Valley Bisa beliefs are explicit that one's failure in kinship duties and obligations is reflected in disturbance of the natural order, and disasters in the natural world are referred to ruptures in normal relations between relatives and the sexes. Successful huntsmanship emphasizes personal bravery, skill, and spiritual merit. By it, an individual may distinguish himself and build up a following of those dependent upon him. Hunters, in their own opinion, are fierce (*bukali*), tough, brave, and above the normal stream of humans. But society norms try to extinguish the idea of meat belonging to the hunter to distribute as he pleases. The Valley Bisa maintain that a hunter receives his prowess from benevolent ancestors who act on behalf of all their descendants, and reminders of ancestral and elder power are writ large in the preceding ritual. The assumption of an important and prestigious role implies rights, expectations, and obligations to one's matrikin.

The consciousness of ancestral dependence begins when a hunter receives his "call" to assume hunting as a profession. It is reinforced at ceremonies commemorating his kills and his rights and obligations to his matrikin are explicit in rites occurring when a young hunter inherits the position and weapon of a deceased elder. This mesh of ritual and rites ensures that each maturing hunter is accountable to his ancestors, to his elders, and through them to his matrilineal relatives. He is graphically reminded that he holds his status as a sacred trust, on the one hand as successor and perpetrator of an important position, and on the other as a representative of his lineage. Rites of passage express the importance which a society attaches to changes in status among its members, and the smooth working of any social system depends upon everyone's knowing and accepting his proper role and the rights and obligations which this assumption of role demands.

Turner (1967) suggests that the transitional period in the rites of passage is important for the edification of neophytes. For it is through the submission to an elder that the neophyte becomes malleable for reflection upon the nature of his society. It was implicit that should both elder and neophyte fail to perform the rites, or should they perform them incorrectly, they would be punished and this would make their community vulnerable to affliction from capricious spirits since they had not sustained traditional orderly behavior. Without these acts, younger generations would be unable to appreciate and grasp the basic values and beliefs of their society and therefore would be unable to conduct themselves properly. It is the esoteric prescriptions and ritual which mature and build hunters into socially acceptable individuals. Ritual transforms a small game hunter into a proven hunter of larger game and impresses him with the duties and obligations and nature of his new state. It is not just the acquisition and knowledge of prescriptions but a change in role which is dramatized.

It may be that in ascribing to the elephant a powerful *chibanda*, capable of afflicting not just the hunter but also his wife, children, and other members of his village, the hunter becomes aware of forces operative in both the natural and social worlds and of the powers which sustain him. Beneath this consideration, however, is the deeper ethic that to persist in customary norms is to live adequately, but to be remiss in one's duties and obligations is to invite disaster.

But it is not just the hunter for whom the rituals have meaning, for the Valley Bisa believe these conventionalized performances help by mystical means to protect, purify, and enrich the members of the group. Members of a village should not quarrel, fight, or curse (i.e., make the village "hot"), and women in particular are under restraint while their husbands are away. Breach of taboos or breaks with traditional patterns affect not only the offender but also other innocent members of the group. The ultimate effect of these sanctions is the preservation of social relationships conducive to human living.

SUMMARY OF PART TWO

Hunting and its organizational forms within the Luangwa Valley has changed through time. In the last century, Valley Bisa hunters employed a variety of techniques and, as exploiters of a major resource, were organized into professional guilds, each under the leadership of magicians. Patterns of belief and rounds of rituals of these guilds reinforced and reflected "traditional" hierarchies and institutions. Although changes in this organizational format were taking place before the establishment of European control, its entrenchment increased the tempo of change in Valley Bisa political and social life as it did elsewhere in Africa. The forms and norms of change shifted from autonomy to national and even international arenas. For valley hunters, this has meant the imposition of outside licensing and yearly payments, restricted takes and seasons, game reserve boundaries, court cases, and resident game guards.

Today hunting is a role assumed by few individuals and the rituals which punctuate their hunting endeavors are functionally related to their society's norms and behaviors. All human beings perceive things in terms of order and patterns, and for the Valley Bisa hunter and his pursuit of game, life is a continuum in which his interpretation of society and life around it share many characteristics in common. Through the extension of familiar categories, both the unfamiliar and unpredictable are given meaning.

In the next section, we examine the interactions of the Valley Bisa with and their influences upon plant and animal populations within the Nabwalya study area. The selection of prey by indigenous hunters reflects the culture and values of the group to which the hunters are responsive. Unlike zoological studies of predators where explanations of selectivity are sought in the behavior or morphology of the beasts, studies of hunting by humans must take into consideration the cultural and technological orientations of their respective groups.

Part Three

CONFIGURATIONS OF THE HUNTING SYSTEM

VIII

Description of Habitats and Bisa Influences

Gun, you discredit me
In the thickets there is game.
Bisa song

THE STUDY AREA AND ITS HABITATS

THE best overview of the Nabwalya study area is from the site of the abandoned government outpost atop Ngala hill. Ngala is the last ridge in a series of escarpment foothills as one follows the tortuous path of the Munyamadzi River from its tumble over the Muchinga escarpment to its confluence with the Luangwa some twelve miles to the east. Its name comes from the hot salt spring which trickles from its base on the eastern side near its midpoint.

A transition in geology and vegetation occurs at Ngala, and its abrupt rise of only a hundred feet above the level flood plain is immediately impressive as one travels west from the Luangwa. These hills so impressed David Livingstone that he speculated they once had formed the shore line of an ancient lake for they reminded him of similar formations along the Zambezi.

But Ngala is one of a series of terminal foothills which stretch at right angles to the view as one gazes down on the winding course of the river below. South of Ngala the transition in topography is less abrupt with the exception of the sharp incline to the pointed peak which bears the ominous name of Kapili Ndozi ("hill of sorcerers"). Atop this incline, it is said, outcasts and those accused of sorcery were decapitated and their bodies abandoned to their animal familiars, the socially repulsive hyenas and vultures. Today, the pointed peak of Kapili Ndozi stands a mute monument to social justice of a bygone era.

Some two miles southwest of Ndozi hill is another series of hot springs called Malanda. Many species of game are attracted to its boiling sulphurous spring which rises in two reedy hillocks at its western end and flows through an area devoid of trees until the water and its concentrates are absorbed in its sandy course.

Gazing north across the Munyamadzi River from Ngala, the next ridge to be seen is called Chongo. Again the name is derived from that of the hot spring at its base. According to legend, the first inhabitants of the valley committed suicide by jumping into this spring rather than submit to a life of servitude under Ngona clansmen. These first settlers were under the leadership of Chongo and it is his name which the spring bears today. Residents say the spring was formerly more extensive and deeper; today it gushes forth as a small hot stream. A colonial officer, P.E. Hall, formerly stationed at Nabwalya, mentions that for him the numerous hot springs were the outpost's most striking feature. Of Chongo spring about 1905 he recalls, it "sent a steady stream of hot water down to a considerable lagoon of warm water in which numbers of hippo lived, and also numerous crocodiles" (Hall 1950).

From between Ngala and Chongo ridges, the Munyamadzi River rushes out over the level plain in its longest straight stretch along its route to the Luangwa. But as if straightness were not a part of its nature, the river soon bends back on itself and begins anew its twisting, tortuous circuit. The instability of the river is visible in the numerous lagoons and depressions spotting its present course. North and west of its first S-shaped bend are two isolated lagoons or oxbows. At one time, they both formed an important link in the Munyamadzi's channel to the Luangwa. Later the river responded to other pressures and cut a new channel, leaving both lagoons to die a slow death under an accumulating burden of sand and decaying vegetation. These two lagoons are called Chinama (the place of animals) by the local population.

South of the river additional lagoons attest to the unsteady nature of the river. All of these southern depressions hold water during the rains. Hippos frequent Mupete Lagoon at this time but return to the river as the water evaporates or is absorbed into the ooze of the depression's bottom. Yet, through the dry season, Mupete remains attractive to waterbuck, scattered warthogs, pukus, and flocks of guineafowl which come to feed on the grasses covering its exposed bottom.

An open habitat flanks both sides of the river. Here a few large trees remain despite the current concentration of cultivation in this area. Behind this open ground the tree canopy closes and blankets the landscape to the far horizon. To the southeast, however, two slender breaks indicate the positions of Chela and Bouvwe grasslands.

The overview from atop Ngala hill changes with the pulse of the seasons. During the dry season, the vista is predominantly a parched pattern of blacks, the charred remains of seasonal fires, and golden browns, the tint of drying vegetation (plate 7). Most trees are deciduous, during the dry season punctuating the river here and there with the light green hues of the few species in leaf. *Cassia siamea*, an exotic evergreen from Asia, marks the sites of some villages.

With last year's grass removed through burning, and with most trees leafless, one looks down on a scorched landscape. The water level in the river continues to drop until it is a mere trickle of its wet season capacity. Fine particles of the alluvial soils are sucked aloft and borne away by brisk whirlwinds. The heavier montmorillonitic clays fissure and crack. Cultivated sites of the previous year stand covered with black ashes or prostrate sorghum stalks, their margins ringed by small huts. No one resides in these field huts, for upon harvest, they return to the more congenial surroundings of their villages.

With the rains of November and December comes the needed element to transform this valley of parched ground into a spring bed of vegetation. Soon the harsh features typical of the dry season are enveloped in a depth of dark greens and the alluvial soils are smothered by a sea of rising sorghums and tall grasses (plate 8). As the Valley Bisa abandon their villages for residence in individual field huts, their parched village pavements sprout opportunistic grasses.

New life and sounds abound as waterfowl and other migrants arrive to inherit a land freshly green and wet. Depressions away from the river fill with water and pulse with life. The river rises, sometimes overflowing its banks and cutting new channels, until its high water mark is reached with the heavy rains of February and March. Thereafter, as the level of the river drops, the land, by degrees, returns to the leanness of the dry season.

At any season the pattern of habitats and different vegetation arrays which one perceives from atop Ngala is a crazy quilt, for both the past history of a wandering river and the shifting agricultural practices of the Valley Bisa have combined to produce a dynamic mosaic. Yet within this mosaic one can define several plant communities or associations of species which appear rather constant in time (fig. 13). The relative proportions of these plant communities for the study area are given in Table 18.

Mopane Woodland (ilambo)

The predominant vegetation on the Luangwa flood plain is mopane woodland. Mopane (*Colophospermum mopane*) is the dominant tree of this association although its degree of dominance depends upon local soil conditions. Mature stands of mopane trees dominate the shallow soils underlain by precipitated clays (plate 9). The surface soil in these areas may be quite sandy with various admixtures of clay, but the transition to the consolidated clays below is normally abrupt. During the rains, water rapidly saturates the top layer of soil and the runoff collects in shallow and

TABLE 18

APPROXIMATE RANKINGS OF MAJOR VEGETATION TYPES OR HABITATS IN STUDY AREA, 1966–67

Habitat Types	Approximate Area (in sq. mi.)	% of Total Area
Mopane woodland	9.4	31.2
Combretum thicket	0.8	2.7
Brachystegia upland	7.3	24.4
Riverine savanna	6.7	22.2
Grassland	1.8	6.0
Land under cultivation	2.4	7.9
Recently abandoned fields	1.7	5.5

often extensive depressions. These same soils lose their moisture quickly after the rains.

Where the topsoil contains a higher proportion of clays and loams as well as sands on a subsurface of mudstone, shrub mopane is the characteristic vegetation. The majority of mopane stems are broken, bent, or browsed by the larger mammals and show loss of vigor. Pockets of these battered stands are scattered and localized. Within these pockets, filtration of water through the surface is extremely slow, resulting in runoff and erosion. Grass cover is sparse on eroded pavements and in the dry season, the topsoil dries firm. The stands of weathered, stunted mopane probably reflect the severity of moisture and nutrient regimes on such soils.

Where the above-mentioned soils integrate with sandier soils, mopane either shares its dominance or gives way to other species. Scattered in these formations are *Cassia abbreviata*, *Berchemia discolor* on old termite mounds, and *Combretum obovatum*. Baobab trees (*Adansonia digitata*) occur singularly. Areas beneath the mopane canopy are normally open, although in some areas a scattered shrub layer comprises wild plum (*Ximenia americana*), native ebony (*Dalbergia melanoxylon*), and occasional thickets of *Combretum elaeagnoides* with small thorn trees (*Acacia nilotica*, *A. mellifera*, and *A. hockii*) dotting the sandy banks of streamlets.

During the rains, the ground is covered with short grasses. *Chloris virgata*, *Urochloa mossambicensis*, *Cynodon dactylon*, *Panicum hippothrix*, *Eragrostis viscosa*, and *Sporobolus festivus* may be locally abundant. Dense mats of *Panicum sociale* are found along the margins of waterfilled depressions. Hunters refer to these soft grasses by the generic term *nswaswa*—an onomatopoeic word for the swishing sound of grass rubbing against one's legs. *Kakonka nswaswa* is a common synonym for hunting.

Mopane woodland changes aspects with the seasons. The fine grasses dry soon after the cessation of the rains and are among the first to be burnt. These fires may burn for days, advancing slowly across the ground,

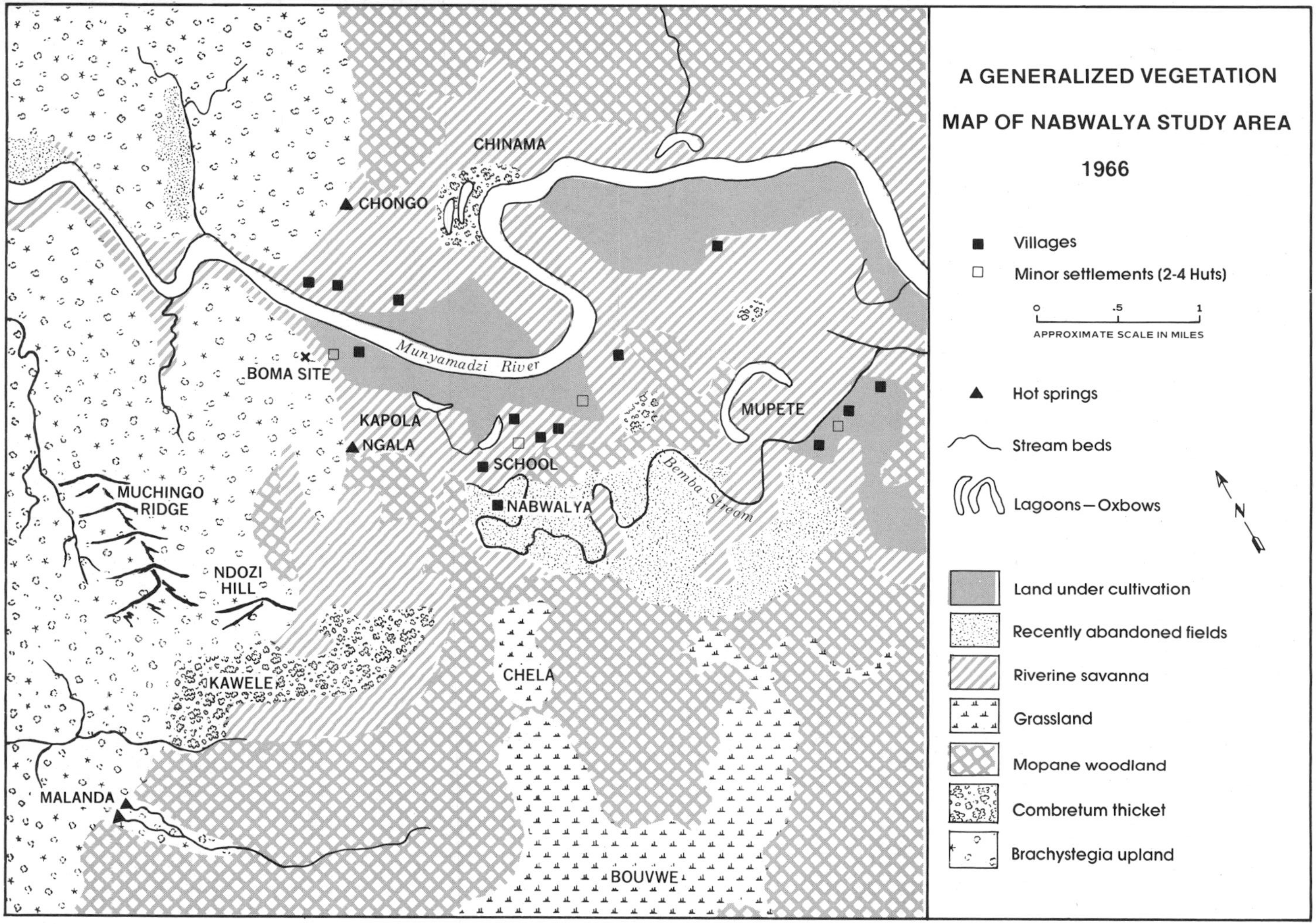

A GENERALIZED VEGETATION
MAP OF NABWALYA STUDY AREA
1966
Villages
Minor settlements (2-4 Huts)
0
.5
1
APPROXIMATE SCALE IN MILES
Hot springs
Stream beds
Lagoons—Oxbows
N
Land under cultivation
Recently abandoned fields
Riverine savanna
Grassland
Mopane woodland
Combretum thicket
Brachystegia upland
CHINAMA
CHONGO
Munyamadzi River
BOMA SITE
KAPOLA
NGALA
SCHOOL
NABWALYA
MUPETE
Bemba Stream
MUCHINGO
RIDGE
NDOZI
HILL
KAWELE
CHELA
MALANDA
BOUVWE

Figure 13.

and do not panic the game as do the hotter fires in the dense taller grasses of riverine savanna. An occasional mopane tree may catch fire and burn for weeks until a skeletal outline in white ash is all that remains.

At no season does mopane woodland become cluttered by leaves or tall grasses obscuring one's view. Perhaps for this reason it is a habitat preferred by hunters and their prey—the buffalo, impala, and warthog. Its openness affords little cover for stalking game directly, but it allows the hunter to see his quarry at a distance, assess its movements, and prepare his strategy.

Grassland (nyika)

An area of extensive grassland lies some three miles south of the Munyamadzi River. Here the grassland is confined to clayey soil overlaid on mudstones. On these areas, the montmorillonite type of clay expands upon the absorption of water in the rains and contracts and fissures under the heat of the dry season. As a result of these seasonal expansions and contractions, the soil surface is distorted and heaved into small mounds. Stands of mopane bordering these grasslands are precluded from invading these areas by the severe physical stresses within the topsoil and the periodic hot fires which sweep across the grasslands each dry season.

In 1967 the northern end of Chela grassland had a scattered canopy of mature camel thorns (*Acacia giraffae*). Some of these were subjected to debarking by elephants. Hunters told me that Malanda at one time had a similar canopy but these too were destroyed by elephants.

The dominant grasses on Bouvwe were *kasense* (*Setaria eylesii*), a tall spiked grass. *Nyelenyele* (*Eriochloa macclonii*) and *Panicum sp.*, both smaller grasses, were relished by game. Scattered among the grasses on Bouvwe were a few weathered mopane, thorn tree saplings, and herbaceous plants.

I have classified the area around Malanda hot spring as a grassland, although its openness is attributable to factors other than those operative at Bouvwe. The salts rising from the two hot springs at its western end may help prevent the establishment of trees, but the herds of grazing mammals attracted by the springs keep the grasses closely grazed and fertilized. The soil is sandy and although the area is ringed by scrub and mature mopane, probably the calcium and sulphur salts, the sandy soil, and browsing pressures combine to give grass the advantage (plate 10).

At Malanda the grass cover is short and composed primarily of *Digitaria milanjiana*, *Dactyloctenium aegyptium*, *Sporobolus marginatus*, and *Cynodon dactylon*. *Cyperus laevigatus* is found growing on the two mounds from which the hot spring issues and within its two channels. Flanked by mature mopane, Malanda is also ringed by a wide band of stunted mopane. The frequency with which mammals visit these springs and the cover provided within the scrub mopane makes Malanda a favorite site of Valley Bisa hunters.

Brachystegia Upland (busenga)

Within this woodland community occur a score or more of trees which characteristically occupy shallow residual soils in hilly country. I refer to this woodland as *Brachystegia* upland, for several species of *Brachystegia* (*B. allenii*, *B. stipulata*, and *B. utilis*) are frequent dominants among its woody components, and the transition between it and other habitats on the study area largely coincides with an abrupt change in topography. In addition to *Brachystegia*, these rolling hills support a woody flora in which *Pterocarpus angolensis*, *Julbernardia globiflora*, *Terminalia sericea*, *Uapaca sp.*, *Lonchocarpus capassa*, *Dalbergia nitidula*, *Pseudolachnostylis maprouneifolia*, and *Lannea discolor* are common. *Khaya nyasica* and *Trichilia roka* occur close to the river.

Shrubs such as *Ximenia americana*, *X. caffra*, *Flacourtia indica*, *Markhamia obtusifolia*, and *Berchemia discolor* dot the slopes and saddles between hills and ridges. In some saddles spongelike mats of grasses on silt soak up the runoff from the rains and become shallow wallows which persist for a short time during the drier months. On the uplands and rolling hills, grass cover may be medium or high, but for the most part is low and sparse. *Hyparrhenia eylesii*, *Andropogon sp.*, *Loudetia simplex*, and *Pogonarthria squarrosa* are the major grasses.

Where erosion is rapid in hilly areas, the surface soil has a lighter, sandy texture with waterworn pebbles and sandstones littering the surface. Within such shallow, porous soils, moisture becomes a critical factor limiting the growth of arborescent forms to widely scattered shrubs. Grass is present in sparse clumps.

Around Muchingo, an undersurface of sloping sandstone resists erosion. The west side of this ridge is densely covered with *Julbernardia*, *Dalbergia*, *Lannea*, *Combretum*, and *Pterocarpus*; its dense tangles are the favored haunts of buffalo, duiker, and elephant. Its eroded eastern exposure offers a vantage point from which one can scan the sparsely vegetated concave terrain below.

The ridges along the Munyamadzi are of hard sandstone; large boulders and stone pavements lie exposed on the surface. The visual aspect of the vegetation atop Ngala hill is noticeably different from that of the valley floor, for here the abrupt change in relief is also reflected in changes in tree species and aspect. Trees rise tall on their precarious perches among boulders. In places, thickets of thorny vines and shrubs cover the abrupt parts of the eastern slopes. These impenetrable places along Ngala were the favored haunts of bushbuck and a leopard during our stay at Nabwalya.

Combretum Thicket (lusaka)

Scattered thickets of varying sizes are found throughout in all the major habitats. Often the occurrence of a thicket indicates a slight shift in soil properties or an anthill, but these, for the most part, are localized and restricted in area. My vegetation map indicates four thickets which were extensive in area; these often harbored game, and consequently were frequented by hunters.

In many of these areas *Combretum elaeagnoides*, *C. ghasalense*, or *C. obovatum* predominated. Shrubs also present were *Canthium zanzibaricum*, *Markhamia acuminata*, *Ximenia americana*, *Phyllanthus sp.*, *Commiphora sp.*, and *Dichrostachys glomerata*.

The largest thicket was called Kawele, a reference to the loud noise one makes in treading upon crisp, fallen leaves during the dry season. From aerial photographs it is obvious that Kawele is an outwash plain derived from erosion of the gravel and sandstones of the adjacent foothills. The surface soil is sandy and in some sites stem density is high. Within Kawele are mixed tree and shrub species commonly associated with both riverine savanna and *Brachystegia* upland. *Pterocarpus angolensis*, *Terminalia sericea*, *Lonchocarpus capassa*, *Sclerocarya caffra*, *Ostryoderris stuhlmannii*, *Combretum elaeagnoides*, *Acacia sp.*, and *Ficus zambesiaca* are found in the canopy layer. The understory is mainly of two species: *Combretum ghasalense* and *Markhamia acuminata*. Ground cover typically consists of short grasses.

Riverine Savanna (chisanze)

Tall grassland with a patchy scattering of large trees occupies the flat land adjacent to the river. The broad strip of riverine savanna below the foothills attests to the shifting course of the river through time, as do the telltale signs of isolated lagoons such as Kapola, Chinama, and Mupete. Today such habitat, with its rich loamy and silt alluvium, has been cleared extensively and used for shifting agriculture. Much of the land east of Ngala has been disturbed in this manner. One must travel some distance from the river and the string of villages to appreciate its former composition and aspect. But once one is away from the river, soil qualities shift quickly so that the species composition of riverine savanna in these areas is generally not as it would be flanking the rivers.

Riverine savanna is a conglomeration of vegetative types along a gradient beginning at the river's edge. On or near the seasonally flooded alluvial flats sausage trees (*Kigelia pinnata*), *Ficus capreifolia*, *Piliostigma thonningii*, white thorn (*Acacia sieberana*), *Dalbergia arbutifolia*, *Khaya nyasica*, and *Albizia adianthifolia* predominate. The winter thorn (*Acacia albida*), a pioneer invader on alluvial flats, is relished by many species of wild game (Feely 1965). Its phenology is the reverse of most trees, and the light green leaves and brownish "apple ring" pods are a welcome view in contrast to the usual bleak austerity exhibited by most trees throughout the dry season.

Away from the river *Diospyros mespiliformis*, *Acacia kirkii*, *Piliostigma thonningii*, and *Ziziphus* form a narrow riparian forest adjacent to lagoons and streams. On sandier soils *Sclerocarya caffra*, *Terminalia sericea*, *Lonchocarpus capassa*, *Combretum imberbe*, *Cordyla africana*, *Lannea stuhlmannii*, and *Ostryoderris stuhlmannii* occur. The fruit of *Sclerocarya caffra* is relished by elephants and other game. Isolated trees are connected by broad elephant trails and the tall grass under their canopies is often flattened by elephants seeking shade or consuming its fruit.

Localized thickets of *Combretum obovatum*, *Commiphora sp.*, and *Markhamia obtusifolia* are met throughout in riverine savanna. Grass growth is luxurious and rapid during the rains, and the height of some species reaches over ten feet. Among the common grasses are *Hyparrhenia rufa*, *Heteropogon contortus*, *Dactyloctenium aegyptium*, *Setaria angustifolia*, *Andropogon*, *Oryza barthii* and *Digitaria milanjiana*. *Panicum maximum* and *Pennisetum purpureum* are found along stream sides with members of *Cyperaceae*.

A narrow band of savanna surrounds Kawele thicket on three sides. Here on poor sandy soils occur a scattering of *Crossopteryx febrifuga*, *Combretum ghasalense*, *Diospyros kirkii*, *Terminalia sericea*, *Markhamia obtusifolia*, and a ground covering of *Digitaria*, *Heteropogon*, *Tristachya*, and *Hyparrhenia* grasses. During the rains these grasses are trodden on and consumed by the herds of buffalo and elephants which frequent Kawele.

VALLEY BISA PERCEPTION AND LABELING OF THEIR ENVIRONMENT

To the human inhabitants of the study area, its landscapes, habitats, and plants are full of meanings and potential products. As is the case with most subsistence cultivators, their gardens are cleared from the surrounding bush and from the bush are gleaned the major components of their material culture. Beyond these pragmatic considerations, the bush is believed full of esoteric properties and figuratively the disorder that reigns there is the antithesis of the order in the village. The bush is said to be populated by frightening spirits and unseen dangers. Thus, metaphorically, the bush means more to the residents than the disorderly tangle which it appears to the eyes of the migrant outsider.

The history of the Valley Bisa is woven into the fabric of the surrounding landscape and the names of most topographic reference points reflect its historical association with some event or person, legendary or otherwise. I have alluded to the significance of Kapili Ndozi and Chongo hot spring, but there are others. A large baobab tree called Kabuswe Yombwe, located between the Munyamadzi and Mupete Lagoon, is named for a prominent Ngona warrior who defended Bisa villages during the Ngoni wars. The local population still renders homage to him at the base of this tree each dry season. Another baobab and small lagoon south of Mupete is called Banakazabwe after a woman who sought refuge from the Ngoni by concealing herself within the hollow of its trunk.

Along the river and Bemba stream, sections of terrain are referred to by the name of the person who in the recent past cultivated it. But in the hinterland where prominent topographic or other features are lacking, pivotal points on the landscape are sites of old hunting camps or villages, a deceased hunter's territory, or the site of an important kill. On the basis of such events, residents label and compartmentalize their environment. These places become the pivotal points for reference to the habitats of their vicinity. Hunting with elders or discussing their movements and routes is akin to reading a few pages in their roll call of heroes and history. One can surmise how this integration of local myth and history within their environment reinforces the hunters' awareness of their past and their consciousness of ancestral help in their pursuits.

To a small group of adepts the bush holds its own esoteric properties for use in prescriptions, magics, or rituals. *Muti*, the generic term for tree is also the term for magic. While the names of some plants may be widely known, knowledge of their specific latent properties and uses is restricted to a few elders or specialists. The nature of these latent powers residing in trees, or in herbs in some cases, is attributable to the color of their bark, sap, roots, or fruits, smell, or name, although there may be other symbolic and therapeutic connotations as well.

Shrubs and herbs are used for a variety of medicinal purposes, and knowledge of these properties and patterns of use belongs mainly to adult men. Knowledge of the types of shrubs, roots, and herbs used to remedy common ailments as diarrhea and other stomach diseases, goiter, eye sores, etc., is for the most part personal lore which is difficult to systematize. But more esoteric lore, involving cures from sicknesses believed caused by possession or affliction, is known to specialists who may demand payment for revealing the curative substances. The following prescription (*muti wakusatamuka*), prescribed for a person suffering from haunting dreams, reveals the therapeutic attributes ascribed to some plants:

> Take the bark of *Munga wa fita* [black thorn tree—*Acacia nilotica*] and the roots of *Munga wa buta* [white thorn tree—*Acacia sieberana*] and place these together with water in a small earthen pot. Then take a small plant, *lwenya* (*Grangea sp.*). It is a green herb with a strong smell. This is also put into the pot. Around midnight, when the afflicted patient is fast asleep, he should be

awakened by dripping cold water on him from the branches of the *lwenya*. When awake, wash him all over with the cold water. This application is repeated several evenings in succession until the haunting spirit (*chibanda*) leaves the patient.

Explanation: A person troubled by haunting dreams is believed possessed by an evil shade, and is said to be "hot" and "black." Whiteness is the color of good spirits (*mipashi*) and when brought together with blackness neutralizes it and drives it away from the person. The *lwenya* herb smells strong and forces the haunting spirit to leave quickly.

The dichotomy between the village and the bush as the respective spheres of major human and animal activities is one which finds expression in Valley Bisa classification and ritual. People live in villages (*mizi*), whereas animals live in the bush (*chonde*). In the villages people should live orderly lives under the protection of their headman and his magic (*nshipa*). The bush (*chonde*) is metaphorically the antithesis of the village. It is not just the haunt of wild animals; evil spirits (*vibanda*), dangerous mammals (*viswango*), and sorcerers (*balozi*) lurk there to snare unsuspecting and unprotected humans. But these two worlds are not totally independent, for most game exist to be the prey of hunters. Hunters pursue their quarry in the bush and under normal conditions are protected there from harm by magic and their ancestral spirits. Should it become necessary to spend the night in the bush, hunters protect their temporary encampment by magic.

In many ways sorcerers are said to operate in a manner reverse to that of hunters. They have turned their backs on village life and kinsmen and their spirits reside in the bush. Here they associate with dangerous animals and return to villages at night to cause sickness or death. Sorcerers also send their animal associates to harm people or to rob them of grain or chickens. But their influence is felt only should ancestral protection be withdrawn as a result of quarrels or through the neglect of kin.

So within the confines of villages live men, women, and their dependents, their domestic stock, chiefly chickens, pigeons, and dogs, and a host of other animals such as rats, mice, and a few birds which have anomalously forsaken the bush. Normally these latter animals are not eaten as food. Within the bush dwell the natural prey of hunters and a host of malevolent beings ready to cause misfortune should "normal" relations break down among village residents.

VALLEY BISA USE OF AND IMPACT ON VEGETATION

The most visible impact by the Valley Bisa on vegetative patterns comes from the clearing of sites for agricultural purposes and their subsequent abandonment, and from the collection of poles, barks, and grasses for building materials. Among residents, the selection of resource components from the bush is partitioned somewhat between the sexes. It is considered women's work to select plants for consumption, grasses for thatching, mud, and firewood, while the selection of trees and reeds to be used in the construction of houses, granaries, mats, hoe handles, etc., is left to the men. However, both sexes assist in clearing garden sites and with the arduous task of hoeing and preparing new sites for cultivation.

On the study area, it is mostly the sandy and clayey soils which support riverine savanna vegetation along Bemba stream, which has been cleared for cultivation sites in the recent past. Only on a few localized sites has the mopane forest been cleared and crops planted on the denser clayey soils; however elsewhere in the corridor, mopane soils are used more extensively for agriculture. Once agricultural sites are abandoned, plant growth on these areas progresses through a number of stages or seres. Disturbed sites in riverine savanna through time become populated by woody plants and grasses characteristic of the site before its disturbance. However, once mopane woodland is cleared and planted the area reverts to grassland. The sequential clearing or opening of mature habitats by humans and their abandonment with the resulting shrubby seres is an important factor in the ecology of some game mammals.

The continuous clearing of land for agriculture and its subsequent abandonment results in an irregular mosaic of vegetation in various stages of regeneration. Today Valley Bisa settlement and fields parallel the Munyamadzi River where their sorghums, maize, and pumpkins flourish on the fertile alluvium. In the recent past, however, fields and villages were mainly along Bemba stream south of the river.

There are many variables which influence the displacement of villages and fields across the landscape at Nabwalya. The more important factors mentioned specifically by residents include:

1. Droughts and the drying of water sources other than the Munyamadzi River. In recent years droughts have made the river the only dependable year-round source of water, and villagers whose residences are at a distance from the river experience inconveniences trekking long distances for water.

2. Social factors such as hostilities and misfortunes. The death of four children in one year was the reason given for a village shifting its site in 1967. Breaches in normal social relations among kinsmen may result in some withdrawing and establishing their own settlement. Depending upon the nature of the conflict and the number of individuals involved, their withdrawal may be temporary or permanent.

3. Exhaustion of soil. The Valley Bisa suggested several indicators of declining soil fertility such as reduction in crop yield and vigor, but apparently shifting sites because of soil exhaustion is not common. I was told of several sites which were cultivated for a few years until their isolation

from other fields and the depredations there by animals dictated their abandonment.

Temporal Succession in Riverine Savanna

A new garden is cleared beginning in June or July. Small trees and shrubs are cut and the branches piled over their stumps. Larger trees are usually left standing. The site is scraped and hoed with the fibrous roots of grasses left exposed to the sun. These roots are consumed by elephants, hippos, and buffalo which visit the cleared fields during the evenings before the crops are sown. Piles of brush are burned preparatory to planting resulting in the liberation of nutrients. After sorghum and maize seeds are planted in November and December, weeding is continuous until February or until such time as the crop emerges in height above its competitors. Following harvest the site is left unattended until clearing and weeding operations begin for the next growing season. An abandoned field is called *chilala*.

The sequence and timing of various stages following its abandonment as a field undoubtedly varies according to the proximity of the wild seed source, soil characteristics, and both the time and intensity with which it was cultivated. To assess succession trends I noted the major species in a series of fields abandoned during different years. In each field, my procedure was to establish a compass bearing near its center; then along this transect line to list the nearest woody plants, herbs, and grasses at each point selected at five- and fifteen-pace intervals. All sites were located in the proximity of Bemba stream. The species list is suggestive rather than definitive.

After one to two years following their abandonment, fields are rapidly invaded by short grasses, herbs, and shrubs although an occasional stalk of sorghum or maize may continue to sprout for a year or so. Among grasses, *Chloris virgata* and *Digitaria milanjiana* dominated on the site sampled, but *Hyparrhenia rufa* and *Heteropogon contortus* were also tallied. Herbaceous plants included *Aframomum sp.*, *Aerva lanata*, *Solanum panduriforme*, *Cucumis anguria*, *Grangea spp.*, and *Corchorus tridens*. The scattering of tree seedlings included *Cassia obtusifolia*, *Dalbergia melanoxylon*, *Combretum obovatum*, *C. ghasalense*, and *Piliostigma thonningii*.

Three to five years after abandonment, the density of woody seedlings increased. All species enumerated in the earlier sere were recorded but with reduced frequency. In addition, *Vernonia petersii* was common. Most trees and shrubs were three feet in height or less; the dominant shrub was *Markhamia obtusifolia*. This shrub was followed, in decreasing order of occurrence, by *Acacia campylacantha*, *A. sieberana*, *Piliostigma thonningii, Lonchocarpus capassa, Combretum ghasalense, C. obovatum*, and *C. elaeagnoides*. Many of these saplings (especially *Piliostigma*) and herbs were browsed by elephants and other game. *Urochloa trichopus, Digitaria milanjiana, Pogonarthria squarrosa*, and *Eriochloa macclonii* were the major short grasses. *Hyparrhenia filipendula*, a tall grass, occurred in scattered clumps.

After six to twelve years saplings were conspicuous and some attained ten feet or more in height (plate 11). *Markhamia obtusifolia* reproduced on sites of this age and incipient *Combretum* thickets were found adjacent to anthills. Prospective dominants such as *Sclerocarya caffra, Ostryoderris stuhlmannii, Combretum elaeagnoides, Acacia sieberana, A. campylacantha*, and *A. goetzei* were found as small seedlings. By virtue of its towering heights and cover value, *Hyparrhenia filipendula* had become the dominant grass, but *Digitaria milanjiana, Hyparrhenia spp.*, and *Urochloa trichopus* were also found. A few herbs persisted.

No fields of more than thirteen years of age were surveyed. Yet with the appearance of dominants in the previous stage, it may be assumed these gradually mature and the area assumes the appearance of undisturbed riverine savanna with tall grasses and scattered tall trees and shrubs. Disturbed areas of this age are difficult for an untrained observer to distinguish from previously "undisturbed" sites especially since most riverine savanna near the river has been disturbed in varying degrees.

Temporal Succession in Mopane Woodland

Mopane is typically found on clayey soils, although on different sites various admixtures of sands are to be found in the surface layer. Despite the small use of these soils for agricultural purposes around Nabwalya, informants considered mopane soils fertile and mentioned they would have utilized these soils more had not distance to the river been critical. They suggested that it was possible to cultivate crops on mopane soils for six to eight years before the soil showed signs of exhaustion.

In clearing mopane woodland preparatory to cultivation, the Valley Bisa pollard the mature trees and pile the cut branches against the stumps. Initial clearing is commenced during the cold season and several months are allowed to pass before the stubble is burned. The fires burn into the root system of the trees.

Once a field has been cleared and abandoned, mopane does not reinvade and establish itself, at least not immediately. Instead grasses *Urochloa mossambicensis, U. pullulans*, and *Digitaria milanjiana* invade these sites. Their fibrous and extensive root systems preclude the establishment of mopane seedlings (plate 12). In Southern Rhodesia, Thompson (1960) found mopane unable to establish itself on soils that supported a good covering of grass.

Bisa to whom I talked said that once mopane was cleared from a site, it never returned. Sites cleared of mopane on the study area were not of sufficient age (six years) to determine the validity of these assertions, but in none of them were there mopane seedlings. Elsewhere in the corridor, old fields abandoned for fifteen years which I examined remained primarily in short grasses. In some of these, *Combretum* thickets were sparse and scattered.

Additional Effects of Valley Bisa Activities on Vegetation

The Valley Bisa influence the composition of the woodlands near their villages in ways other than through agricultural clearings. Craftsmen know the physical properties of most trees, and accordingly select specific trees for use in construction of their houses, granaries, drums, mortar and pestles, hoe handles, gunstocks, etc. Mopane is one of the harder, more durable, and readily available woods. As a consequence it is sought for many of their constructions. The tree itself is differentiated into two classes—*kapani mamba* and *mupani mumana*—on the basis of bark quality. Only the latter has pliable bark suitable for tying. In addition, the Valley Bisa prefer this species for firewood (see table 19); it produces a hot fire and burns slowly. There are other hardwoods, of course, and many less durable or pliable trees to choose from for differing constructions.

TABLE 19

SELECTION OF WOODS FOR FIREWOOD OBSERVED IN FOUR BISA VILLAGES (28 APRIL–7 AUGUST 1967)

Species	Percentages Selected by Each Village *Village*			
	1	2	3	4
Colophospermum mopane	91.0	56.2	36.4	64.7
Acacia albida	4.5	4.2		
Acacia sp.	1.5	14.6	9.1	11.8
Combretum sp.	3.0	20.8	54.5	17.6
Cassia abbreviata		4.2		5.9

Note: Each observation represents a bundle of firewood brought back to a village by women on separate occasions. Total observations were as follows: Village 1, 66; Village 2, 48; Village 3, 11; and Village 4, 17.

Within the study area several plant resources have been depleted or diminished within the memory of those now living. The leaves of a small ground palm (*Palmaceae*) are used extensively for tying and basket weaving. These small palms are fed upon by various animals which when added to the quantities needed in construction greatly exceeds the capacity of the small palm to reproduce itself in local areas. In 1967, some villagers were traveling ten miles roundtrip to collect their bundles of ground palms. In 1830, Gamitto (1960:148–49) found that these palms were scarce on Chewa lands across the Luangwa; yet the demand for their leaves remained so great that they were bartered from others.

The reeds (*Phragmites*) that formerly flanked the Munyamadzi on both sides have disappeared and are now found only surrounding Chinama lagoon. These reeds are used for making mats and baskets. Several interacting factors including a general drying trend within the valley, heavy utilization by man and beast, and the agicultural clearings along the flanks of the river account for its reduction on the study area.

The two instances above were mentioned to me by men in response to my inquiry about vegetation changes they had noted during their lives. However, in their opinions the factor responsible for depletion of these resources was depredations by elephants. When I suggested agricultural clearings along the riverbanks or heavy collection by man in the past, none of my informants found these suitable explanations, nor did they show a willingness to entertain my ideas.

In recent years the distance which those south of the river travel to obtain mopane poles in sufficient quantity has also increased. Roundtrip distances of six or eight miles are not uncommon for these villagers. For villages close to the river's edge on the eastern edge of the study area, it is more convenient to cut poles north of the river and ferry them across, than to find poles in the cutover woodlands south of the river.

Residence in a village confers to the individual the right to cultivate land and exploit the natural resources within its vicinity. Since no individual has priority rights to plant resources, there is no restraint against the culling of desirable woods close to the village. It was expected that the gathering of woods by the Valley Bisa in the vicinity of their villages would produce in time a mosaic of species different from similar woodlands more distant from their habitations. Therefore I assumed that woody species of frequent utility would be collected and removed near village sites, leaving mainly those species of little or no value and size categories of preferred species not suitable for use.

To illustrate this impact I selected for study two areas of riverine savanna (sites A and B) and two areas of mopane woodland (sites C and D). Sites A and C were removed from villages and showed no signs of human activities whereas the other two were close to villages and showed signs of disturbances. Control and disturbed sites of both habitats were compared for species composition, growth form, and density of woody plants.

In comparing the two sites of riverine savanna, it was apparent that the site close to villages (B) had been culled of its major woody species of usable size. *Combretum ghasalense*, a dominant on both sites, occurred mainly as seedlings on the disturbed site. The larger *Combretums* and other trees near villages if accessible to climbers had one or more of their canopy branches removed. Likewise, mopane, an important canopy species on the undisturbed site, was found only as a seedling near villages. Valley Bisa selection against these dominants opened the areas adjacent to villages to an invasion of *Dichrostachys glomerata*, a small, thorny shrub which forms dense tangles and is of no use to the local inhabitants. Selection of woods near their villages resulted in a noticeable increase in the density of woody stems per acre (see table 20). This effect endures for some time because abandoned village sites were often surrounded by shrubby vegetation.

TABLE 20

SPACING AND DENSITY OF WOODY PLANTS IN RIVERINE SAVANNA AND MOPANE WOODLAND

	Riverine Savanna		*Mopane Woodland*	
Sites	A Control	B Disturbed	C Control	D Disturbed
Mean distance (ft.) between woody plants	14.7	8.4	31.3	7.3
Density of woody plants (stems) per acre	201.0	621.8	44.6	816.3[1]

1. Seventy-nine percent of all mopane was cut or utilized.

One's impression within an undisturbed mopane forest is of tall towering tree trunks with a scattering of shrubs. Young mopane seedlings are sparse and restricted to the ground where gaps occur in the overhead canopy. On the study site, disturbance by humans occurred mainly along its edges and within small patches.

The main human influence in this habitat is the cutting of straight limbs in the canopy. Where this disturbance occurs, mopane retains its dominance and reproduces itself, but in opening the canopy, the ground layer is invaded by two shrubs, *Ximenia americana* and *Capparis rosea*. According to informants, these shrubs and their fruits are relished by game, which together with the overall increase in cover makes these sites more attractive for some species.

The interactions of any society with its environmental resources are multiplex and those for the Valley Bisa are no exception. My limited samples permit only subjective conclusions, but these suggest some ways in which the local inhabitants through their various activities affect the constitution and composition of their vegetative environment. Through their clearings for agriculture, selective consumption of woods, and recurrent grass fires, they also influence the distribution and abundance of game in their immediate environs. The opening of the canopy layer in mopane woodland and the clearing of lands for agriculture and its subsequent abandonment in riverine savanna increase the amount of plant material on the ground and in the shrub layers of these habitats. During the dry season, this increase in food and cover together with the water in the river, accounts for the high density of game, particularly impala and zebra, in the vicinity of villages. Whereas at this season, water is a crucial environmental variable, these other factors probably play a larger role than one might suspect, for the Valley Bisa, through their activities, create a more diverse and structured environment than would exist otherwise. In the next chapter I present some evidence which shows heavy use by game within these habitats during the dry season.

My mention of this effect on vegetation in a treatise on hunting is to suggest that whereas some men in their roles as hunters do kill game, these same individuals together with others in their building and agricultural chores engage in activities which bring about changes in the structure of the vegetation which increases the use of these same areas for game. Although my description does not allow me to qualify these associations, it suggests that the number of Valley Bisa presently on the study area did not necessarily mean less game.

IX

Population Structure and Ecology of the Larger Mammals

> Hide near the animal's crossing point. There will be a noise.
>
> Bisa Song

IMPRESSIONS OF GAME ABUNDANCE IN THE MUNYAMADZI CORRIDOR

THE varieties and abundance of wild animals inhabiting the central Luangwa Valley have impressed Europeans for more than a century. Therefore, reviewing the notes of the early explorers and administrators and the tour reports of game rangers provides a historical perspective for assessing population trends of mammals in the Munyamadzi Corridor.

Dr. Lacerda in 1798 (Burton 1873) and Gamitto in 1831–32 (1960), both Portuguese explorers on a mission to King Kazembe of the Lunda, encountered Bisa hippo trappers encamped along the Luangwa. Gamitto's party offered to kill hippos with their guns, but the Bisa refused because the explosions would have scattered the hippos into less accessible places. Gamitto was impressed with the numbers and variety of game which he found along the banks of the Luangwa which included "all species of tropical quadrupeds" with the exception of the giraffe. The abundance of lions and crocodiles there astonished him.

Subsequent explorers such as Livingstone in 1866, Thomson in 1890, Glave in 1894, and Hoste in 1897 were impressed by the number of tracks and actual game which they saw. It is significant that Livingstone found wildebeest plentiful west of the Luangwa and even killed one, whereas the others did not mention this species at all. During the last decade of the nineteenth century, rinderpest, an epizootic, swept through the Luangwa Valley decimating large numbers of ungulates. This epizootic was severe particularly for buffalo and wildebeest. Hall (1910) a commissioner for three years at Nabwalya recalled that the Valley Bisa mentioned how plentiful the wildebeests were around their villages before this epizootic and Melland (1938), who arrived in the valley shortly thereafter, remembered that "the remains of buffalo that had succumbed were common."

Beginning in 1901, J. E. Hughes spent two years as assistant commissioner of the Nabwalya Division, which then comprised the upper Luangwa Valley. Hughes (1933) described his division as "a hunter's paradise of about 10,000 square miles." According to him all mammals were increasing rapidly in the valley. He describes the tall grass along the Luangwa River as "trodden into paths or tunnelled by rhino, elephant, hippo, or buffalo." In areas where the grass had been burned, he noted "many kinds of game," notably hartebeest, zebra, eland, impala, and reedbuck. On his tours throughout his district in 1902, Hughes killed eleven elephants and mentions that the Mufungushi River north of Nabwalya as "still good elephant country." According to Hughes, impala, puku, and reedbuck were common around Nabwalya.

If Hughes' (1933) recollections that reedbuck were numerous at the turn of the century near the Luangwa and at Nabwalya were correct, then this species has suffered a considerable reduction in range. None of the other hunters or administrators who hunted around or resided at Nabwalya during the same decade mentioned the occurrence of reedbuck in either place. Since Hughes' hunting notes were written many years after his experiences, he may have confused or exaggerated some of his impressions. Rather, it would seem that reedbuck have never been plentiful in the corridor, and that their habitat requirements are mostly met around Chifungwe Plains, nearer the base of the escarpment where they are still found in numbers today.

On 25 September 1905, Lyell, a big game hunter, left Fort Jameson for his shooting grounds in the valley northwest of Nabwalya. By the time of his return to Fort Jameson on 31 October, he had shot forty-nine head of game including three elephants, one rhino, two zebra, one kudu, seven warthog, two hartebeest, two reedbuck, three roan, fourteen puku, five waterbuck, six impala, one bushbuck, one klipspringer, and one crocodile (Lyell 1910). In another volume Lyell (1913) records shooting six hippo from a single pool of the Luangwa.

During September and October 1909, Letcher (1911), another hunter, encountered forty-nine elephants on nine separate occasions; the largest herd contained eight animals. He found buffalo tracks common in places but the few survivors of rinderpest were shy. Rhinoceros, roan, eland, and hartebeest were widely distributed but plentiful. Letcher estimated the average size of the eland herds he observed in the valley at thirty. He encountered between 150 and 200 roan antelopes, mostly in small herds ranging from eight to thirteen each. He saw two small herds of wildebeests and secured a trophy with difficulty. Female kudus were numerous but Letcher saw only six males. Of zebra, Letcher says "there are more zebra in North-Eastern Rhodesia than any other animals" and mentions their annoying habit of getting in his way when stalking more prized game. He found impala "plentiful" in the riverine belts, and also puku and waterbuck.

Between 1910 and 1940, there is little information on wildlife populations in the Munyamadzi Corridor. Because of sleeping sickness, the valley was closed to hunting and outsiders from 1912 to 1925 and 1927 to 1934 (Pitman 1934). What few references there are suggest that game was abundant.

In 1931, Captain C.R.S. Pitman, Game Warden of Uganda, was employed to make a faunal survey of Northern Rhodesia. His reports on game numbers, gathered from officials and through correspondence, suggest that all species in the valley were increasing, with the exception of the rhino which was "wickedly poached and undoubtedly decreasing rapidly" (Pitman 1934). Another species for which Pitman showed concern was the Cookson's wildebeest of Saidi's country. Elephant he found "abundant," buffalo "everywhere," klipspringer "noticeably plentiful among the Muchingas," and kudu "and the usual antelopes with the exception of the sable, abounded in the valley" (Pitman 1934). He suggested that Mpika District contained more game in greater variety than any other in Northern Rhodesia save possibly Namwala.

Pitman's survey, the results of which are contained in a lengthy publication, defies an easy summary. But one of his strong recommendations was that the greater part of the unoccupied land between the west bank of the Luangwa River and the base of the escarpment should be set aside as a game sanctuary. He suggested that a corridor be established between the two sections of this game reserve and that this area should continue to be occupied by its inhabitants. The two sections of the Luangwa Valley Game Reserve were established on 27 May 1938 (Denman 1957).

In 1934, C. Ross was appointed elephant control officer for Mpika District and in 1937 was credited with averaging seven elephants a month (Mpika District Notebook). But in the valley on 29 May 1938, while attempting to kill his 350th elephant, Ross was himself killed. Another elephant control officer, Langham (1953) mentions the hazards of elephant hunting in the middle Luangwa Valley, for according to him, "every elephant carries suppurating sores from muzzle-loader gun shots" and "the harassed herds charge as soon as the hated scent of man is sensed."

Although the Luangwa Game Reserves were created prior to 1940, proper staff for their protection was not assured until after the conclusion of the Second World War. One of the first game rangers stationed at Mpika was E. Poles. His term of service covered the period from 1946 to 1958 and to his credit belongs the first attempt to systematize the numbers of game sighted while on tour. In his reports, Poles was repeatedly of the opinion that populations of eland, roan, kudu, rhino, and hartebeest were decreasing and he suspected local hunters were responsible for reductions in their numbers. Other game species were either holding their own or increasing.

The next estimates of game within the corridor were provided by L. D. C. Allen who replaced Poles at Mpika. Allen's tour of duty at Mpika extended from 1959 to 1964 although his stay at Mpika was not continuous throughout this period. Allen noted apparent increases in buffalo, elephant, hippopotamus, bushbuck, duiker, eland, hartebeest, warthog, and reedbuck and decreases in impala, kudu, oribi, puku, roan, zebra, rhino, and waterbuck.

THE STATUS OF MAMMALS ON THE STUDY AREA

Of the more than twenty different species of large mammals on the study area, I found elephant, hippo, buffalo, impala, waterbuck, warthog, and zebra to be abundant. Others, while conspicuous, were rare in actual number and played a minor role as targets of Valley Bisa hunting. As a consequence, the major part of this section is devoted to describing the population structure, behavior and movements of these major species. I do not deny the importance in the ecology of the area of the less frequently observed mammals, but I shall mention them only briefly.

Elephant

As the largest terrestrial mammal, the elephant needs no introduction. Despite their huge size, it was surprising to me how silently elephants can move. Oftentimes the only evidence I had of the proximity of these large beasts was the sound of their rumbling stomachs or tree branches being stripped.

Old bulls are found as solitaries or in small groups accompanied by other males. Normally cows associate in larger groups which contain one or more cows and their offspring of various sizes. For classifying elephants into size categories, I used a drawing of age classes furnished me by W. F. H. Ansell. I used four of his five size categories which were subjectively described with reference to individuals of adult size. These four classes and a brief description of each follow:

Size Class	*Brief Description*
Infant	Very small, no visible tusks, capable of passing beneath adult cow at forelegs
Juvenile	Larger than infant. Incapable of passing underneath adult cow
Subadult	Slightly smaller than adults, tusks small but visible
Adult	When accompanied by others, these were obviously the larger

Adult cows are smaller in size than bulls and generally carry smaller and thinner tusks. In bachelor herds the larger were classified as adults; those smaller in size were listed as subadult, although some of these may have been adults as well. Using these subjective categories of size and sex, the categories of elephants observed on the study area are given in Table 21. Since I was unable to determine the sex of subadults, juveniles, and calves in cow herds, some of which were undoubtedly males, the number in each of these categories for female herds includes both sexes. The percentage composition of male and female herds differ since my classifications of male herds contains only males sufficiently old to be "bachelors" while the composition of female herds contains adult and young females, as well as young males.

TABLE 21

ELEPHANTS OBSERVED IN STUDY AREA
(BY SEX AND SIZE CATEGORIES)

	Sex and Size Categories						
	Male Herds		Female Herds				
Period	Adult	Sub-adult	Adult	Sub-adult	Juvenile	Calf	Uniden-tified
1966 August–December	17	8	18	12	8	8	20
1967 April-August	28	10	41	37	15	11	16
Total	45	18	59	49	23	19	36
% of Total	18.1	7.2	23.7	19.7	9.2	7.6	14.5

Elephants appear to have poor vision but their senses of smell and hearing are excellent. Normally they are docile, but when annoyed their stance with trunk held high, ears out, and making shrill screams is a stereotyped posture in many tourists' memories. The Valley Bisa say cows with offspring are extremely bad tempered and may charge with little or no provocation. Also reputedly dangerous are tuskless elephants which are not infrequent in the valley. A resident returning from the Copperbelt was killed by an elephant just outside the chief's village in June 1966, and in December a school teacher's bicycle was mangled by an enraged cow.

Elephants move great distance at night or when feeding. Because of their mobility, elephants are likely to be encountered in all habitats. They usually rest during the heat of the day in shade. Elephants consume grasses and occasionally dig for roots and chip bark from trees. Hunters refer to these latter activities as collecting magical substances for protection against enemies.

Buffalo

When wounded, the buffalo is generally acknowledged by European hunters as the most dangerous mammal. As formidable as they are in appearance and by reputation, I find buffalo in herds shy and retiring rather than aggressive. But once wounded or alone their pugnaciousness and cunning are legendary. In adult bulls the horn bosses are massive, covering the top of the cranium. The horns sweep outward and then upward. The horns of females and subadults are smaller and not as expansive. Only adult males are fully black in color; females are usually light brown.

Buffalo are gregarious and are usually encountered in herds of more than twenty individuals. Herd size is larger during the rains than at other seasons; the largest herd which I counted contained 380 individuals. Infrequently bulls are encountered as solitaries, but more often they consort in small groups of three to five. Since buffalo herds are compact units and often several tiers deep, when viewed from the ground it is not possible to assess the numbers hidden by those closest to the viewer or to sort their members into sex and age classes. The mean percentage of calves in six small herds was 26.4 percent, which suggests adequate recruitment.

Movements of buffalo to water are largely nocturnal during the dry season. A buffalo herd on the move is a noisy band, and their grunts and coughs are often audible in the early evenings as they sweep past the tier of villages in the direction of the river. Feeding usually occurs in the early morning and late into the evening. During the heat of the day, buffalo usually lie in shade. Buffalo are most often sighted in mopane woodland but their wide movements do not restrict them to this habitat.

Buffalo have poor vision, but possess keen senses of hearing and smell. They are inquisitive and their attitude while being stalked is one of suspicious curiosity. Only rarely are hunters able to approach a herd without being noticed, and frequently the last part of their stalk is under the intense scrutiny of the buffalo. These encounters always end in a sudden stampede, either triggered by the explosion of a gun or by some other stimulus before the hunter can fire. If the hunter or cause of alarm is not located, the herd might stampede in his direction, and hunters on several occasions have had to climb trees to escape such an onrush. Generally after a short rush the herd stops and turns to face its danger before making off again with loud snorts. Once startled by the sight or scent of man, a herd becomes suspicious and restless and is generally unapproachable by hunters for a number of hours thereafter.

Impala

Often described as the most beautiful and graceful of the African antelopes, the impala is the most frequently encountered game species on

Plate 9. Mopane woodland west of Bouvwe plain. Note the lack of undergrowth in areas where the canopy is complete and the abundance of mopane seedlings and saplings under open canopy in the foreground. A herd of buffalo can be seen in the center of the picture. (May 1967)

Plate 10. *Digitaria milanjiana* and *Cynodon dactylon* grassland surrounding Malanda hot spring. In the background, note the border of scrub mopane surrounding the grassland and farther back the taller trees of mature mopane. Two zebra and three hartebeest graze on the short grasses attended by a flock of cattle egrets. (December 1966)

Plate 11. Field succession six years after abandonment on sandy soils of riverine savanna habitat. Bushy shrubs to left of picture are *Markhamia obtusifolia*; other stems, mostly *Acacia* have been browsed by elephants. In the background, the taller *Acacias* and *Combretums* border Bemba stream. (December 1966)

Plate 12. Field succession six years after abandonment on clayey soils of mopane woodland. Note absence c mopane reproduction and elephant prints in front center of photograph. (December 1966)

the study area. Horns occur on males only; those of adults are lyrate, curving outward, backward, then upward with an inward twist.

Impala are gregarious and for the most part are encountered in herds in which one sex predominates. Ewe herds average larger than those of rams; the largest in 1967 contained seventy-five individuals. This herd was observed in August when impala were concentrated near the river and may have contained several groups. Larger impala herds have been recorded elsewhere in Africa. In East Africa, Schenkel (1966) encountered herds of over one hundred impala and in Southern Rhodesia, Dasmann and Mossman (1962a) recorded herds of two to three hundred individuals. The largest number of rams observed in a single herd at Nabwalya contained ten calves, six yearlings, and nineteen adults.

Impala herds vary in size throughout the year and appear more flexible in sex composition at some seasons than at others. Following the rut in April and May, mixed groups containing individuals of all ages and both sexes are common. Such large groups are frequently found in open bush near the rivers, and undoubtedly their numbers contribute to their safety in these areas. With the first rains in November, large herds break into smaller bands and retire from the river to mopane woodland. As the time for parturition approaches, ewes become extremely wary and are seen as singles or in small groups. Few of these groups retain a male escort, and my observations for December show 17 percent of all males observed were with ewes (see table 22).

Another change in herd composition occurs during the rut in April and May. Observations of solitary males increase and these apparently com-

TABLE 22

SEX RATIOS AND GREGARIOUSNESS OF IMPALA IN STUDY AREA

Month	Number Classified	Ratio of Rams to Ewes	Total Ram Observations for Month: % Single Rams	% Rams in Bachelor Groups	% Rams with Ewe Bands
1966 August	207	53:100	2.2	10.8	87.0
September	232	46:100	2.7	17.8	79.5
October	101	63:100	0.0	48.7	51.3
November	181	192:100	5.9	71.4	22.7
December	402	42:100	8.4	74.8	16.8
1967 April	127	59:100	17.0	21.3	61.7
May	192	49:100	20.6	68.3	11.1
June	182	36:100	5.3	57.3	36.8
July	224	57:100	3.7	64.2	32.1

pete for dominance over the ewe groups. At this time each group of ewes has one adult male associated with it; adult males become intolerant and shepherd their ewe groups closely. Only 11 percent of the rams observed during May were with ewes. Following the rut, mixed groups containing both sexes and all ages are common once again. Single rams are observed in most months but are most frequent during late April and May (see table 22) when most adult males are defending their territories. At this season bachelor herds contain nonbreeding adults and subadult males. Single ewes are a common sight in November at parturition time and are occasionally seen thereafter.

Impala are nervous and noisy animals. When alarmed, they utter a distinctive snort which may alert neighboring game. Other individuals within a herd snort as they also sense the disturbance, until suddenly, the whole herd becomes alarmed and reels away from the danger. Such an alarmed band of impala seems to explode in all directions with some of its members jumping high in the air. Such behavior has value in confusing predators, for it is impossible to focus on an individual in the shifting melee of colors.

When in large herds, impala are difficult to approach on foot, for while some members graze or browse, other members, particularly those on the periphery, maintain their vigilance. Alarmed individuals assume a rigid posture and this posture is assumed by others in a herd until all note the danger or it passes. At other times, suspicious impala may lower their heads as if feeding, then suddenly look up and stare in the direction of danger. This behavior is often noted by hunters, who characteristically stalk game when its head is lowered for feeding.

Although impala were one of the more plentiful antelopes around Nabwalya, I found ewe bands extremely sensitive to human proximity. Therefore I was unable to separate all individuals observed into adult and subadult categories. Ewe groups are compact units and the constant movements and shifts of individuals made it difficult to separate those in a herd which were classified from those remaining. For large herds I normally scanned the herd to estimate its numbers and to count and classify the males associated with it. However, I made a special effort to classify all individuals in smaller groups. Apparently, hunters knew the odds against a successful stalk of large herds for they rarely paused upon encountering one, and in most cases, animals within these herds knew of our presence before we were conscious of theirs. Such vigilance on the part of ewes is common behavior where impala are frequently disturbed by humans (Schenkel 1966).

Ram groupings averaged smaller than those for ewes (see table 23), maintained a spread formation, and most individuals could readily be classified as calves, yearlings, or adults on the basis of horn length and

TABLE 23

SIZES OF RAM AND EWE GROUPS OBSERVED IN STUDY AREA

Predominant Sex in Group	No. of Observations of Each Group Size									
	1	2	3	4	5	6–10	11–15	16–20	21–30	31+
Ram	52	22	21	10	5	17	7	2	...	1
Ewe	12	10	7	13	4	26	18	9	18	23

Note: Although sexes were found together during all seasons, groups were assigned a sex according to the sex predominating in each group.

shape, and to a lesser degree on body size. Adult males with tall lyrate horns were identifiable in all groups. Yearling males older than twelve months, with horns which curved outward at the base and then inward at the tips, could be differentiated from adults through their second year (Child 1964). By April, male calves showed small spiked horns and if still with their natal herds could be identified, provided the herd was not prematurely spooked.

The ram to ewe ratio presented in Table 22 should be interpreted in reference to their seasonal pattern of behavior. The high ratio of males recorded for November reflects the difference in visibility of the two sexes, for during November and early December, adult females are scattered and secretive. In November the largest ewe group I recorded contained sixteen and seven of these were rams. Several days after parturition ewes and calves apparently regroup into herds again, for in December large ewe herds are a common observance.

Because of the vigilance of ewes, I could determine the sex and age only of small groups and have used these observations to estimate the adult ewe/calf ratio. In December counts, 39 percent of all ewes observed were accompanied by fawns (50 females:19 fawns). This low percentage suggests that most ewes had joined large groups, that these smaller groups contained a disproportionately larger number of barren or still pregnant ewes, or that these groups contained a number of yearlings which had not bred. By contrast small ewe groups observed from April to June 1967 showed a sex and age ratio of 21 males: 100 females: 84 fawns.

A preponderance of females in the sex ratio is typical of many ungulates. In their study of deer in California, Taber and Dasmann (1954) found a differential sex mortality among fawns and yearlings with appreciably more males dying before becoming reproductively active in the population. If male calves are separated from ewe bands in the May rut following their birth the previous November or December, as has been suggested (Dasmann and Mossman 1962a), whereas female calves are retained within these herds, such unequal stress may be the cause of the greater vulnerability among males. Further, since males for the most part associate in smaller herds, they may be more vulnerable to predators and hunters.

For males, survival of calves to yearlings in 1966 seemed sufficient for recruitment purposes (see table 24). From August to December 1966 calves comprised 20.6 percent of the total population of males classified at Nabwalya. During November and December these become yearlings and this cohort comprised 21 percent of all males classified from April to August 1967. The low percentage of male calves noted for this latter period may reflect breeding failure, although my previous figure of 84 percent of females with calves would not support this conclusion. It may be that the 1966 calf population remained with groups of ewes and were not separated in my counts. The percentage of adults in the population remained surprisingly consistent over the two census periods, suggesting a high mortality rate among the young.

TABLE 24

AGE COMPOSITION OBSERVED FOR RAM IMPALA IN NABWALYA STUDY AREA AND THE MUNYAMADZI CORRIDOR

				Percentages in Each Class		
Year	Period	Location	No. of Observations	Calf	Yearling	Adult
1966	August–December	Nabwalya	310	20.6	8.7	70.6
		Corridor	121	11.6	8.3	80.2
1967	April–August	Nabwalya	216	9.3	20.9	69.9
		Corridor	116	16.4	12.9	70.7

Note: The relative age of males was determined by the shape and length of horns (see text).

During the latter part of the dry season, impala concentrate in mopane woodland, riverine savanna, and regenerating agricultural lands near the river. Movements across the open fields to drink at the river takes place at night. At this season the sandy bars flanking the shallow channel of the Munyamadzi River reveal the hoof prints of impala drinking there the previous evening.

Impala become restless as the rainy season approaches, and once the rains begin, they abandon the habitats frequented throughout the dry season. After a trace of rain fell during the evening of 8 November 1966, I counted twenty-five impala tracks crossing the cleared track joining the government school with the game guard camp atop Ngala Hill. Following a rainfall of .63 inches the night of 10 November, I counted only sixteen impala tracks in the soft mud of this road and none thereafter, although I continued to count the tracks of other game watering at the river during the evenings. A hunter, explaining this behavior, asserted that impala did not tolerate mud on their hooves.

Dasmann and Mossman (1962a) suggest that impala are a successional species which thrive in circumstances which open up forest, dense woodland, and tall grassland. My observations (see figure 14) suggest a preference by impala for short grassland and open mopane forest during the rains and a return to riverine savanna and abandoned agricultural land when these areas have been burnt and water in the hinterland becomes a limiting factor. Impala are both grazers and browsers. In the abandoned agricultural land where they concentrate from June to October, they were often seen in areas from which most of the grasses have been removed through burning and along the margins of the other types of vegetation.

In his study of the mammal distribution in the Tarangire Game Reserve, Tanzania, Lamprey (1963) shows the distributions of impala is strongly related to the boundary between two types of vegetation. He suggests that the advantages gained in such ecotones are a greater variety of food plants and escape cover from predators. Impala were rarely seen in the center of open areas. Rather they were encountered along the edge where shrubs and trees offered quick access to cover. Even in mature stands of mopane, impala were encountered mainly in those sections where breaks in the tree canopy or soil–water relationships were such that shrub growth was encouraged.

Waterbuck

The common waterbuck is found throughout the Luangwa Valley. Only the males possess horns and these horns are strongly ringed for most of their length.

Waterbuck were frequently seen in small herds (table 25). In 1966, small herds of two to five waterbuck comprised 42 percent of my observations, and in 1967, 63 percent. Sightings of individuals of either sex for the same periods were 20.6 and 18.5 percent, respectively.

Female herds were for the most part without adult male escort (76

TABLE 25

FREQUENCY DISTRIBUTION OF WATERBUCK GROUP SIZE FOR STUDY AREA AND CORRIDOR, 1966–67

	No. of Animals in Each Group											
	1	2	3	4	5	6	7	8	9	10	11–15	16–20	20+
Observations	20	14	15	8	10	3	5	2	5	4	5	1	8

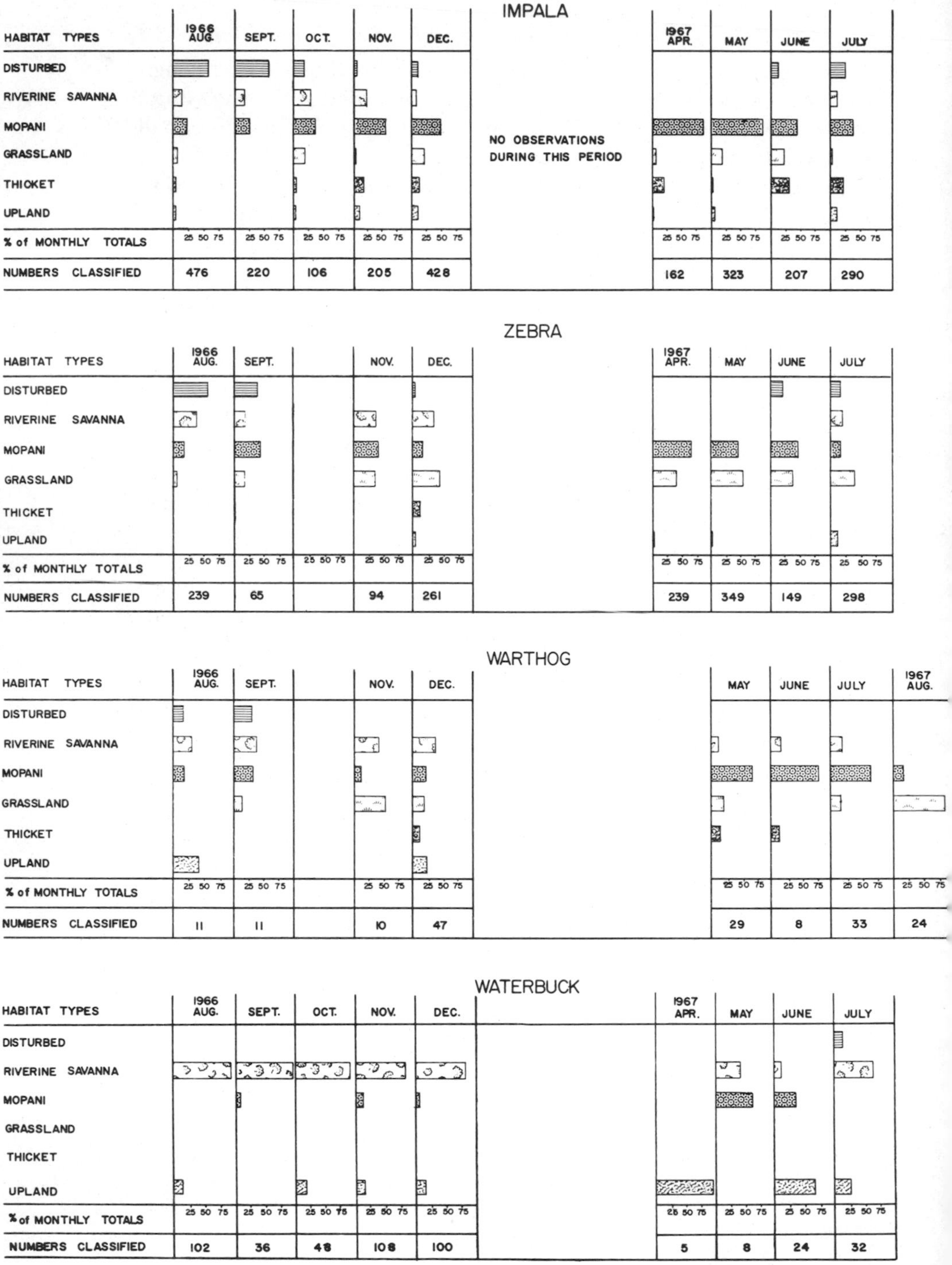

IMPALA

HABITAT TYPES	1966 AUG.	SEPT.	OCT.	NOV.	DEC.		1967 APR.	MAY	JUNE	JULY
DISTURBED						NO OBSERVATIONS DURING THIS PERIOD				
RIVERINE SAVANNA										
MOPANI										
GRASSLAND										
THICKET										
UPLAND										
% of MONTHLY TOTALS	25 50 75	25 50 75	25 50 75	25 50 75	25 50 75		25 50 75	25 50 75	25 50 75	25 50 75
NUMBERS CLASSIFIED	476	220	106	205	428		162	323	207	290

ZEBRA

HABITAT TYPES	1966 AUG.	SEPT.		NOV.	DEC.		1967 APR.	MAY	JUNE	JULY
DISTURBED										
RIVERINE SAVANNA										
MOPANI										
GRASSLAND										
THICKET										
UPLAND										
% of MONTHLY TOTALS	25 50 75	25 50 75	25 50 75	25 50 75	25 50 75		25 50 75	25 50 75	25 50 75	25 50 75
NUMBERS CLASSIFIED	239	65		94	261		239	349	149	298

WARTHOG

HABITAT TYPES	1966 AUG.	SEPT.		NOV.	DEC.		MAY	JUNE	JULY	1967 AUG.
DISTURBED										
RIVERINE SAVANNA										
MOPANI										
GRASSLAND										
THICKET										
UPLAND										
% of MONTHLY TOTALS	25 50 75	25 50 75		25 50 75	25 50 75		25 50 75	25 50 75	25 50 75	25 50 75
NUMBERS CLASSIFIED	11	11		10	47		29	8	33	24

WATERBUCK

HABITAT TYPES	1966 AUG.	SEPT.	OCT.	NOV.	DEC.		1967 APR.	MAY	JUNE	JULY
DISTURBED										
RIVERINE SAVANNA										
MOPANI										
GRASSLAND										
THICKET										
UPLAND										
% of MONTHLY TOTALS	25 50 75	25 50 75	25 50 75	25 50 75	25 50 75		25 50 75	25 50 75	25 50 75	25 50 75
NUMBERS CLASSIFIED	102	36	48	108	100		5	8	24	32

Figure 14. Percentage distribution among habitat types of impala, zebra, waterbuck, and warthog

percent all observations). The largest group of females seen at Nabwalya consisted of thirty-eight animals. Attached to this group were two adult males, which suggests that it may have been a temporary union of two smaller herds. Males are territorial during the mating season (DeVos and Dowsett 1966; Kiley-Worthington 1965). The highest percentage of single males (33.3 percent) was observed during the 1966 dry season.

Large groups were apprehensive of human proximity; however, smaller gruops were quite curious and I found this species to be the easiest of the antelopes to stalk consistently within firing range for rifle or shotgun. The usual reaction to humans for waterbuck was to stand and stare; if alarmed they would run a short distance before turning once again to stare.

Several researchers have remarked on the unbalanced sex ratios observed for this species. In 1953, Verheyen (1955) estimated the waterbuck population in the Ishango section of Albert National Park to contain 20.6 percent males. Later Bourliere and Verschuren (1960) estimated the percentage of males at 30.5 in the same park. On their study areas in Southern Rhodesia, Dasmann and Mossman (1962b) found the sex ratio varied from 31 males: 100 females to 109 males: 100 females. In the South Luangwa Game Reserve during two periods of observations (July and September–October), DeVos and Dowsett (1966) found females predominated in the July counts (51.8 males: 100 females), but males predominated in the September and October count (190 males: 100 females). When their two counts are averaged, the sex ratio was balanced among adults; among subadults, there were slightly fewer males than females. Single territorial males were obvious during their second count.

Several reasons may be suggested for the low numbers of males recorded for Nabwalya during 1966–67 (see table 26). Males may be more vulnerable to predation since they are usually found singularly or in small groups. Verheyen (1955) thought this was the case for Albert National Park, and of the nineteen waterbuck killed by lions and examined by him,

TABLE 26

SEX AND AGE RATIOS OBSERVED FOR WATERBUCK IN STUDY AREA AND WITHIN CORRIDOR

Year	Period	Location	Numbers Classified	Males per 100 females	Immatures per 100 females
1966	August–December	Study Area	341	10.4	43.9
		Corridor	154	42.7	30.3
1967	April–August	Study Area	71	89.7	55.2
		Corridor	31	166.7	77.8

Note: Male calves with spike horns were included with immature totals.

eighteen were adult males. Of the thirteen waterbuck killed or reported wounded at Nabwalya, eight were males, three were females, and two were unreported as to sex. The preponderance of males in hunter kills suggest this sex is more vulnerable, and the low proportion of males on the study area indicates hunting may be a factor in their survival.

Young males, when first excluded from their natal herds during the rut, may face adjustments and patterns of stress to which females are not subjected. Yet the even sex ratios observed by DeVos and Dowsett (1966) on an unhunted population in the South Game Reserve would not seem to substantiate this conclusion.

Another possibility is that male and female waterbuck have separate habitat preferences or patterns of movement and my study may not account for these differences. Kiley-Worthington (1965) found the daily movements of waterbuck in East Africa to be different in parts of their range. In some areas she suggests hunting as the cause for a diurnal to nocturnal shift in activity patterns. If males were more vulnerable, they might show patterns of movement and activity different from females. The hunters whom I accompanied afield may have consciously avoided thickets and areas frequented by males, although kill ratios do not support this conclusion.

Large herds of females might be more readily perceived than bachelor herds which normally contain fewer individuals. Stevenson-Hamilton (1947) noted that waterbuck blend within their environmental background under certain conditions. The largest male herd contained four calves, two yearlings, and three adults. However, I frequently encountered larger female herds. One of these was often encountered early in the morning and evening in the open glades surrounding Ngala hot spring. Since Ngala was located along the route which some hunters often used when leaving their villages, the over-representation of this one large group in my sample may account for some bias in the observed sex ratios.

Waterbuck lambs are apparently born near the middle of the rainy season in February (Stevenson-Hamilton 1947; Dasmann and Mossman 1962c). An adult female shot on 31 December 1966, and examined by me contained a completely developed fetus. After birth, lambs are often seen in company with their mothers. Although I obtained no conclusive information as to when male lambs become independent of their mothers, it apparently occurs for some during their first year. During May, I encountered several groups of male calves either by themselves or in the company of older males. The button horns on males are visible during the latter half of their first year. On sight I estimated the age of each male by comparing its length of horn with that of its ear. Using this criterion individual males were grouped into one of four age classes defined as follows:

Class	*Approximate Age*
Horns less than ears	Less than 1 year
Horns equal to ear length or slightly longer	Yearling
Horns equal to twice ear length	Subadult, 3 or 4 years old
Horns more than twice ear length	Adult

I had no means of judging the accuracy with which horn length correlated with age, but Spinage (1967) found that length of horns was a useful field technique in identifying Uganda waterbuck up to three years of age. The asymptotic length of horn was not reached in this population until age six, but the overlap of values between males aged three to six years made his field estimates unreliable. Such evidence suggests a possible error in my field observations separating subadult from adult categories.

If the percentage of calves recorded in late 1966 is compared with the percentage of yearlings in the first half of 1967 (see table 27), my figures suggest a high survival rate for calves once past the critical period of isolation from their natal herds. This survival rate is also reflected in my sample of male age classes for the corridor.

TABLE 27

AGE COMPOSITION OF MALE WATERBUCK POPULATION IN STUDY AREA AND CORRIDOR

				Percentage of Observations			
Year	Period	Location	No. of Obser- vations	Calf	1–1½ Yearling	2–2½ Sub- adult	3+ Adult
1966	August–December	Study Area	35	28.6	11.4	17.1	42.9
		Corridor	30	26.7	16.7	23.3	33.3
1967	April–August	Study Area	45	15.6	26.7	28.9	28.9
		Corridor	24	20.8	25.0	20.8	33.3

Note: Age was estimated from comparison of horn length to ear length (see text). Thus, 1 to 1½ is equal to or slightly longer than ear length.

The age pattern observed among male waterbuck indicates between 40 and 45 percent of the population consisted of immatures two years of age and under. Such a high percentage of young suggests a high rate of turnover, at least for males.

Waterbuck favor sites where water is found year-round and are seldom encountered far from such sources. On 6 May 1967, I encountered three yearling males in mopane woodland about three miles from water and one of this group was secured by a hunter.

Unlike other antelopes, waterbuck prefer areas where tall grass flourishes in the rains. The sparsity of my observations during April and May suggest they camouflage themselves well in these dense grasses. Their main habitat (see figure 14) is riverine savanna, although they may be found in the rough and stony country in the escarpment foothills close to the river.

Waterbuck actively feed from just before until several hours after sunrise. During the heat of the day they are usually found lying in dense grass cover or in the shade of trees. Feeding begins again two or three hours prior to sunset and may continue into early evening.

Zebra

Burchell's zebra which inhabits much of Central Africa is the species found within the Luangwa Valley.

For the most part, zebra were found in small groups containing between two and six animals (see table 28). During the dry season large groups were rare and the largest group observed contained twenty adults and eight subadults. But during the rainy season zebra were frequently seen in large groups of up to seventy-five animals.

TABLE 28

FREQUENCY DISTRIBUTION OF ZEBRA GROUP SIZE
OBSERVED ON STUDY AREA, 1966–67

	No. of Animals in Each Group													
	1	2	3	4	5	6	7	8	9	10	11–15	16–20	20–30	30+
Observations	4	10	13	23	25	19	10	6	8	3	20	9	12	7

I found zebra inquisitive and easy to approach. But this species is one which hunters seemed least interested in hunting. Although hunters were quite cognizant of the approachability of the species. I never observed any attempt to stalk them. When approached by curious zebras, hunters frequently referred to their stupidity (*chali chiatumpa chipuba*).

Zebras survive close to villages and at night their high pitched shrills and neighs in the bush are common sounds. They are active grazers at all times during the day. During the dry season their trek to the Munyamadzi is made at night or in the early morning.

Although I was unable to determine the sex of these mammals in the field, I did count the numbers in each group and note the presence within each herd of foals and subadults. These data provide some basis for estimating the sex ratio if the composition of groups for this species is the same as that reported for the Plain's zebra.

In his study on the plain's zebra in East Africa, Klingel (1965) found it associated in herds of two types. One type, the family group, contained a stallion, a group of females, and their young. The second group included surplus stallions. He found the former stable in numbers and composition, whereas stallions occurred either individually or in small groups. Small herds containing up to ten Burchell's zebra which I watched closely on the short grass plain of Malanda seemed consistent in composition to those noted for the Plains zebra by Klingel.

If I am correct in assuming that Burchell's zebra shows a tendency to group by sexes, then sex ratios of this species at Nabwalya can be estimated by comparing my observations of herds containing foals and subadult animals with those primarily adult in composition. On this basis my figures for August through December 1966 show 211 males to 229 females (92 males:100 females). If large groups containing over thirty animals were excluded from the April to August observations, the sex ratio is almost unity—365 males to 374 females (98 males:100 females). On the Henderson Ranch in Southern Rhodesia, where Dasmann and Mossman (1962b) collected eighty-eight Burchell's zebra, they secured slightly more males than females (109:100). Of the dead zebra I examined in 1966–67, three were male and two female.

Small zebra foals accompanying adults were observed every month. The greatest number of new foals was seen in May through July (forty-four foals) although twenty-seven were noted in December. Two pregnant mares were observed at Malanda during December, and in the same month I observed a stallion mounting a mare. Throughout the year the percentage of foals by months within the total population observed varied from 4.8 (August 1966) to 23.5 (January 1967). The percentage of subadults observed each month varied from 3.3 to 25.8. Both observations suggest suitable recruitment of young.

The habitat preferences of zebra mirror those of impala. Zebra are frequently observed within disturbed and riverine savanna throughout the dry season. During the rains, they are usually found in grassland or mopane woodland. Zebras are fond of sandy areas where they roll and toss in the dust. Such dusting areas frequented by zebras are common in mopane woodland, old fields, and at Malanda. Although zebra appear to be primarily grazers, the Valley Bisa say that they also occasionally dig for roots and consume browse.

Warthog

Some writers consider the warthog, with its sloping forehead, large curving tusks, and prominent fleshy warts, as one of the continent's ugliest species. The young lack the prominent skull features of the adults and are reddish brown.

Several studies have been published on growth and development of warthogs; unfortunately these were not available at the time of my field research. The population studied in most detail (Child, Sowls, and Mitchell 1965; Roth 1965) is in Southern Rhodesia, and the methods developed for age determination there would seem applicable to warthog populations in Zambia.

Gross field observations permit only generalizations about the population structure. In determining the sex of warthogs afield I was never sure unless I could see the genitals of the males. In adult males these are prominent when they run directly away from the observer. Large single warthogs were assumed to be males, and adult animals accompanied by smaller animals were assumed to be females with young. It was frequently difficult to assess the sex of single animals.

The observed adult and subadult sex ratio of 108 males:100 females is not unusual for warthogs (see table 29). Child, Roth, and Kerr (1968) recorded a sex ratio of 43 males and 35 females from a sample of fetuses and quoted sources showing sex ratios approached parity for wild populations. The sex ratios of warthog populations studied by Dasmann and Mossman (1962b) in Southern Rhodesia varied from 47 males:100 females to 108 males:100 females. Bourliere and Verschuren (1960) and Child, Sowls, and Kerr (1968) report a predominance of females in other areas. Similarly, a large proportion of young in the population is not unusual for this species. Dasmann and Mossman (1962b) showed the percentage of young of the year in various populations varied from 42 to 58 percent.

Ansell (1960b) mentions that the farrowing time in the Luangwa Valley

TABLE 29

SEX AND AGE COMPOSITION OF WARTHOG POPULATION IN STUDY AREA

Year	Month	Total Observed	Total Sexed	Male	Female	Juvenile
1966	August[1]	35	31	11	11	9
	September	30	30	13	10	7
	November	10	8	1	3	4
	December	49	39	21	13	5
1967	January–February	31	28	13	13	2
	April–May	29	25	9	13	3
	June	8	8	5	3	...
	July	33	32	11	12	9
Total		225	201	84	78	39

Note: Observations include those supplied by Bisa hunters.

1. Includes 1967 totals for August.

is from late September to December, with a possible peak in October and November. My observations support a more restricted farrowing season and suggest it begins earlier than September. In mid–September a hunter shot a large sow accompanied by two piglets, which measured approximately seven inches at the shoulder.

Most warthogs were observed singularly or in pairs (see table 30). Larger groups were predominantly a sow and her recent litter, or those remaining from a previous litter, and an adult male. During the breeding season warthogs are monogamous (Child, Roth, and Kerr 1968).

TABLE 30

FREQUENCY DISTRIBUTION OF WARTHOG GROUPS IN STUDY AREA, 1966–67

	No. of Animals in Each Group					
	1	2	3	4	5	6
Observations	39	15	17	8	3	1

On the study area warthogs are encountered in all habitats. They are diurnal and normally feed in early morning or late evening. Warthogs appear to relish grass, roots, and rhizomes which, during the dry season, are often found in depressions. When feeding, warthogs rest on their front knees. With their head lowered at an angle, their tusks can be advantageously used for digging. Hunters know their preoccupations with feeding and stalk only when they find their prey's head lowered. During midday warthogs usually rest, retreating to antbear's burrows or dense shade. I found them attracted to the hot springs and mud baths of Malanda at all times of the day.

Other Mammals

Eland. The largest antelope is the eland. Like cattle, eland are often found in herds. The largest herd encountered at Nabwalya contained thirty-six animals; this herd was encountered in July and August 1967. Both this herd and a smaller one containing twenty-four eland were adequately stocked with subadults. On occasion small groups of eland or singles were seen accompanying impala, zebra, and buffalo. Infrequently, bulls and cows were encountered alone.

Eland are wary antelopes and almost constantly remain on the move. They never seem to stand or rest as do other game, and when disturbed flee at a fast trot. When walking, the tendons of the legs make an audible clicking sound which hunters compare to static heard on radios. In the wild, I never heard them utter a sound, but when shot and dying they utter a deep guttural groan which Valley Bisa hunters consider ominous.

I encountered eland infrequently and often at such a distance that determinations of age and sex were impossible. Since cows also bear horns, it is necessary to be close to a herd to differentiate between subadult males and cows. As far as I could determine eland herds were not decreasing, and hunting, irrespective of its influence on herd levels in the past, was not a critical factor during my residence at Nabwalya.

Hippopotamus. Hippopotami are large, weighing up to five thousand pounds, semiaquatic mammals which spend most of the daylight hours sleeping in deep river pools or lagoons. During the evening they exit from the water along well-defined trails and spread out into the surrounding bush to feed. In an evening these large beasts can consume large quantities of vegetation and where their wallows occur in the proximity of cultivated sites they do considerable damage to gardens. Toward morning, they return to their pools.

Hippos are gregarious and are encountered in large groups during the day but occasional solitaries are also seen. With the desiccation of most lagoons and a drop in the water level of the river during the dry season, the hippo population of the study area in 1966–67 was confined mainly to Chinama lagoon. In October 1966 I counted 161 hippopotami from one spot along the shoreline of this lagoon, and in November, 181. During the rains, hippos scatter and take up stations in the river and other lagoons.

Apparently populations of hippopotami are vulnerable to overhunting especially in areas where they are restricted to few wallows during the dry season. With legal protection from hunting, their population in some valley streams is now high (Attwell 1963; Ansell 1965) and may be "approaching maximum density" (Grimwood, Benson, and Ansell 1960).

Kudu. Kudu are shy and their fawny grey coats with faint white striping on the sides blend with the background of vegetation in which they are frequently encountered. Bulls are encountered individually and if in cover remain stationary unless approached closely. This behavior coupled with their solitary tendencies may account for the underrepresentation of males in my samples (47 adult males per 100 adult females). Females are more gregarious and often consort with other adult females and offspring. At Nabwalya kudu could not be considered plentiful; yet my counts suggest that they were holding their own in population numbers (68 juveniles per 100 adult females).

Puku. Puku are about the same size as impala but more substantially built. Puku are found in riverine savanna, closely associated with habitats flanking the river and lagoons. On the study area, they were found along the river, around Chinama and Mupete lagoons and infrequently in the open glade to the east of Ngala ridge. Puku were more frequently encountered at Chinama than elsewhere, and here I counted nineteen in a single herd. Elsewhere they were usually observed as singles or in small groups of up to three. This species is more common along the Luangwa and Mupamadzi flood plains than on the study area. My observations on puku elsewhere within the corridor shows a more even sex ratio than that recorded at Nabwalya (79 adult males versus 56 adult males per 100 adult females).

Bushbuck. Although bushbuck (*Tragelaphus scriptus*) are common, their distribution is limited to thickets and dense brush; they are largely nocturnal. Whereas I saw bushbuck only eight times, I frequently noticed their hoofprints along paths and in the fields. Bushbuck are shy and wary by nature, and when alarmed they utter a sharp, deep bark similar to a dog's.

Lichtenstein's Hartebeest. These antelopes are rather large, up to four feet at the shoulders, with high shoulders and sloping quarters. They are readily recognized by their long "melancholy" faces. Both sexes bear horns which are heavily ringed and thick at the bases and rapidly attenuate to backfacing points.

On the study area hartebeests were seen on four occasions. Their favored haunts were in the hinterland, back from the river, and along and in the escarpment foothills. At Nabwalya I encountered them around Malanda hot springs and I was told that they were more common to the south. A small herd of hartebeest seen at Malanda on 8 December 1966, contained a young calf, and on 28 September 1966, I observed two young hartebeests unaccompanied by adults between Nabwalya and Kazembe.

Rhinoceros. At the turn of the century the black rhinoceros was "met with everywhere especially in the Muchingas from the slopes by Mpika to the foothills of the Luangwa side" (Mpika District Notebook). Although extirpated throughout much of their former range in Zambia (Grimwood, Benson, and Ansell, 1958), they seem to be holding their own in numbers in the Munyamadzi Corridor. Ansell (1969) estimates a population of forty-three to fifty rhino for the corridor—undoubtedly a minimal estimate. I saw rhino on five occasions around Nabwalya. Twice I observed them singly and three times in groups of two. One of these latter groups included a female and subadult.

The curiosity of rhinos is well known and when found without their almost continuous escort of tick birds they can be approached closely. Game ranger reports contain several references to rhinos which were shot when they charged caravans in the corridor. A hunter confided that he had shot one in the Ngala foothills in 1963 and I know of one that was killed in 1967 near Malanda. But because rhinos are infrequently encountered in the bush and I could detect no predetermined efforts to kill rhino, my impression is that they are not shot commonly nowadays.

Giraffe. Although I did not see a giraffe on the study area, there is evidence that giraffes are occasionally sighted as far north in the valley as

Nabwalya. Recent game reports have documented a gradual northward extension of their previous range in the South Game Reserve. In a note in the game file dated 7 March 1947, Lancaster notes "a few years ago there was an odd giraffe or two wandering along the west bank of the Luangwa near Nawalia (*sic*)." In the annual game reports of 1961 and 1966 there were "unconfirmed reports" of giraffes near the Munyamadzi confluence with the Luangwa. While walking to Mwanya in May 1967, I spotted a giraffe footprint on the sands about eight miles east of Nabwalya. Later, upon returning to Nabwalya and inquiring if anyone had seen giraffes, I was told that the previous year several hunters had seen a male giraffe in the mopane woodland north of Bouvwe Plain. Whether these observations represent the itinerant wanderings of a single individual or a northward expansion of their range remains to be shown.

Blue Wildebeest. Blue wildebeests were common before the turn of the century, for Hall (1910) mentions their abundance around Nabwalya before they were decimated by rinderpest. Until recently wildebeests were confined to the east bank of the Luangwa. Poles (Mpika Tour Report, 1952) mentions their appearance on the west bank in the North Game Reserve in 1948. Today this species is numerous in the Luambe and North Luangwa Game Reserves and my observations of a single wildebeest on three occasions in 1967 on the plains south of Nabwalya may indicate a slow recovery of its former range.

Roan Antelope. Roan antelope were infrequent visitors to the study area. I sometimes saw their tracks in the sands of Malanda and in the mopane forest flanking both Malanda and Bouvwe Plains. I encountered roan only twice, each time near Bouvwe Plain. One herd contained two adults; the larger herd contained sixteen individuals.

Smaller Antelopes. The smaller antelopes were seldom encountered. The common duiker was seen on four separate occasions—two males and two females. These usually travel alone and seem partial to open grassy glades and rocky hills. The first sign one usually has of the presence of Sharpe's grysbok is a sudden explosion on the far side of cover. These small antelopes were seen ten times. They are secretive and inconspicuous and I never saw one that had not been disturbed. Grysbok were fairly common along the river in the thickets of abandoned agricultural lands and in riverine savanna.

Predators and omnivores. Although seldom seen, predators and scavengers were not rare. Most are nocturnal and remain secluded during the day.

I saw lions on two occasions, but their guttural roars were frequently heard in the evenings and early mornings. During our residence, one lion was killed near Chinama lagoon by a safari group and another along the Mupamadzi by valley residents. An indication of lion activity on the study area is suggested by the number and kinds of mammals killed by them. Carcasses or skulls listed in Table 31 were examined by me and suggest the selectivity of these predators.

TABLE 31

PREDATOR KILLS (MAINLY LION) IN EACH SEX AND DENTITION WEAR CLASS RECORDED IN STUDY AREA, 1966–67

	SEX			WEAR CLASS				
Species	Male	Female	Unclassified	Slight	Medium	Heavy	Undetermined	% of Total
Buffalo	7	11	1	7	4	6	2	44.2
Zebra	...	1	15	2	6	...	8	37.2
Waterbuck	1	2	1[1]	1	2	...	1	9.3
Impala	1[1]	...	...	...	...	...	1	2.3
Eland	1	...	...	...	...	...	1	2.3
Warthog	...	...	1[1]	1	...	...	...	2.3
Porcupine	...	...	1[1]	...	...	...	...	2.3
Total	10	14	19	11	12	6	13	99.9

1. Leopard or wild dog.

Signs of leopards were not seen as frequently as were those of lions. A troop of eight wild dogs was seen only once. The tracks of the smaller carnivores, serval, wild cat, genet, and civet, were frequently seen in the fields, villages, and along paths. Several species of mongooses, and the striped polecat were recorded. Honey badgers were seen twice. Signs and sounds of the spotted hyena were nightly occurrences around villages. Hyenas were seen four times in the early mornings.

HABITAT UTILIZATION AND ABUNDANCE OF GAME

The previous discussions of the common game species showed the monthly frequencies with which some of these species were observed in each habitat. Some species, notably impala, zebra, and warthog, showed a preference for particular habitats at different seasons, and waterbuck and puku were confined in their distribution to areas flanking the rivers. Elephants and buffalo show no preference. These sight records do not provide a quantitative measure of the utilization by mammals of the habitats in which they were encountered.

Use of Habitats by Game

For this assessment I measured the density of game trails along five transects, each three hundred feet in length, within several habitats. Since it was impossible to determine the species responsible for the trails or the frequency of use, I made the following assumptions: (1) the figures assigned the three classes of trails in each habitat were proportional to game density, and (2) the use of trails by game either for feeding or movement was reflected by trail cover values. As suggested by Agnew (1966), I weighted game trails by assigning them to one of three subjective classes based upon their definition.

All measurements were made between 27 July and 2 August 1967. By this time the grass had been burnt from large areas, making it impossible to assess use within the major grasslands and abandoned fields. No transects were attempted in *Brachystegia* uplands.

High trail values were recorded for Malanda hot spring, *Combretum* thicket (Kawele), and mopane woodland disturbed by human activities (see table 32). These values imply greater utilization by game of these habitats than for either undisturbed riverine savanna or mopane woodland. Although comparative values were not obtained for three habitats, I would expect *Brachystegia* uplands to show low trail values, and grassland and abandoned fields to show intermediate values.

TABLE 32

GAME TRAIL COVER IN SEVERAL HABITATS IN STUDY AREA

Habitat Type & Location	Range of Cover Values	Mean Cover Value (Percent)	Game Signs Observed Within Trails
Combretum thicket (burned) Kawele	9.75–14.0	12.0	kudu, zebra, impala, elephant, buffalo
Combretum thicket (unburned) Kawele	13.0 –18.5	15.5	
Riverine savanna (unburned) north of Kawele	6.5 –11.75	9.3	zebra, impala, elephant, buffalo, warthog
Malanda grassland (burned) north side	13.75–20.25	17.9	eland, zebra, impala, elephant, buffalo, warthog, hartebeest
Malanda grassland (unburned) south side	13.5 –22.5	19.1	
Mopane woodland (unburned) between Chela and Kawele	5.25–13.0	8.0	impala, buffalo, elephant, zebra
Disturbed mopane woodland north of Chela	15.5 –22.75	18.1	impala, buffalo, zebra, elephant, warthog, grysbok

Note: Sample consisted of five transects, each 300 ft. in length.

The main vegetation types do not support game in the abundance with which it is found in the more restricted associations or early successionary stages of riverine savanna and mopane woodland. Several factors may account for this uneven spread of game, at least during the dry season when the transects were made. Mature mopane forest and riverine savanna composed mainly of canopy trees are largely unreachable by mammals other than elephants and there is little food and cover for most species in these habitats. On the other hand, these same habitats when disturbed by human activities which open up the canopy and make clearings for agriculture result in a diversified plant environment of small and medium height shrubs. A second factor is the availability of water near pasturage. During the rains depressions away from the river fill with water and the short grasses flourish in mopane woodland. At this season impala and zebra prefer the openness of mopane to the dense cover of the tall grasses of riverine savanna. Later, grass burning is uneven, and whereas slow-moving fires in mopane woodland consume much of the ground vegetation, the hot rapid fires that sweep across the savanna near the river often leave grass stalks from which new shoots may sprout. Therefore, during the dry seasons, cover and food for most game is found in the successionary stages and thickets near the main rivers. In the previous chapter I showed how the activities of the Valley Bisa along the river create conditions favorable for game, and the densities of zebra and impala on the study area are in part due to these human wrought changes in the environment.

The highest cover value for trails was recorded at Malanda hot springs. The combination of food, water, and minerals together with the dense band of cover surrounding the open grasslands make this area attractive to game at all seasons. Both burned and unburned sections of this grassland showed comparable trail values.

Relative Abundance of Game

Wildlife investigators use a variety of methods to make a census of game. Aerial surveys have proven useful in determining numbers of game in open grasslands and in spotting dark-colored ungulates in savanna type woodlands. From the ground, numbers of ungulates have been counted in strips from vehicles moving along tracks with the effective width of the strip determined by averaging the distance from the middle of the track to the spots where ungulates were seen. Dasmann and Mossman (1962d) found that this method underestimated game numbers when tested with a known population in Livingstone Game Park. Lamprey (1964) counted the numbers of game within a circumscribed area by transversing three transect lines on a daily basis for four years. Since each of these transects was marked he was able to establish a visibility profile in each habitat. In census techniques employing direct counts, sufficiently similar conditions must be maintained so that the comparison of counts is meaningful and valid.

Early in my study I was faced with the choice of how to make a census of game on the study area and several important factors influenced my decision on how to proceed. A prime determining factor was my interest in the Valley Bisa as a people and their role in the overall ecology of their environment. The local attitude toward Europeans was that they were more interested in game than in the welfare of the local people. Since initial impressions are always difficult to change, I was concerned that this prevailing stereotype would be applied to me and my research. To show an immediate and overriding interest in wildlife and hunting would certainly have alienated me from the Bisa and precluded my gaining their confidence.

Secondly, because of the emergency conditions then existing between Zambia and breakaway Rhodesia, gasoline was severely rationed and expensive when obtainable. These restrictions limited the use of my vehicle to infrequent journeys to nearby towns. As a result of this rationing, my maneuvering was restricted mainly to the study area, and most of my travel was done on bicycle or on foot. In my opinion this restraint worked to our advantage and made my wife and me more dependent upon local hospitality than would otherwise have been the case.

In the end I decided to count game as it was encountered on hunting forays. This approach seemed the most innocuous while remaining the most practical in terms of my overall emphasis. Any census figure of wild animals is ultimately only a momentary expression of a dynamic situation and there are limitations to all methods. As I did not dictate the time or duration of these hunts, the time spent each month in observance varied from 5.5 to 44 hours. For comparison between months, these figures are reduced to the number of game observed per hour (see table 33) and monthly percentages for each of the major species (see figure 15).

The study area was a small unit of a much larger space over which game traveled at will. Impala, waterbuck, and zebra probably spent most of their time within the area demarcated but the movements of buffalo, elephant, and some others covered a much greater area.

To determine whether the probabilities of encountering game were similar for each month I used a chi-square test. Values of all game observed per hour for August through December were not significantly different from expected values but those for April and May were significant. Figures as low as those observed for June and July were expected for five out of every one hundred samples.

The numbers of buffalo, impala, zebra, waterbuck, and warthog observed on each hunt were subjected to a two-way analysis of variance to

TABLE 33

RELATIONSHIP BETWEEN TOTAL HUNTING TIME AND MAMMALS OBSERVED IN STUDY AREA

Month	Year	No. of Hunts	Total Hours	Total Mammals Observed	Mammals/ Hour
August	1967	12	31.50	950	30.2
September	1966	7	12.25	372	30.4
October	1966	4	5.50	158	28.7
November	1966	7	18.75	571	30.5
December	1966	13	44.00	1,190	27.0
April	1967	4	20.50	1,219	59.5
May	1967	9	37.50	1,522	40.6
June	1967	8	30.00	708	23.6
July	1967	13	38.75	895	23.1

1. Only personal observations used.
2. Hours rounded to nearest quarter hour.

determine variation in the numbers of each species observed per hour for each month and for time of day (morning or afternoon). All tests indicated a very significant relationship between numbers observed by months and time of day. With the exception of waterbuck, the mean number of those species encountered during the morning was nearly double those of the afternoon (see table 34). These tests and the percentage composition of the game observed each month (figure 15) suggest that populations on the study area were subject to considerable flux, at least between wet and dry seasons.

In addition to the above count, game numbers were assessed on two other occasions. While estimating game populations within the Luangwa Valley along transect lines from the air in June 1967, David Patton estimated the populations of elephant and zebra within a fifty square mile

TABLE 34

COMPARISON OF NUMBERS OF SPECIES OBSERVED AND FREQUENCY OF ENCOUNTER BETWEEN MORNING AND AFTERNOON HUNTS, NABWALYA STUDY AREA

	Number of Hunts on which Species were Encountered[1]		Mean Number Observed Per Hour on Each Hunt	
Species	Morning	Afternoon	Morning	Afternoon
Impala	35	25	13.9	6.6
Buffalo	16	5	10.2	2.8
Zebra	32	20	8.8	4.2
Waterbuck	20	15	1.4	5.4
Warthog	23	9	0.7	0.3

1. Sample includes 42 morning and 35 afternoon hunts.

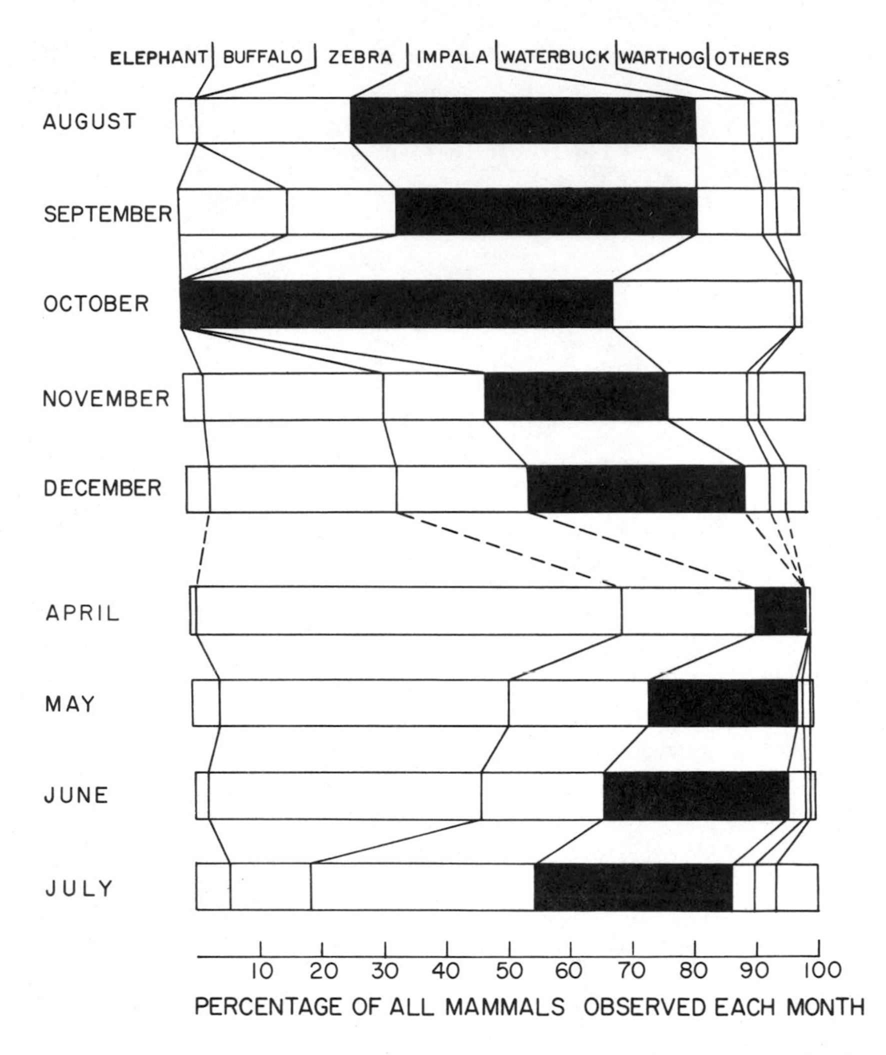

Figure 15. Individual species of mammals observed each month (in percent), Nabwalya Study Area, 1966–67

radius of Nabwalya Village at thirty-five and one hundred, respectively (D. Patton, personal communication, 12 March 1968). These figures were computed using a sample four-mile radius centered on the chief's village. Patton's estimates of 4.2 elephants, 3.3 buffalo, and 2.3 zebra per square mile for the area west of the Luangwa River to the escarpment and south of the Munyamadzi River including the northern third of the South Game Reserve were the highest densities for these species observed in this survey of the Luangwa Valley.

In the early morning following each of the afternoon or evening rains in November and December, I counted the numbers and kinds of tracks crossing and recrossing the road leading from the school to the game guard camp atop Ngala hill (see table 35). Since this road parallels the course of the river, counts of tracks indicate numbers of game passing between Ngala hill and the school on their way to the river during particular evenings.

TABLE 35

COUNTS OF GAME TRACKS[1] (1966)

	9 Nov.	11 Nov.	24 Nov.	29 Nov.	5 Dec.	14 Dec.
	Rainfall (Inches)					
Species	Trace	.63	.15	1.1	.53	.29
Elephant	–	–	–	–	1	3
Hippo	–	3	3 [33]	5	16 [9]	8 [9]
Rhino	–	2	–	–	–	–
Buffalo	17	10	6	4	27 [24]	380 [337]
Waterbuck	2	7	46 [32]	15	22 [17]	21 [20]
Impala	25	16	–	–	–	–
Zebra	3	4	33 [4]	7	10 [10]	14 [14]
Puku	–	2	2	–	–	2 [2]
Bushbuck	–	4	2	–	5 [3]	4 [3]
Antbear	–	–	1	1	–	1
Hyena	2	2	1	1	1	1
Small cats	2	3	8	4	6	5 [1]

Note: Game tracks counted were those crossing a one mile strip of road between Nabwalya Government School and Ngala Hill. The counts were made in the early morning after afternoon or evening rains had obliterated previous tracks.

1. Figures without brackets represent counts of tracks pointed in the direction of the river and those within brackets, the tracks pointed inland from the river.

Recent studies indicate that mammals observed in transects bear little or no relationship to the actual numbers of animals within an area. In a North American study, Van Etten, Switzenberg, and Eberhardt (1965) suggest that the true relationship between the numbers of deer seen by hunters and the actual population is not a straight line for there are proportionally fewer deer observed when their population is low than when deer are at higher densities. Since I did not assess the ease with which each of the major game species was visible to hunters nor determine by an independent method the numbers of game at Nabwalya, I am unable to calculate density figures for these species. My technique indicates their relative numbers and suggests a ranking of various game. In terms of total numbers observed, buffalo was the most abundant species on the study area. This species was followed in rank order by impala, zebra, waterbuck, elephant, and warthog. However, numbers alone do not reflect the availability or vulnerability of a species to hunters and the important variables in this interaction are left for the next chapter.

X

Valley Bisa Hunters and Their Prey

I consume as lightning (God)
The lion with difficulty downs his prey.
Bisa proverb

THIS chapter examines characteristics of the Valley Bisa hunting system as it was observed to operate during 1966–67. It considers hunters both as individuals in terms of their respective ranks and their general contributions to the meat supply of local residents, and as a group in their interactions while in search of prey within the various habitats. In order to do this, we integrate materials assembled in Part II on the ideology of hunters and within the previous two chapters.

THE HUNTERS

Although many men hunted during the thirteen months of my study, these may be sorted into four groups based upon their length of stay at Nabwalya during my residence and the location of their village. On this basis, "resident" hunters were those whose primary village of residence was among the fifteen villages or settlements studied and who spent six or more months living there during 1966–67. The residency of "transient" hunters was likewise among the same villages, but they spent less than six months in residence. These individuals either returned to Nabwalya between periods of employment or because of their marriages to several wives (one or more of whom lived in villages other than those in which records were kept) spent half or more of their time in these other villages. The domicile of "occasional" hunters was not among villages on or adjacent to the study area. For the most part, "officials" who hunted were not Valley Bisa but representatives of government either in residence or on short visits.

I recorded 1605¼ hours of hunting for the study area from 1 August 1966 to 7 August 1967. The fifteen resident hunters contributed 75 percent or 1202¼ hours of this total, but not all of these hunted to the same extent, for seven residents each spent eleven hours or less in hunting during the year and accounted for only 2.5 percent of all hunting time. Among this group were three young men, all residents of the same village, who made a single kill when they discovered a young cow buffalo mauled by a lion and dispatched it with their spears. The eight remaining residents inhabited the larger villages. Four of these were elders and the headmen of their respective villages. The younger men, Lubeles and Timothi, were the most diligent hunters. Together they accounted for 38 percent of all hunting time.

The six transients hunted 119¾ hours or 7.5 percent of all time recorded for this activity. In this group was Mwape, a novice with no previous training as a hunter. He had spent most of his life in a copperbelt town and returned briefly to Mponde for marrriage. During his three-month stay, he kept his uncle's gun, but this was destroyed when his field hut mysteriously caught fire at night. Shortly thereafter he returned to town.

Katwishi, the son of a renowned hunter who had died several years prior to my study, came in mid–May. He was uncertain whether to return for work in the city or remain in the valley. Lusefu was the headman of a village west of Nabwalya. In January he married a woman at Nabwalya and subsequently divided his time between that village and that of his new wife. Zikomo also was married to another wife off the study area, which accounted for his prolonged absences. Londoni and Frank hunted for brief periods while on leave from their jobs in the city.

No individual in either resident or transient groups restricted his movements throughout the year to the study area; even residents spent some time away for various reasons. Figure 16 depicts periods of absenteeism of a week or longer for the major hunters.

The five occasionals spent seventy hours pursuing game at Nabwalya. Individuals in this category were the chief, two of his councilors, and two visitors from elsewhere in the corridor. Although the chief maintained a residence for official purposes near the government school he moved his compound to the Mupamadzi River in October 1966.

Officials included three resident game guards and government officials from Mpika and elsewhere. Together they hunted 213¼ hours or 13.3 percent of the total recorded time. Although the game guards' main concern was the control of local hunting and the enforcement of the Faunal Ordinances, they were called upon by residents to protect their crops and granaries from depredations by elephants and buffalo. Twice they were allowed to hunt for meat rations. Official parties were occasionally dispatched to Nabwalya to secure game for government ministers visiting Mpika.

Nineteen of the sixty-five adult males recorded in my 1966 census of

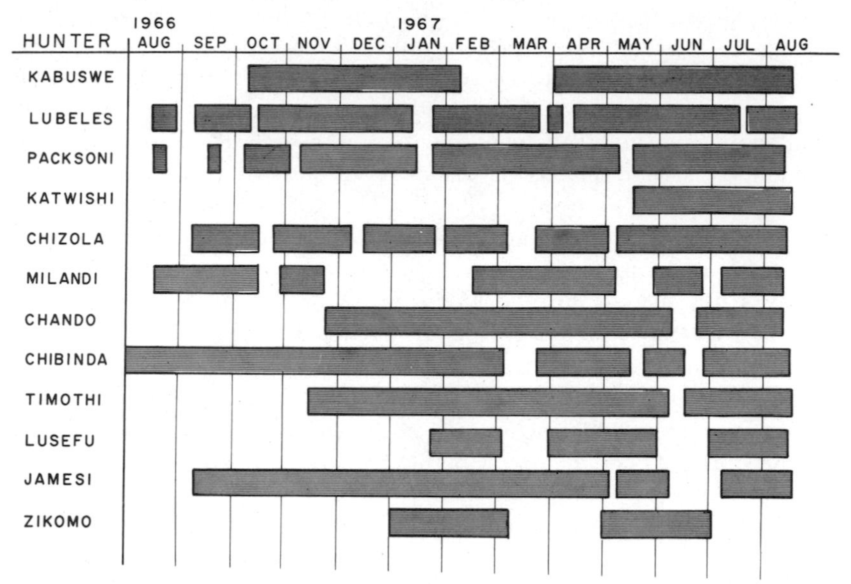

Figure 16. Periods of residence (in weeks) for hunters on Nabwalya Study Area, August 1966–August 1967

fifteen villages on the study area hunted big game during the year. How does this compare with data from other rural areas in Zambia? For an Ushi village on the Plateau, Kay (1964) found that all but one of the twenty men whose activities he followed for a year did some hunting. In this region where game is scarce, these individuals spent as much time chasing and trapping small mammals and birds as hunting for the larger mammals. Only four men, three of them under forty-five years of age, spent more than one hundred hours hunting. Kay found little difference between the contribution of young and old hunters, but unfortunately he does not provide a list of game killed. Kapferer (1967) in his occupational survey of eighty males in Plateau Bisa villages around Lake Baka Baka, listed five individuals (6.3 percent) as hunters. The main occupation of these males was fishing. Although other estimates of the numbers of hunters and their activities were not found in the literature, the mention of hunters and the local esteem for their endeavors in many ethnographic accounts (Richards 1939; Turner 1957; White 1956; Stefaniszyn 1964b) suggests a widespread enthusiasm for hunting in many areas of rural Zambia.

Ranks and Effectiveness of Hunters

A cultural tradition is a body of information and knowledge shared by members of a group. As times and conditions change, some components of this information become inappropriate and if the tradition is to persist, new materials must be found to modify it without destroying its essential coherence or unity. Previously, I mentioned that hunters were ranked by their possession of magics and the kinds of prestigious mammals slain. This system of ranks and other hunting behaviors are not exactly "things of the past" for change has been uneven and slow. The range in behaviors and values among those who hunted centered mainly on the type of weapon each employed.

The majority of hunters possessed muzzleloading guns and for these, the risks in killing game were such that most followed the traditional system previously described. On the other hand, a few former or current civil servants as well as the chief possessed breechloading shotguns. In addition, the game guards and the chief had rifles. With the exception of the chief, these individuals, by virtue of their transient status and affiliation with government, were cosmopolites; being immediately responsible to no local constituents their hunting efforts were unencumbered by local norms.

Inquiring about the personal achievements or rank of individuals in a society other than one's own requires the sensitivity to discriminate between assertion and accomplishment. To obtain information on the ranks of hunters, I asked older men which individuals I should contact for information on the types of magics and the ritual components to placate the spirits of eland, lion, and elephant. If an individual's hunting accomplishments were known to two or more of these persons and the hunter himself acknowledged the claim, I accepted this as evidence of his rank. However, recording the numbers of prestigious game slain posed a different problem for numbers do not have the same meaning for the Valley Bisa as for us. Therefore, rather than ask individuals only for the numbers of these game slain, I requested they mention also its specific kill site and recorded only those for which a kill site was given. My ranking of hunters according to the traditional scheme is given in Table 36.

Having assessed the traditional ranking of hunters, I next sought to evaluate their relative efficiency in the pursuit of game. For evaluation of a hunter's success I chose two criteria:

1. The ratio of an individual's successful trips to his total hunting attempts. A hunt was successful if the individual returned with a head of game. Hunts of short duration and those of infrequent participants were eliminated from this analysis.

2. The yield of biomass per hour of an individual's recorded hunting time. Weights for this analysis come from the carcass yields for various mammals provided in Appendix B. Adjustments in the weights listed were made for subadults and those unlisted as to sex. Carcasses salvaged from lions were evaluated at one-half normal carcass yield.

TABLE 36

USE OF MAGICS AND NUMBERS OF PRESTIGIOUS GAME REPORTED KILLED BY VALLEY BISA HUNTERS

Hunter	Estimated Age	Magics[1]	No. of Game Killed		
			Eland	Lion	Elephant
Chongo	55	CH, UL, MF	3	. . .	5
Lubeles	33	CH	0	0	1
Katwishi	38	CH	0	0	0
Chief	65	CH, UL, MF	many	many	many[2]
Wisdomi	65	CH, UL	4	0	8
Kazembe	55	CH, UL, MF	4	. . .	3
Paulo	47	CH, UL	0	1	6
Chizola	53	CH, UL, MF	11	0	0
Chando	63	CH, UL, MF	4	0	2
Chibinda	60	CH,UL, MF	3	0	4
Timothi	38	CH	0	0	0
Lusefu	45	CH, UL	. . .	0	. . .
Zikomo	55	CH	. . .	. . .	. . .
Packsoni	50	CH, UL	0	0	0

1. CH = *chilembe*; UL = *ulwito lia nama*; MF = *mfenzi*.
2. Killed two elephants raiding fields in 1966–67. As a prerogative of his status, numbers are not mentioned, only that he has killed many (*yavula*).

These criteria seem functionally related to an individual's skill in stalking, knowledge of game, and its movements, as well as the limitation imposed by his weapon. An important component of success and yield was the type of weapon used. Breechloading weapons, the 12 guage shotgun and .375 magnum rifle, are superior in killing power, accuracy, and effective range to the muzzleloading guns employed by most resident and transient Valley Bisa. The major disadvantages of the muzzleloader are its lack of accuracy and power and the time consumed in recharging it. These factors result in the wounding and loss of almost as many large mammals as are killed or eventually retrieved. I recorded that the Valley Bisa wounded twenty-six buffalo in addition to the thirty-three which they killed and retrieved. But this one record may underestimate the number of those which escape with wounds from these weapons.

Before firing at game, hunters with muzzleloaders generally close to within twenty paces or less of their prey. In spite of the greater range of modern weapons, I found that those with modern weapons also considered the same range optimal and sought to obtain the same general distance from their prey before firing. Since there was little, if any, savings in time or skill recorded between the users of modern and muzzleloading weapons, the increases in yield and success recorded for the former weapons appear mainly as a function of their killing power and mechanical efficiency.

The success experienced for hunters with muzzleloaders ranged from 0 for Packsoni, to 50 percent for Zikomo, but most were between 9 and 33 percent (see table 37). I am unable to offer a satisfactory explanation for Packsoni's lack of success. It may have been his lack of skill or luck or both. In 1967, he fired at close range at a warthog and missed. This incident quickly became a source of amusement to those who knew of it. Since the success ratios of some transients and occasional hunters are higher than those of residents, it seems likely that the total efforts of individuals in the former two categories were underrepresented. Since the village in which Zikomo spent some of his time was not on the normal rounds of my assistant, his frequent shifting between this village and another a short distance away may account for some of his hunts on the study area going unreported. However, it is unlikely that any of his kills escaped notice. To a lesser extent, similar circumstances may explain the high success ratios of Timothi and Lusefu.

Success ratios of hunters with modern weapons ranged between 33 and 57 percent, and the case of Lubeles who hunted with both types of weapons is instructive. When I joined him on hunts, he had access to my weapons, a rifle or a shotgun, although he ordinarily carried a muzzleloader as well. His success with modern weapons was 45 percent, but on hunts during which he used his muzzleloader exclusively, his success dropped to 13 percent. The game guards were the most efficient group, since their hunts were restricted mainly to the killing of rogue game.

At this point it is instructive to compare stalking success of the Valley Bisa with studies of natural predators. Biologists have commonly suspected a low rate of success among natural predators, although few studies show this quantitatively. During five years of observations on four European raptors, Rudebeck (1950, 1951) found that only 7.6 percent of 688 attempts by these birds to secure prey were successful. The success for each of the four species ranged from 3.5 to 10.8 percent. Of twelve complete stalks by Indian tigers observed by Schaller (1967), only one was successful. He speculated that the majority of tiger stalks ended in failure with probably twenty unsuccessful stalks for each prey captured. On Isle Royale, Michigan, Mech (1966) reported that of the seventy-seven moose which he observed tested by wolves, only six, or 7.8 percent, were killed.

In contrast to the above are the high rate of success documented for carnivores which outrun their prey after closing within striking distance. Estes and Goddard (1967) report a success ratio of 85 percent for the African hunting dog; Hornocker (1970) 82 percent for the mountain lion, and Schaller (1968) 50 percent for the African cheetah. Elsewhere Schaller's (1972) summary of recent information on the hunting success experienced by various species of carnivores shows a wide range between 8 and

82 percent. As more of these studies are made of individuals rather than combining observations of the same species, it is probable that the success ratio for a species will be shown to vary, as illustrated be Eaton (1970) for the cheetah, and as this study has shown for individual hunters.

From the viewpoint of the local constituents, a seemingly better indication of a hunter's effectiveness would be the amount of meat he made available for their consumption. The timely kill of an occasional buffalo would be more likely to satisfy the "meat demands" of one's relatives than the killing of several head of smaller game over the same interval, although smaller game are sought for its variety.

The yields with muzzleloaders ranged from 1.3 to 53.5 pounds per hour while those with modern weapons ranged from 16 to 635 pounds per hour (see table 37). It should be noted that most of the meat from the hippo killed by Jamesi was not consumed by resident Valley Bisa; therefore meat yields for muzzleloaders were much less than this figure would seem to suggest. Whereas Chibinda's success ratio was only 13 percent, by concentrating on large game (four buffalo, one waterbuck) he managed to achieve a respectable yield. On the other hand Milandi, who had a shotgun, sought mainly impala and consequently his yield was low. At the other extreme, the game guards whose primary targets were elephants, show the highest yields.

Frequency of Kills and Meat Supply

The frequency with which hunters killed game varied. The few mammals I killed are credited to the hunters who accompanied me, for on each occasion they received most of the meat. In terms of total game killed throughout the year, Lubeles was the most successful, with twenty-three kills to his credit (see figure 17). Milandi, with eighteen kills was next, followed in decreasing number of kills by Timothi, Chizola, and the game guards. The possibility that an individual's efforts to secure game would be reduced following a kill is not supported by my data. The fewest kills were made in March; the most in July.

A total of 60,392 pounds of game carcasses (carcass yield) were made available to residents at Nabwalya during the year through the efforts of all hunters. Although carcass yield includes bone in addition to meat, I use this figure as the amount of consumable meat the Valley Bisa derived from each carcass, for they consumed meat from the head and many of the internal organs. I assume these weights compensate for the pounds of bone embedded in a flayed carcass.

If we assume that the population figures assembled in Table 2 represent a stable population and that four children are given the status of one adult, then there were three hundred adult units on the study area during the year. If we further assume that the total meat supply was equally

TABLE 37

SUCCESS AND YIELDS CALCULATED FOR FIFTEEN HUNTERS IN STUDY AREA

Hunter	Weapon[1]	No. hunts	Hours	Success[2] (%)	Mammals killed or retrieved	Biomass[3] (lbs.)	Yield = Biomass/Hours
Residents							
Packsoni	m	9	51 ½	0	0	0	0
Lubeles	m	32	174 ¾	12.5	4	1,797	10.3
	s, r	42	150 ¼	45.2	20 ½	9,497	63.2
Chizola	m	43	178 ½	23.2	12	4,413	24.7
Kabuswe	m	16	50 ¼	18.8	3	304	6.0
Chando	m	24	109 ½	12.5	3	1,092	10.0
Chibinda	m	40	141	12.5	5	2,644	18.8
Timothi	m	49	276 ¼	28.6	13	5,478	19.8
Jamesi	m	11	26	9.1	1[4]	1,390	53.5
Transient Residents							
Zikomo	m	8	50 ½	50.0	4	807	16.0
Katwishi	m	7	27 ¾	14.3	½	37	1.3
Lusefu	m	6	28 ½	33.3	2	924	32.4
Occasional							
Wisdomi	s,r	6	38	33.3	2	894	23.5
Officials							
Pilsoni	s, r	6	24	50.0	3	1,487	62.0
Milandi	s	30	95	46.6	18	1,550	16.3
Game guards	r	14	37 ¾	57.1	8	23,972	635.0

1. m = muzzleloader; s = shotgun; r = rifle.
2. $\text{Success} = \frac{\text{successful hunts}}{\text{total hunts}} \times (100)$
3. See biomass conversion, Appendix B; adjustments made for subadults and carcasses retrieved from lion kills.
4. Hippo killed in field (see text).

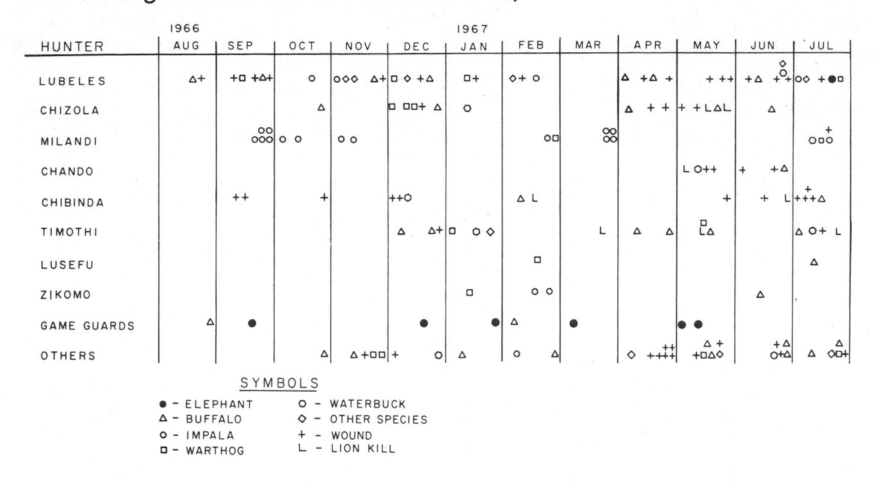

Figure 17. Individual hunters' success, August 1966–July 1967

distributed among these adult units (not an inaccurate assumption in the case of elephant and most buffalo carcasses), this amounted to 201 pounds of meat per adult for the year.

The monthly mean of meat per adult ranged from 6.2 to 28.5 pounds with a mean value of 16.8 pounds. Of this total, the game guards contributed 40 percent (23,971 pounds) of all meat supplied to local villagers or 80 pounds of fresh meat per adult. All other hunters together contributed 36,421 pounds or 121 pounds per adult. Lubeles and Timothi provided 51 percent of the meat attributable to the latter group.

The meat from game killed by Valley Bisa hunters was apportioned primarily among their matrikin, although depending upon its size and the hunter's commitments, meat in varying amounts was partitioned among others not related by descent to the hunter. It was impossible to detail the exact distribution of meat for each game carcass, especially the larger forms such as buffalo. Villages with one or more hunters in residence seemed to fare better in terms of total animal protein consumed, and enjoyed a greater variety of game than those villages which did not have an active hunter in residence. Although I have no comparable data for the larger villages, the yearly composition of meat side dishes for three small settlements shows that more than 90 percent of the meat which they consumed was elephant and buffalo.

INTERACTIONS BETWEEN HUNTERS AND THEIR PREY

All predators show preferences in their selection of prey, and the selectivity of many natural predators corresponds to their structural and behavioral adaptations (Kruuk and Turner 1967). Valley Bisa hunters are

Plate 13. A herd of waterbuck grazes on sorghum sprouts in a recently harvested field. Two zebra approach the field from the bush. The hut on stilts enables its owner to hear animals as they approach his field prior to the harvest of his crops.

Plate 14. Hunters sometimes scavenge meat from kills made by predators. This hunter, having earlier retrieved a buffalo foreshoulder from a predator kill, inspects a buffalo herd as it moves through an abandoned field.

Plate 15. The Valley Bisa have retained many traditions, in addition to hunting lore, which were once widespread in Zambia. In this photograph, villagers sit on the ground and clap their greetings to Chief Nabwalya.

Plate 16. Hunting occurs predominantly in the morning. Here a Valley Bisa hunter, with his muzzle-loading gun over his shoulder, scans for game while shielding his eyes from the rising sun.

also selective predators. Unlike studies of natural predators, however, studies of man's environmental relationships must take into account variables other than biological attributes. Between man and his environment is interjected a "middle term"—technology and belief-based perception which influences his selectivity and use of resources. Beliefs and values of a culture channel the perception and use of environmental products by its members, and for the Valley Bisa these at least partially explain their selectivity of mammals.

Species of Prey Selected

Among the variety of mammal life which surrounds them, hunters have a predilection for certain kinds which they kill for food. These preferences were articulated for me by an elder hunter when he said:

> First is *bamunjili* [warthog]. Second is *namavwamba* [female impala] and third is *mboo* [buffalo]. These animals we call *nama sha buBisa*, and when the *lupunga* grass is ripe in the water-filled depressions, these types of meat we relish with porridge made from *lupunga* flour. These two substances go well together. We do not like the meat from kudu, bushbuck, or waterbuck; since their meat tastes "cold" these are hardly worthy of a shot. Although we do eat the flesh from these animals, its taste is not as well liked as the former ones.

All of the former three species are normally fat, which in Valley Bisa idiom connotes health. According to them the flesh of other game requires salt as an additive to remove its "coldness."

My records of game killed or retrieved by Valley Bisa hunters (see table 38) during the period of study substantiate their verbal statements but not necessarily in the order indicated by the above statement. My list includes four buffalo and four zebra retrieved by hunters from lions and two buffalo killed by hunters but stolen by hyenas. The numbers of game crania (see table 39) tallied in the bush or adjacent to village sites provide information on the composition of kills prior to my study. Each of these crania was identified as a kill by a specific hunter. In this list, buffalo, impala, and warthog crania dominate, although the number of elephant crania may appear as an exception. During my study, the Valley Bisa killed only one elephant and wounded ten others raiding their fields. In recent times the pursuit and destruction of elephants beyond the confines of garden sites has become the responsibility of the game guards, and during the year these guards killed six of these large beasts within the confines of the study area. The mammoth crania of elephants persist for eight or more years before deteriorating, and because of this the time interval represented by their presence is longer than that for other species.

Predation among nonhuman carnivores is sometimes dependent upon the density options of their prey, and the preference quotient of relative

TABLE 38

CHRONOLOGICAL REVIEW OF MAMMALS KILLED OR RETRIEVED BY BISA HUNTERS IN STUDY AREA

Month	Buffalo	Impala	Warthog	Waterbuck	Zebra	Others
August 1966	2	. . .	. . .	(2)	. . .	. . . .
September	3[1] (2)	5	1 (1)	. . .	. . .	. . . .
October	2 (1)	3	. . .	. . .	. . .	. . . .
November	2	3 (1)	2 (1)	. . .	1	1 puku
December	4 (3)	. . .	4 (1)	2	. . .	1 bushbuck
January 1967	1	. . .	3	2	1	(1 puku)
February	4	5	2	(1)	. . .	. . . .
March	. . .	4 (1)	. . .	. . .	1	. . . .
April	5 (2)	. . .	. . .	. . .	. . .	1 hippo (6 elephants)
May	4 (5)	(1)	2 (1)	1 (2)	1	1 puku
June	6 (8)	1	. . .	1	1	(1 elephant)
July	5 (5)	2	3	2	1	1 elephant 1 bushbuck 1 eland (2 elephants)
August (2 wks.)	1	. . .	. . .	. . .	1	. . . .
Totals	39 (26)	23 (3)	17 (4)	8 (5)	7	7 (10)

Note: Numbers of mammals wounded are given in parentheses.
1. Two buffalo stolen by hyenas at night while carcasses lay in the brush.

TABLE 39

SELECTION OF GAME BY HUNTERS IN NABWALYA STUDY AREA

Species	Sex			Wear on cheek teeth				
	M	F	Undetermined	Slight	Medium	Heavy	Undetermined	%
Elephant	12	5	8					37.3
Buffalo	13	7	5	8	12	2	3	37.3
Impala	3	1	2	2	3		1	9.0
Warthog	. . .	1	4					7.5
Waterbuck	1	1	. . .		1		1	3.0
Bushbuck	2	. . .	. . .		1		1	3.0
Zebra	. . .	. . .	1		1			1.5
Rhino	. . .	. . .	1					1.5
Total	31	15	21	10	18	2	6	100.1

Note: Proof of selection was indicated by game crania or bones discovered near villages or in the bush.

frequency of kill divided by relative frequency of abundance is used by biologists studying the preferences of predators. For this assessment, a quotient of unity suggests that the species is taken in proportion to its abundance and reflects no selection, while quotients greater than this figure indicate preference or vulnerability of a species, and a figure less than unity indicates indifference. This index shows a value of 1.0 or greater for buffalo, bushbuck, warthog, waterbuck, puku, and for elephant, impala, zebra, and eland values less than unity.

The application of this index of preference shows that relative availability is not the only factor determining the prey selection of hunters. This index discriminates against those species which are solitary, restricted in habitat, or which infrequently occur within the confines of the study area. For example, the highest value of preference recorded (20) for bushbuck does not reflect preference for this species by the Valley Bisa, but rather that this species was rarely encountered during day hunts. Since most hunts I accompanied were directed toward the Bisa's major prey, the buffalo, the habitats of other game such as the thickets along the river in *Brachystegia* upland favored by bushbuck, and riverine savanna near the river, the haunts of puku and waterbuck, were bypassed. For the most part, hunts were directed away from the river rather than along its course. But the occurrence of a prey species in the kill at a higher percentage than its abundance may also indicate its vulnerability. Although a facultative predator may have a strong preference for a particular species, it may turn to an alternative, less palatable but more abundant species which at the time provides more profitable hunting. Such prey are called "buffer species." For the Valley Bisa at Nabwalya, species of low palatability but high vulnerability were the waterbuck and the bushbuck. Similar species might be the puku and waterbuck for inhabitants of the flood plain along the Mupamadzi.

Although the zebra is an abundant and frequently encountered species, it is not actively sought by hunters despite its vulnerability. I discount the fact that a supplemental license is required to take zebra west of the Luangwa River as a deterrent causing them to refuse this species. Should residents wish to kill zebra they could easily do so while minimizing the possibility of their detection by the game guards.

Of the seven zebra recorded in my table, four were retrieved from lions, two were killed at my request on my license, and one was discovered dead of unknown causes. A negative attitude toward an abundant species calls for an explanation. In my opinion, this rejection reflects the anomalous position of the zebra in Valley Bisa classification. In this view hunters normally kill only those mammals whose flesh does not carry the taint of social stigma. A zebra killed by a lion or found dead in the bush would be another case, for in their idiom the location of such carcasses reflects the benevolent guidance of their ancestral spirits.

Some selection is attributable to prey behavior. Although the major species of game were visible on most hunts, less than half of the encounters with these species elicited a stalk response from the hunter. For each encounter the hunter must read many situational variables in deciding whether or not to attempt a stalk and the odds associated with various species, as suggested by their success ratios (see table 40), were probably a major determinant. Warthog and buffalo show the highest values for attempted stalks per encounter, reflecting their stalkability relative to other species. Whereas the retrieval or recovery rate for wounded warthogs was comparatively high, those recorded for impala and buffalo were low.

TABLE 40

RATIO OF SUCCESS EXPERIENCED BY HUNTERS WITH DIFFERENT SPECIES OF PREY (IN PERCENT)

Species	Stalk/Total Encounters (× 100)	Kill & Wound/Total Encounters (× 100)	Kill/Stalk (× 100)	Kill/Total Kill & Wound (× 100)
Impala	36.5	3.0	2.9	33.3
Zebra	9.0	1.6	9.1	50.0
Waterbuck	53.7	13.9	11.1	42.9
Warthog	66.7	17.5	18.4	70.0
Buffalo	84.0	60.9	26.0	35.8

Note: Data given in App. C.

All game killed by hunters and examined by me appeared healthy. As suggested by the amount of wear on the cusps of their cheek teeth, most were adults in the prime of life. Moderate parasite loads within their digestive tracts and tapeworm cysticerci were typically notable in all carcasses. Since residents show no concern over the presence of these entities, did not understand parasite life cycles, and frequently consumed half-cooked meat, the presence of these parasites constituted a major source for human infection.

Sex and Age of Prey Selected

Valley Bisa hunters also discriminate in their selection of sex and age categories of their prey (see table 41). For this analysis I eliminate the eleven prey not catalogued as adults or subadults, although most of these were undoubtedly adults. Eighty-eight percent of the game taken by hunters were adults. Of the subadults, five were males, two were females, and four were undetermined as to sex. The majority killed were males (52m:34f). Since males are the largest in body size, and since Valley Bisa classification stresses maleness, hunters probably consciously selected large mammals since they provided larger returns for their hunting efforts. Males may also be the more vulnerable sex.

TABLE 41

PREY SELECTION BY HUNTERS[1] ACCORDING TO SPECIES, SEX, AND AGE

Species	Undeter-mined	Adult male	Adult female	Juvenile subadult	Young	Total
Elephant	...	1	...	...	...	1
Buffalo	6	21	9	2	1	39[2]
Impala	2	11	7	3	...	23
Warthog	2	7	8	...	...	17
Waterbuck	...	3	3	2	...	8
Zebra	1	2	2	1	1	7
Puku	...	1	...	1	...	2
Bushbuck	...	...	2	...	...	2
Hippo	...	1	...	...	...	1
Eland	...	...	1	...	...	1
Totals	11	47	32	9	2	101

1. Excluding game guards
2. Total includes two buffalo taken from hunters by hyenas and four retrieved from lions by hunters.

Successful stalks were generally dependent upon the prey's remaining unaware of the hunter's presence at least at the start of the stalk. Large herds of impala were generally aware of a hunter's presence at the beginning of the encounter and often moved ahead of the hunter. By their behavior these groups alerted other prey until the hunter moved out of their vicinity. Buffalo and smaller groups of waterbuck and impala were generally aware of the hunter only toward the end of a stalk, and before the escape response jelled among all group members, the hunter was usually able to select a particular prey and attempt a shot.

To determine whether the herd size of various game was an important factor in the stalk of these mammals by hunters, a chi-square table was constructed to compare the size distribution of herds stalked by hunters with the distribution of group size of the four principal prey observed. Both sets of observations were sorted into five arbitrarily selected herd sizes (see table 42).

For impala, significantly more smaller groups were stalked than expected. For this species, rams composed 71 percent of my observations on groups of five or less. Since rams constituted 36 percent of the observed impala population, eight rams would be expected in a kill sample of twenty-three animals if hunters selected these randomly, according to their assortment by sex. The kill record of thirteen males and eight females suggests that males were more vulnerable and that the larger herds of ewes and young offered a more efficient predator alarm system than the smaller groups of bachelor males. Despite the stated preference

TABLE 42

FREQUENCY DISTRIBUTION OF ENCOUNTERS AND DISTRIBUTION OF STALKS OF SELECTED GROUP-SIZE CATEGORIES FOR WATERBUCK, IMPALA, WARTHOG, AND BUFFALO

	GROUP SIZE					
WATERBUCK	1	2–5	6–10	11–20	21+	Total
No. of Times Encountered	20	47	19	6	8	100
Groups Stalked	9	13	3	3	1	29
$X^2_{4df} = 4.602 \quad P < .40$						
IMPALA						
No. of Times Encountered	64	92	43	36	42	277
Groups Stalked	24	31	9	7	1	72
$X^2_{4df} = 15.387 \quad P < .005$						
WARTHOG						
No. of Times Encountered	39	43	1	...	...	83
Groups Stalked	15	23	0	...	...	38
$X^2_{2df} = 1.472 \quad P < .50$						
BUFFALO						
No. of Times Encountered	0	3	3	6	17	29
Groups Stalked	0	3	3	4	15	25
$X^2_{3df} = 0.406 \quad P < .95$						

for female impala, six of the ewes killed during our residence were taken on two occasions by a single hunter with a shotgun. On separate occasions, he fired into a large ewe band, killing and wounding three. Hunters with muzzleloading guns sought individuals and small groups rather than large herds of impala.

For apparently similar reasons, more solitary waterbuck than expected were also stalked. Solitary males defend territories during the late rains and early dry season and at these times are quite conspicuous. Although adult males constituted only 20 percent of the observed waterbuck population, the majority killed by hunters were of this sex.

A stalking response was elicited in hunters more often for warthogs and buffalo in terms of their frequency of encounter than for the other species. For warthog, hunters stalked groups of two to five more frequently than expected and singles less frequently, but for buffalo size of the group was unimportant. Buffalo usually consorted in herds, and groups of all sizes were equally approachable, unless the herd had been previously disturbed by another hunter.

Effect of Predation on Prey Populations

What was the effect of Valley Bisa hunting on the prey populations at Nabwalya? This question is not easily answered after only one year of study, for humans were not the only predators operating on the study area and the study area was not a closed system for the prey. Therefore, departures from "normal" sex and age structure among species in the prey population cannot be ascribed exclusively to the Valley Bisa, for lions, wild dogs, hyenas, jackals, and smaller carnivores were abundant. Yet a tentative answer may be valuable as a means of placing human and nonhuman predation in some perspective.

It is almost impossible to generalize about the influence of predation upon a prey population for its effect depends in part upon the interaction of many variables. There is rarely, if ever, a one-to-one relationship between predator and prey numbers, and for this reason predation should be studied from a community perspective rather than from the viewpoint of an individual predator or prey species. Theoretically at least, a predator can regulate or control the numbers of its prey if it can increase its density or effectiveness as the abundance of prey increases or vice versa, but other studies (Errington 1963; Wynne-Edwards 1962) show that some prey species are capable of controlling their own population levels.

Leopold (1933) classified the variables of predation into five groups: (1) density of prey populations; (2) density of predator populations; (3) characteristics of the prey in response to predation; (4) density and quality of alternate foods available to predators; and (5) characteristics of the predator as revealed by its food preferences, efficiency of attack, etc. Following this scheme proposed by Leopold, Holling (1961) classified these predatory factors into universal and subsidiary variables. Universal variables are always present in predator–prey interactions and include predator and prey densities. Subsidiary variables were either constant or absent and included environmental, prey, and predator characteristics.

If we limit this analysis to the two universal components, prey and predator density, suggested by Holling, my data indicate two points: (1) most prey species have increased in numbers during the past thirty years; and (2) human and carnivore predation are complementary. During this same interval, the number of hunters has decreased and the spectrum of species harvested by them has declined and today is confined to the larger and more numerous species. Of the four species most actively sought by the Valley Bisa, my data show that kills are largely confined to adults in good health and that the majority of these are males. So long as their selection is confined to these groups any notion that hunters are a serious mortality factor in the survival of any ungulate population can be disregarded. Studies by Wilson and Roth (1967) in eastern Zambia and by Graham (1967) in Botswana show that saturation hunting by Africans armed with modern weapons was unable to clear game from good habitat or to change significantly its sex and age structure.

According to my records, wild carnivores at Nabwalya took mainly zebra and female buffalo. The highest mortality among ungulates usually occurs among the young through either disease or their inexperience in detecting and avoiding predators. Since my field classifications indicate high calf mortality among impala and waterbuck, predation by wild carnivores is the most likely cause, since I found no evidence of disease. Even when actively sought by investigators, the numbers of young killed by predators are often underrepresented in their samples, for the fragile remains of the young are difficult to locate and their bones disintegrate rapidly or are consumed by scavengers. During this study I found the fresh remains of two buffalo calves, one juvenile warthog, and one calf waterbuck which were killed by carnivores. Evidence from hunters suggests that predators cull mainly the young and less fit, including those wounded by hunters, and those from large herds.

Some other studies of predators suggest preferences similar to those which I propose for the study area. Eight impala killed by predators in East Africa and examined by Schenkel (1966) were all female and juveniles (three females, five juveniles). Dasmann and Mossman (1962a) describe predation as an important mortality factor on impala populations in Southern Rhodesia. Most of this species killed by leopards were old females.

In Kafue National Park in Zambia, Hanks, Price, and Wrangham (1969) found lions the most important predator on waterbuck, for this predator killed sixty-eight waterbuck in comparison with nine killed by wild dogs and two by leopards. In this park, lions killed more males than females and juveniles, although these investigators indicate lions consumed little meat from the carcasses. Kiley-Worthington (1965) also observed that in areas where waterbuck populations were dense, this species was not relished by predators. These observations indicate that both lions and the Valley Bisa treat waterbuck as a "buffer species" and kill it only when other more desirable species are not vulnerable. Since adult males are the most vulnerable category of this species, the low number of males recorded in the waterbuck population on the study area may not be due exclusively to hunters.

INTERACTION BETWEEN HUNTERS AND THE HABITATS

Although many factors contribute to the odds that an individual prey will be killed by a hunter, here we are mainly interested in habitat as an environmental variable. From the standpoint of the hunter, any choice of a search pattern which brings him into close contact with his prey increases his chances of making a kill. Since hunters know the habitat types preferred by a species, we may assume that they have evolved reasonably efficient search routines which maximize prey–man contacts and provide opportunities for testing game of various sorts.

Duration of Hunts and Seasonal Patterns

Both hunters and game respond in their movements to environmental changes. Game moves seasonally in response to changes in the location of its requirements for food, cover, and water and as hunters search for game, their wanderings correspond to those of their prey.

The monthly mean duration of Valley Bisa hunts (see figure 18) shows a bell-shaped curve with generally fewer and longer excursions during the wet season months. At all times, much travel appears necessary for hunters to locate susceptible prey, for most encounters do not provide the opportunity for a stalk. Although game is visible to hunters throughout the year, hunters seek a particular set of conditions which permit them to approach close to their prey. It seems plausible that at times when game is widely scattered in the hinterland and cover is dense, as during the wet season, hunters must spend more time searching for susceptible prey than during the months when game is concentrated near the rivers and their villages. Dampness of powder and on firing caps are additional reasons why fewer hunts are mounted during the rains, for in March when most rain fell, only six hunts were recorded.

While hunting on relatively open terrain, the Valley Bisa typically walk at a brisk pace. This is lessened slightly in cover. Using the conversion

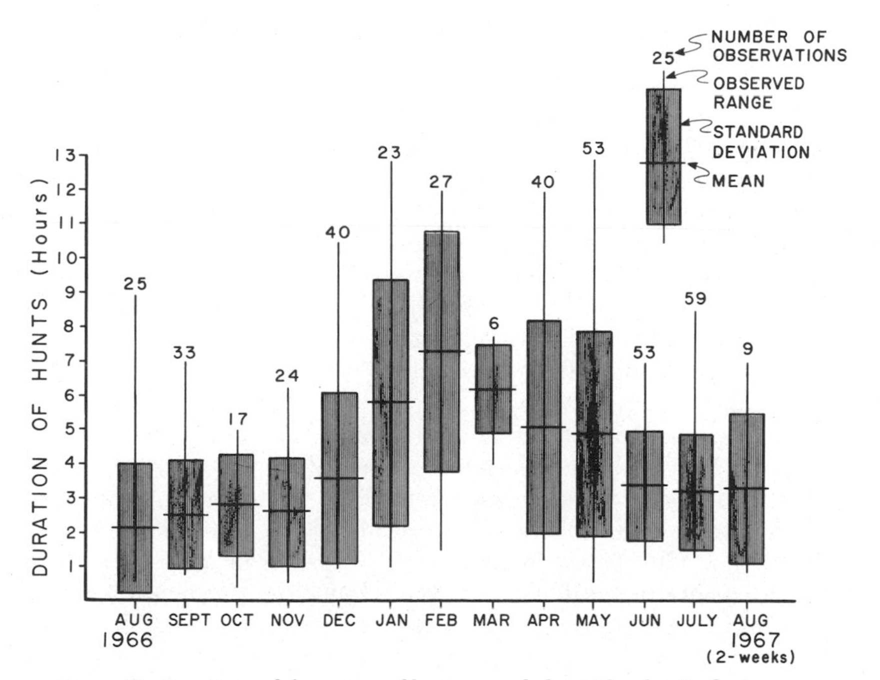

Figure 18. Duration and frequency of hunts recorded at Nabwalya Study Area

factor of fifteen minutes for each mile traveled, the mean distance traveled ranged from nine miles in August to twenty-nine miles in February. The longest distance recorded for a single day's hunt, forty miles, occurred in May.

On the study area, there were no set territories for hunters, although some areas, by virtue of their proximity to an individual's residence, were more frequented by him than by others. This contrasts with conditions on the plateau where game is relatively scarce. There a few individuals using magic are reported to protect their favorite sites from the successful intrusions of others. Although local hunters at Nabwalya knew of these practices, they apparently felt no need for these restrictive magics (*muti wakukaike mpanga*) while game was so plentiful.

Distribution of Hunting Time Among Habitats

Which habitats did hunters prefer at which seasons? Seeking to answer this question, I compare the percent distribution of habitat types on the study area with the percent seasonal distribution of hunting time recorded in each habitat (see table 43). I assume that if the percent distribution of hunting time coincides with the percent values for a given habitat, then this agreement suggests hunters choose that habitat in proportion to its availability. A higher percentage of search time invested within a habitat indicates a preference, while a lesser percentage suggests an avoidance by hunters. Since I was unable to map all hunting routes and the habitats are distributed in a crazy-quilt fashion, it is unlikely that hunters' choices of routes were selected entirely in terms of availability. Yet this typology provides a method for making the question operational.

The percentage time invested by hunters in mopane woodland (both seasons), disturbed bush (dry season), riverine savanna (wet season) mirrors their percent distribution on the study area. Higher percent values for time than for habitat distributions were recorded in riverine savanna (dry season), grassland (both seasons), and *Combretum* thicket (both seasons); lesser values of time were recorded for disturbed bush (wet season) and *Brachystegia* upland (both seasons). What then do these data suggest about hunter search patterns?

Mopane woodland offers two advantages to hunters: openness in searching for game, and cover for stalking along its border with other habitats. Because mopane covers much of the hinterland and extends in long arms almost to the river, it provides open access to most other habitats, for with the exception of localized stands of scrub mopane and thickets along drainage lines, the ground and shrub layers remain uncluttered throughout the year. As a consequence, mopane is used by hunters for moving from one habitat or site to another.

Abandoned fields and riverine savanna during the rains are covered

TABLE 43

COMPARISON BETWEEN PER CENT DISTRIBUTION OF HABITAT TYPES AND RECORDED HUNTING TIME IN EACH HABITAT BY SEASONS

	Distribution of habitat types					
	Disturbed Bush	Riverine Savanna	*Mopane* Woodland	Grass-land	*Combretum* Thicket	*Brachy-stegia* Upland
	13.4	22.2	31.2	6.0	2.7	24.4
	Distribution of hunting time					
Dry season[1] (276 hrs.)	13.1	36.5	30.3	8.6	5.9	5.6
Wet season[2] (348¾ hrs.)	5.9	23.2	31.1	13.0	8.0	18.8
Both seasons (624¾ hrs.)	9.1	29.1	30.7	11.0	7.0	13.0

Note: Data was taken from App. D and Table 18.

1. Dry season: August, September, October, November, 1966; July, August, 1967.
2. Wet season: December, 1966; January, April, May, June, 1967.

with tall rank grasses which makes the spotting of game difficult and restricts hunters' movements to the game trails which crisscross them at intervals. The amount of time invested in the habitats during the dry season by hunters reflects the abundance of game close to the villages and the opening of these areas following the dry season fires.

Hunters show a preference for grassland and thickets, albeit for somewhat different reasons. Shrubs around the periphery of grasslands offer hunters a vantage point from which they can scan the open terrain of the grasslands while remaining concealed, and from which game approaching or leaving the grassland may be ambushed. Thickets offer year-round cover for both large and small game.

Brachystegia upland covers nearly a quarter of the study area, and its low use by hunters reflects not only its distance from their villages but also its low productivity for game. A resident of a village near Ngala ridge spent 30 percent of his hunting time in this habitat during the rains but only 10 percent during the rest of the year. This individual used the uplands for access to other habitats, for like mopane, the uplands remained relatively uncluttered by rank vegetation during the rains.

Location of Kill Sites

A subsidiary question relates to why hunters might prefer some habitats over others. Hunters' choice of habitat may reflect not only their knowledge of the habits of preferred species and the visibility profile within certain habitats, but also their past successes within certain areas or habitat types. Unlike cheetah, wild dog, and wolves, which rely upon speed to overtake their prey, the Valley Bisa hunter often depends upon the location of susceptible prey at a distance and upon stealth and surprise for closing the distance requisite for discharging his weapon.

The major plant communities in which hunters killed or wounded game are given in Appendix E. Since few prey are killed outright, game wounded in one habitat often died in another. To overcome this classificatory problem, I sorted each kill attempt by the habitat in which the prey was initially wounded. Then, a chi-square test was made to test the hypothesis that prey actually killed or wounded in each habitat was proportionate to the number of prey expected to be killed or wounded based upon the percent distribution of habitat of that type on the study area (see table 44). Admittedly such a test is of limited value since the number of game killed or wounded throughout the year was not predetermined, and the categories of habitat eliminate the phenomenon of the *edge effect*. According to this analysis fewer prey than expected were wounded or killed in *Brachystegia* upland and mopane woodland, and more than expected in riverine savanna, disturbed sites, and thickets. Few mammals were killed on agricultural land. The numbers in this category were mainly elephant and buffalo wounded while raiding crops at night.

These tests indicate that a complexity of factors influence the choice of hunting routes, and the location of kill sites (see figure 19) illustrates an important complication in the typology used. The majority of game (71 percent) were slain in "ecotones," areas in which two habitats interface. Such areas commonly show a greater variety of food and cover plants than the major communities on either side. Where a species in its distribution shows a marked preference for such areas, the phenomenon is called the *edge effect* (Odum 1959). Although I did not determine its significance in the distribution of species at Nabwalya, Lamprey (1963) found the edge effect significant for impala, buffalo, warthog, and waterbuck in his distributional studies within the Tarangire Game Reserve, Tanzania.

Since hunters seek several species, we might expect their routes to represent a compromise between the habitat preferences of these species and that their hunts, directed toward the procurement of one species, would be switched toward the pursuit of another species appearing vulnerable at the moment.[1] In terms of time and yield, the most efficient target for hunters with muzzleloading guns was buffalo, and it was mainly toward this species that most hunts were directed. Detecting buffalo at a distance and preparing strategy for its stalk were important objectives and mopane woodland was ideal habitat for spotting large herds. Other prey, such as herds of impala, waterbuck, and warthogs were relatively safe in

1. My research in 1973 was concerned with both the selection and knowledge of buffalo and their movements and variables in Valley Bisa hunting behavior and strategies.

TABLE 44

COMPARISON BETWEEN OBSERVED AND EXPECTED NUMBERS OF MAMMALS KILLED OR WOUNDED BY HUNTERS IN HABITAT TYPES

	Habitat Types						
	Disturbed Bush	Riverine Savanna	*Mopane* Woodland	Grass-land	*Combretum* Thicket	*Brachy-stegia* Upland	Total
Observed	20	40	32	7	7	9	115
Expected	15.4	25.4	35.9	6.9	3.1	28.1	115
X^2 values	1.37	8.39	0.42	0.00	4.91	12.98	28.07
			$X^2_{.005(5)} = 16.75$				

Note: Expected values were derived by multiplying the percentage of habitat types on the study area (see table 18) by the total number of mammals killed or wounded. Observed values of kills in each habitat are given in Appendix E.

open habitat. However, smaller herds of these same species were vulnerable near its edge where there was cover for a stalking hunter. Since large herds of buffalo appeared on the study area at irregular intervals, an efficient search routine for the Valley Bisa hunter would seem to include the mopane woodland to check movement to and from game haunts and to detect buffalo, and the ecotones to use for cover should a vulnerable band of impala and warthog be spotted.

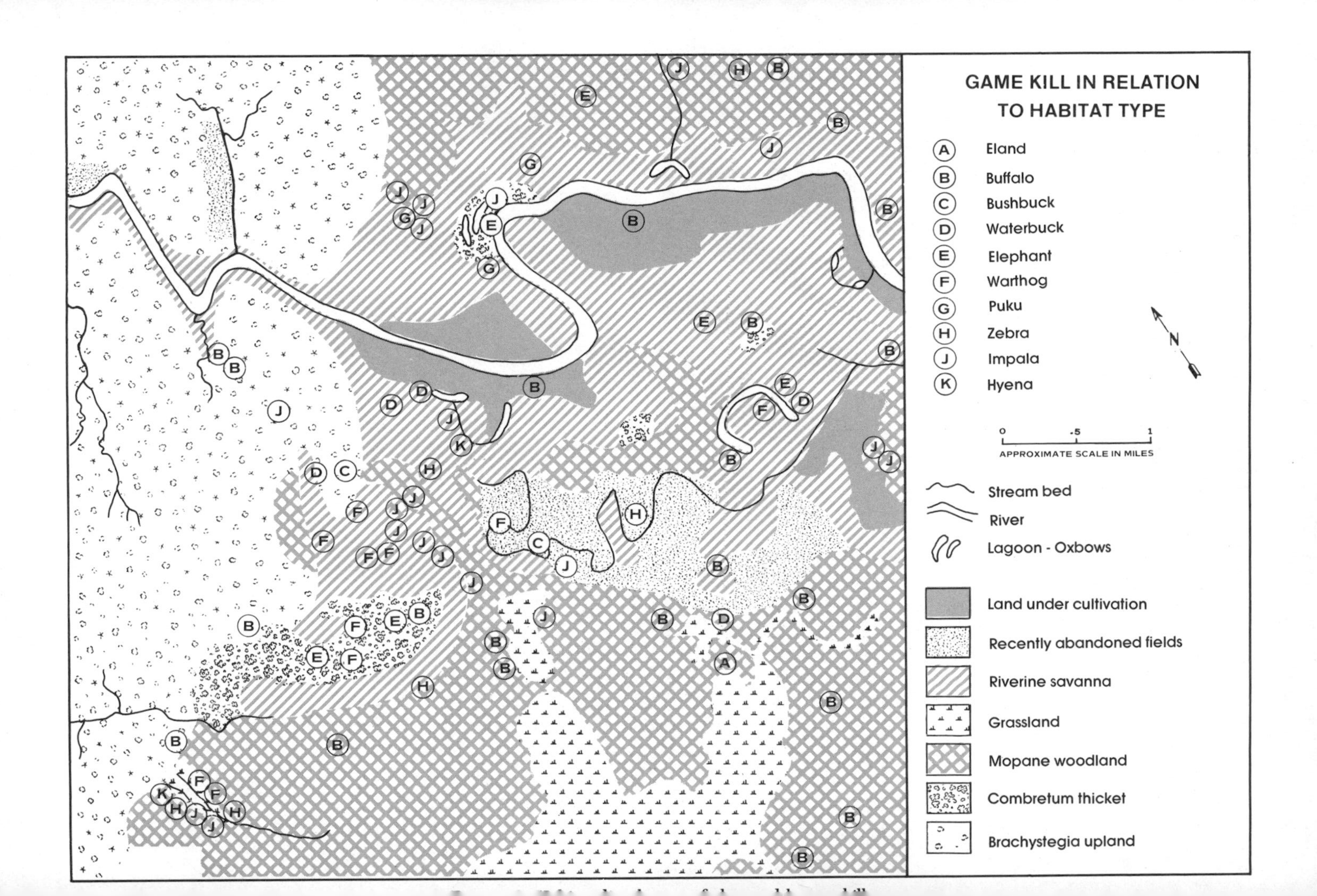
GAME KILL IN RELATION TO HABITAT TYPE
A Eland
B Buffalo
C Bushbuck
D Waterbuck
E Elephant
F Warthog
G Puku
H Zebra
J Impala
K Hyena
N
0 .5 1
APPROXIMATE SCALE IN MILES
Stream bed
River
Lagoon - Oxbows
Land under cultivation
Recently abandoned fields
Riverine savanna
Grassland
Mopane woodland
Combretum thicket
Brachystegia upland

XI

Prospects for the Future

Fellow searchers for meat (vultures)
I also belong to the chase
Wherever I wander, remain
For I also belong to the chase
A skillful hunter.

Bisa song

My own approach in this study has been eclectic, and thus has often involved painting over with broad brushstrokes some areas in my analysis where sufficient data were lacking. To admit this is not to apologize for the inadequacies of the present volume. Defining the characteristics of all cultural and environmental variables is beyond the capacity of a single investigator in a short field study. Since it is impossible to study the whole range of phenomena affecting an ethnic group, this study has focused primarily upon the hunting system and its processes as defined for the Valley Bisa of Zambia. Conceptual distinctions among the various aspects of a cultural system are a useful device provided they can be shown to have value in predicting and explaining the behavior of a group of people, and one does not lose sight of the interconnectedness of what one is studying with other systems in the overall cultural matrix. Valley Bisa men are aware that their ideological involvement with game is at variance with the facts of subsistence, yet for some their hunting activities serve to define the strongest distinction between the sexes in symbolic terms. This has been reported of other groups in Zambia, for the Bemba (Richards 1939), Luvale (White 1956), and Ndembu (Turner 1957) value hunting more than agriculture, and yet in no case is hunting the basis of their economies.

In defining the Valley Bisa hunting system, I described the following components: (1) aspects of the cultural system that define the role of the hunter, and the ideology of the cultural system which fixes the hunter's cognitive patterns and provides an assortment of techniques by which the hunter exploits mammalian resources; (2) the environment which provides the physical setting and the resource units consisting of various species of game and plants; and (3) the interrelationships between the population of hunters and environmental components.

In this study, I have found it useful to make a distinction between "operational" and "cognized" environments (Rappaport 1963). The operational environment is composed of units in the natural environment which are specified by the investigator as important variables within the system he is studying. Components of the physical–biological environment relevant in this study were described in Chapters Four, Eight and Nine, and the relationships between these variables and the Valley Bisa sociocultural system were diagrammed in Chapter One (see fig. 1) and discussed in Chapters Three, Six, and Seven and Ten. The "cognized" environment describes how the Valley Bisa perceive, classify, and organize their world of phenomenal experience. Although my operational categories of climate, habitats, and mammals share many characteristics in common with their cognized model, the animistic and anthropomorphic concepts of the Valley Bisa and their interpretations of cause-and-effect relationships between events are not the same. But this much should be expected for the Valley Bisa, like people everywhere, have unique interpretations of the world and life around them, and as long as these explanations and ideas do not impair the maintenance of appropriate and viable ecological relationships, they may prefer to retain their own interpretations and meanings rather than adopt those supplied by others.

It is reasonable to assume that a people's cognition of environmental phenomena is an important mechanism producing the observable behavioral patterns within their environmental setting, and therein lies its relevance to ecological studies. Thus in this study, the refusal of the Valley Bisa to hunt and consume abundant species such as the zebra and hippopotamus was explained in part by reference to the cognitive patterns of the group. But the search for mechanisms should not cease here, for other determinants of cultural traits should be sought in the interplay between environmental and cultural factors. Although articulated in terms of the approachability of the spirits, the timing of most hunts in the morning nevertheless coincides with the abundance and nearness of game at this time. In a similar manner, their predilection toward the selection of buffalo reflects their accumulated knowledge about the predictability, approachability, and vulnerability of this species as well as the high return of meat for their efforts.

As Rappaport (1967) suggests, the real issues involved with the cognized models are not the extent to which it may conform to "reality" as defined in the operational model, but the extent to which the observed behavior elicited is appropriate and adaptive to the "material situation of the actors." The hunting system as depicted does not reside in a vacuum, but is related to and influenced by other components of the Valley Bisa cultural system. What is changing and will continue to change are the conditions within which the cultural system has and will operate, for such systems are never static. They are affected by external forces stemming from other groups and the environment and internal forces, such as changes in the status of individuals, the processes of urbanization, and the diffusion of new ideas and tools. Perhaps because of my orientation toward a more "traditional" aspect of their cultural system, I have tended to overlook the inconsistencies and conflicts within the broader matrix and have depicted the Bisa in the Luangwa Valley as simple hoe cultivators and hunters living a rather precarious existence in what was until very recently an isolated and insulated environment. Yet the same values and beliefs were viable and apparent in almost every Valley Bisa endeavor, activity, and ceremony during the course of my study. What has been left unstated in this analysis is the future and changes in this system; yet it is not difficult to imagine what the impact of newer and more radical conditions and ideas will have upon their lives. A real difficulty is that of explaining the appearance of these new variables, for my residence in the valley was not a good vantage point from which to assess changes in individuals occurring in the cities nor the future plans of government for the area.

I do not have access to the details of the development plans the various governmental agencies will pursue for the Valley Bisa. One plan rumored and discussed during 1967 was their removal from the valley to a new environment on the plateau where they would be more amenable to government plans for their economic and social development. This plan would call for radical changes in the Valley Bisa way of life. However if they are allowed to remain in the valley, as most Valley Bisa themselves seem to prefer, many of the gradual changes described by Long (1968) for the Plateau Lala and the development of cooperative farms in the valley should not be far in the future. The implementation of such plans would accentuate some signs already apparent in 1967. Agricultural cooperatives would bring about changes in settlement patterns and the basic unit of residence along with the emergence of new patterns of social status and work arrangements. Wealth and leadership would accrue to those in positions in these nonindigenous associations and the status positions of former times, such as that of village headman, would be reduced to titles which few individuals would feel inclined to strive for. With such cooperatives in operation, the government would find better ways of protecting farmlands from game depredations and would hire game guards and arm them for protection work. In order to ensure some governmental control over such operations, these employees would most likely be outsiders rather than local residents. The maintenance of a post of Zambian police in the corridor would hasten the demise of "traditional" forms of social control. The position of the subsistence hunter amidst all these marked social and economic changes would be hard to predict. With improved lines of communication with the plateau and the construction of roads necessitated by the cooperative farms, hunters might be attracted to supplying game meat to the relatively meatless populations on the plateau. And one would expect that with the building of the oil pipelines and railroad on the plateau, such developments would cause entrepreneurs on the outside to look temptingly at the game supplies in the valley and would thereby supply the incentive for the commercial marketing of the valley's rich wildlife populations.

If this change appears demeanable, it should be evident from the conditions I have described in this volume that change and process have always been the norm. The high percentage of meat acquired from outsiders is indicative in many ways of the magnitude of change during the last eighty years. For in the past, hunting guilds were responsible for providing both animal protein and the means of exchange for the local population. The operation of these guilds was intimately related to the functioning of the social, political, and economic systems. An essential variable maintained in the past was a cadre of local huntsman to provide sufficient meat for the resident population. During these times, hunters in residence were a desirable asset and their presence may have been an important factor in keeping villages together, for a group without hunters was assured neither animal protein nor protection. The hunter's rituals and role reflected his alignment within the social, political, and economic spheres. His intimate involvement within each of these systems made him a suitable candidate for leadership.

Today migrant labor and outside markets provide the major means of exchange and almost half the protein consumed locally is derived from the efforts of outsiders—either the game guards or safari clients. While it may still be true that the successful hunter is esteemed by his fellow men, the prestige which formerly went with that position is being eroded by the emergence of new criteria of evaluation on the local scene.

New criteria of evaluation, such as the mastery of the English language, operation and maintenance of machinery, awareness of the outside world, carpentry, store ownership and management, and wage earning are becoming more significant in determining how the relative contributions of various relatives on the local scene are appraised. The felt needs of the community include more than animal protein, for clothing, salt, and other commercial goods are available for the most part only to those men and subsequently to their dependents who work in labor markets outside the corridor.

Individuals returning from their work in the cities bring with them new ideas and the means (money) to implement new life styles. Some who elect to remain in the valley establish stores and use their accumulated capital to invest in stocks of goods for resale. Most of those to whom I talked during my study found little value in "traditional" ways, and young people in particular either sought to withdraw from the influence of their elders and establish their own settlements, or quickly returned to the cities. Through their work in the city it is possible for some individuals to acquire the means and contacts to acquire modern weapons which are more efficient than the muzzleloading guns largely in use up to now. It is unlikely that individuals armed with these precision weapons will be saddled with the same behavioral abstentions that have hindered the hunter using muzzleloading guns.

Today the opportunity to gain rank through killing mammals such as eland, lion, and elephant is diminished by the presence of the game guard enforcing government game laws with respect to the taking of these species. In addition, the quantity of game killed each year in the corridor by game guards and by outsiders on safari and its free distribution has removed the former monopoly of hunters over this resource, and as a consequence has cut deeply into their former prestige and status. Because of these and other factors, the configuration of future changes for Valley Bisa society is in large measure dependent on a much larger social entity, for it determines the economic activities and technological training for the majority of its men. So whatever the outcome, change among the Valley Bisa will be the result of external policies and practices which are largely undirected and unplanned from the point of view of the local constituency. These changes will entail shifts in "traditional" orientations, technological improvements, and new political interests and pressures. And these changes will undoubtedly bring their associated problems as the Valley Bisa adapt themselves to new interests and pressures. In time, human predation coupled with environmental changes induced by an expanding human population will become the major factors decreasing game populations within the corridor. In this light, the hunter with his archaic weapon and rounds of rituals is but a throwback upon a passing era.

Appendix A

COMMON AND SCIENTIFIC NAMES OF WILD MAMMALS AND BIRDS MENTIONED IN THE TEXT

MAMMALS* (after Ansell 1960a, Walker, 1964)

Order Lipotyphla (Insectivora)	
Elephant Shrew	*Petrodromus tetradactylus
Shrew	*Crocidura hirta
Order Primates	
Bush baby	*Galago sp.
Vervet monkey	*Cercopithecus aethiops
Baboon	*Papio sp.
Order Pholidota	
Pangolin	Manis temmincki
Order Carnivora	
Wolf	Canis lupus
Side-striped jackel	*Canis adustus
Wild dog	*Lycaon pictus
Cape polecat	*Ictonyx striatus
Honey badger, ratel	*Mellivora capensis
Civet	*Viverra civetta
Genet	*Genetta genetta and G. tigrina
Slender mongoose	*Herpestes sanguineus
Marsh mongoose	*Atilax paludinosus
Banded mongoose	*Mungos mungo
Spotted hyena	*Crocuta crocuta
Puma (mountain lion)	Felis concolor
Wild cat	*Felis lybica
Serval	*Felis serval
Caracal	*Felis caracal

Tiger	Panthera tigris
Leopard	*Panthera pardus
Lion	*Panthera leo
Cheetah	Acinonyx jubatus
Order Tubulidentata	
Antbear, aardvark	*Orycteropus afer
Order Proboscidea	
Elephant	*Loxodonta africana
Order Perissodactyla	
Black rhinoceros	*Diceros bicornis
Burchell's zebra	*Equus burchelli
Plain's zebra	Equus quagga
Order Artiodactyla	
Bush pig	*Potamochoerus porcus
Wart hog	*Phacochoerus aethiopicus
Hippopotamus	*Hippopotamus amphibius
Giraffe	*Giraffa camelopardalis
Common duiker	*Sylvicapra grimmia
Sharpe's grysbok	*Raphicerus sharpei
Whitetail deer	Odocoileus virginianus
Mule deer	Odocoileus hemionus
Moose	Alces americana
Reedbuck	Redunca arundinum
Waterbuck	*Kobus ellipsiprymnus
Defassa waterbuck	*Kobus defassa
Puku	*Kobus vardoni
Impala	* Aepyceros melampus
Roan antelope	*Hippotragus equinus
Sable antelope	Hippotragus niger
Hartebeest	*Alcelaphus lichtensteini
Blue wildebeest	*Connochaetes taurinus
Bushbuck	*Tragelaphus scriptus
Kudu	*Tragelaphus strepsiceros
Eland	*Taurotragus oryx
Cape buffalo	*Syncerus caffer
Order Rodentia	
Porcupine	*Hystrix africae-australis
Cane rat	*Thryonomys swinderianus
Bush (mopane) squirrel	*Paraxerus cepapi
Bushrat	*Aethomys chrysophilus
Multimammate rat	*Praomys (Mastomys) natalensis
Gerbil	*Tatera leucogaster

*An asterisk indicates a mammal occurring in the Nabwalya Study Area.

BIRDS (after Mackworth-Praed and Grant 1962–63)

Cattle egret	Bubulcus ibis
Maribou stork	Leptoptilos crumeniferus
Lappet-faced vulture	Torgos tracheliotus
White-backed vulture	Pseudogyps africanus
Black kite	Milvus migrans
Bateleur eagle	Terathopius ecaudatus
African goshawk	Accipiter tachiro
Helmeted guinea fowl	Numida meleagris
Go-away bird	Corythaixoides concolor
Violet-crested Turaco (lourie)	Gallirex porphyreolophus
Racquet-tailed roller	Coracias spatulatus
Ground hornbill	Bucorvus leadbeateri
Gabon nightjar	Caprimulgus fossii
Pennant-wing nightjar	Semeiophorus vexillarius
African pied wagtail	Motacilla aguimp
Fork-tailed drongo	Dicrurus adsimilis
Straight-crested helmet shrike	Prionops plumata
Retz's red-billed shrike	Sigmodus retzii
Oxpecker (tick bird)	Buphagus africanus and B. erythrorhynchus
Red-billed quelea	Quelea quelea

Appendix B

ESTIMATED ADULT WEIGHTS AND EDIBLE MEAT FOR IMPORTANT ANIMALS IN THE STUDY AREA

		Robinette 1963		Sachs 1967				
Species	Sex	Average of	Weight (lbs.)	Average of	Weight (lbs.)	Estimated Adult Weights This Study	Carcass Yield for Both Sexes (%)	Edible Pounds of Meat Each Carcass
Elephant	M	5	11,405			11,000	40	4,400
	F	1	5,997			5,950	. . .	2,380
Hippo	M	4	5,560				. . .	1,390
Buffalo	M	10	1,343	8	1,655	1,343	60	806
	F	4	952	2	1,483	1,000		600
Eland	M	3	933			933	65	
	F	1	483	6	662	550	. . .	358
Zebra	M			13	546	550	55	303
	F	1	619	8	483	500	. . .	275
Waterbuck	M	1	520	7	500	500	55	275
	F			3	387	400	. . .	220
Warthog	M	16	181	16	191	181	65	118
	F	9	125	2	117	125	. . .	81
Puku	M	1	144			140	65	91
	F	3	135			135	. . .	88
Impala	M	1	135	28	125	135	65	88
	F	2	84	12	93	90	. . .	59
Bushbuck	M	8	96			96	65	62
	F	11	63			63	. . .	41

Appendix C

FREQUENCY OF HUNTING SUCCESS EXPERIENCED BY BISA HUNTERS WITH DIFFERENT SPECIES OF PREY*

Species	No. of Encounters	Attempts to Stalk	Wound	Kill
Impala	197	72	4	2
Zebra	122	11	1	1
Waterbuck	54	29	4	3
Warthog	57	38	3	7
Buffalo	87	73	34	19

*Data for buffalo derived from hunters' reports and personal records; for other species, only personal observations are used.

Appendix D

MONTHLY DISTRIBUTION OF HUNTING TIME AMONG HABITATS*

			Habitat Types					
Month	No. of Hunts	Hours	Disturbed Bush	Riverine Savanna	*Mopane* Woodland	Grass-land	*Combretum* Thicket	*Brachystegia* Upland
August 1966–67	29	70.75	8.50	23.75	21	11.50	2.25	3.75
September	27	63	6.75	20	23	3.75	5.50	4
October	13	37	3.50	16.50	12.50	1.50	1	2
November	18	39.75	8	19.50	5.75	1.25	3	2.25
December	27	89.50	2.75	22.50	20.50	15.75	9.25	18.75
January 1967	10	49.25	1	10	9.75	1.50	3	24
April	13	61.50	3	10	25.50	7.25	3.75	12
May	21	90.25	6.50	15.75	38.25	13.75	7.50	8.50
June	21	58.50	7.50	22.75	14.50	7.25	4.25	2.25
July	26	65.50	9.50	21	21.25	5.75	4.50	3.50

*Hunting time recorded to the nearest quarter hour.

Appendix E

HABITATS IN WHICH MAMMALS WERE KILLED OR WOUNDED BY HUNTERS DURING WET AND DRY SEASONS, 1966–67

Habitat	Season*	Elephant	Buffalo	Warthog	Impala	Waterbuck	Zebra	Others	Total	%
Disturbed	Dry	1	7	1	–	–	–	1	20	17.4
Bush	Wet	7	2	–	–	–	–	1		
Riverine	Dry	1	1	3	9	3	1	3	40	34.8
Savanna	Wet	2	6	2	–	6	1	2		
Combretum	Dry	1	–	–	–	–	–	–	7	6.1
Thicket	Wet	2	–	3	–	–	–	1		
Mopane	Dry	1	6	1	4	–	1	1	32	27.8
Woodland	Wet	–	10	1	6	1	–	–		
Brachystegia	Dry	–	2	–	1	–	–	–	9	7.8
Upland	Wet	–	5	1	–	–	–	–		
Grassland	Dry	–	2	2	–	–	–	–	7	6.1
	Wet	–	–	–	1	–	1	1		
Total		15	41	14	21	10	4	10	115	

*Dry season: August–November 1966; July, August 1967.
Wet season: December 1966; January–June 1967.

Bibliography

Agnew, A. D. C.
1966 "The Use of Game Trails as a Possible Measure of Habitat Utilization by Large Mammals," *East African Wildlife Journal* 4:38–46.

Ansell, W. F. H.
1960a *Mammals of Northern Rhodesia*. Lusaka: Government Printer.
1960b "The Breeding of Some Larger Mammals in Northern Rhodesia," *Proceedings Zoological Society of London* 134(2):251–74.
1965 "Hippo Census on the Luangwa River, 1963–1964," *Puku* 3:15–27.
1969 "The Black Rhinoceros in Zambia," *Oryx* 10(3):176–92.

Attwell, R. I. G.
1963 "Surveying Luangwa Hippo," *Puku* 1:29–49.

Beattie, J.
1964 *Other Cultures*. New York: Free Press of Glencoe.

Beachy, R. W.
1962 "The Arms Trade in East Africa in the Late Nineteenth Century," *Journal of African History* 3(3):451–67.

Bourliere, F., and Verschuren, J.
1960 *Exploration du Parc National Albert, introduction a l'ecologie des ongulés du Parc National Albert*. Brussels: Institut des Parcs Nationaux du Congo Belge.

Brelsford, W. V.
1956 *The Tribes of Northern Rhodesia*. Lusaka: Government Printer.

Burton, R. F., trans.
1873 *The Lands of Cazembe: Lacerda's Journey to Cazembe in 1798*. London: John Murray.

Child, G.
1964 "Growth and Ageing Criteria of Impala, *Aepyceros melampus*," *Occasional Papers of National Museums of Southern Rhodesia*, no. 27B, pp. 128–35.

Child, G., Sowls, L., and Mitchell, B. L.
1965 "Variations in the Dentition, Ageing Criteria and Growth Patterns in Warthog," *Arnoldia* (Rhodesia) 1(38):1–23.

Child, G., Roth, H. H., and Kerr, M.
1968 "Reproduction and Recruitment Patterns in Warthog (*Phacochoerus aethiopicus*) Populations," *Mammalia* 32:6–29.
Cory, H.
1949 "The Ingredients of Magic Medicines," *Africa* 19(1):13–32.
Cunnison, L.
1959 *The Luapula Peoples of Northern Rhodesia*. Manchester: Manchester University Press.
Dasmann, R. F., and Mossman, A. S.
1962a "Population Studies of Impala in Southern Rhodesia," *Journal of Mammalogy* 43(3):375–95.
1962b "Abundance and Population Structure of Wild Ungulates in Some Areas of Southern Rhodesia," *Journal of Wildlife Management* 26(3):262–68.
1962c "Reproduction in Some Ungulates in Southern Rhodesia, *Journal of Mammalogy* 43(4):533–37.
1962d "Road Strip Counts for Estimating Numbers of African Ungulates, *Journal of Wildlife Management* 26(1):101–4.
Denman, E.
1957 *Animal Africa*. London: Robert Hale Ltd.
DeVos, A., and Dowsett, R. J.
1966 "The Behavior and Population Structure of Three Species of the Genus *Kobus*," *Mammalia* 30(1):30–55.
Doke, C. M.
1931 *The Lambas of Northern Rhodesia*. London: George G. Harrap & Co. Ltd.
Douglas, M. M.
1966 *Purity and Danger*. New York: Frederick A. Praeger.
Dowling, J. H.
1968 "Individual Ownership and the Sharing of Game in Hunting Societies," *American Anthropologist* 70:502–7.
Eaton, R. L.
1970 "Hunting Behavior of the Cheetah," *Journal of Wildlife Management* 34(1):56–67.
Estes, R. D., and Goddard, J.
1967 "Prey Selection and Hunting Behavior of the African Wild Dog," *Journal of Wildlife Management* 31:52–70.
Errington, Paul
1963 *Muskrat Populations*. Ames, Iowa: Iowa State University Press.
Evans-Pritchard, E. E.
1937 *Witchcraft, Oracles, and Magic among the Azande*. Oxford: Clarendon Press.
Feely, J. M.
1965 "Observations on *Acacia albida* in the Luangwa Valley," *Puku* 3:67–70.
Forde, C. D.
1964 *Yakö Studies*. London: Internataional African Institute.

Gamitto, A. C. P.
1960 *King Kazembe*. I. Cunnison, trans. vols. 1 and 2. Lisbon: Estudios de ciencias politicas e socias, nos. 42 and 43.
Gluckman, M.
1965 *Politics, Law, and Ritual in Tribal Society*. Oxford: Basil Blackwell.
Gouldner, A. W.
1960 "The Norm of Reciprocity: A Preliminary Statement," *American Sociological Review* 25:161–78.
Gouldsbury, C., and Sheane, H.
1911 *The Great Plateau of Northern Rhodesia*. London: Edward Arnold.
Graham, P.
1967 "An Analysis of the Numbers of Game and Other Mammals Killed in Tsetse Fly Control Operations in Northern Bechuanaland 1942 to 1963," *Mammalia* 31(2):186–204.
Grimwood, I. R., Benson, C. W., and Ansell, W. F. H.
1958 "The Present Day Status of Ungulates in Northern Rhodesia," *Mammalia* 22(3):451–67.
1960 "The Present Day Status of Ungulates in Northern Rhodesia," in *Wildlife in an African Territory* by F. F. Darling. London: Oxford University Press, pp. 138–51, App. 3.
Hall, P. E.
1910 "Notes on the Movements of *Glossina morsitans* in the Lundazi District, North-Eastern Rhodesia," *Bulletin of Entomological Research* 1(3):183–84.
1950 "Memories of Abandoned Bomas No. 2; Nawalia," *Northern Rhodesia Journal* 1(5):55–57.
Hanks, J., Price, M. S., and Wrangham, R. W.
1969 "Some Aspects of the Ecology and Behavior of the *Defassa* Waterbuck in Zambia," *Mammalia* 33(3):471–94.
Holling, C. C.
1961 "Principles of Insect Predation," *Annual Review of Entomology* 6:163–82.
Hornocker, M. G.
1970 *An Analysis of Mountain Lion Predation Upon Mule Deer and Elk in the Idaho Primitive Area*. Wildlife Monographs, no. 21.
Hughes, J. E.
1933 *Eighteen Years on Lake Bangweulu*. London: Field.
Junod, H. A.
1962 *The Life of a South African Tribe*, vols. 1 and 2. New York: University Books.
Kapferer, B.
1967 *Cooperation, Leadership, and Village Structure*. Lusaka: Institute for Social Research, Zambian Papers, no. 1.
Kay, G.
1964 *Chief Kalaba's Village*. Lusaka: Rhodes–Livingstone Paper, no. 35.
Kiley-Worthington, M.
1965 "The Waterbuck (*Kobus defassa* Ruppel 1835 and *K. ellipsiprimnus*

Ogilby 1833) in East Africa: Spatial distribution; A Study of the Sexual Behavior," *Mammalia* 29:177–204.

Klingel, H.
1965 "Notes on the Biology of the Plains Zebra *Equus quagga boehmi,* Matschie," *East African Wildlife Journal* 3:86–88.

Kruuk, H., and Turner, M.
1967 "Comparative Notes on Predation by Lion, Leopard, Cheetah and Wild Dog in the Serengeti Area, East Africa," *Mammalia* 31(1):1–27.

Lagercrantz, S.
1934 "The Harpoon Downfall, and Its Distribution in Africa," *Anthropos* 29:793–807.

Lamprey, H. F.
1963 "Ecological Separation of the Large Mammal Species in the Tarangire Game Reserve, Tanganyika," *East African Wildlife Journal* 1:63–92.
1964 "Estimation of the Large Mammal Densities, Biomass and Energy Exchange in the Tarangire Game Reserve and the Masai Steppe in Tanganyika," *East African Wildlife Journal* 2:1–46.

Lane-Poole, E. H.
1956 "The Luangwa Valley in 1918," *Northern Rhodesia Journal* 3:154–63.

Langham, R. W. M.
1953 "Memories of an Elephant Control Officer," *Northern Rhodesia Journal* 2(2):3–16.

Laughlin, W. S.
1968 "Hunting: An Integrating Biobehavioral System and Its Evolutionary Importance," in *Man the Hunter*, R. B. Lee and I. DeVore, eds. Chicago: Aldine Publishing Co., pp. 304–20.

Leach, E.
1964 "Animal Categories and Verbal Abuse," in *New Directions in the Study of Language*, E. H. Lenneberg, ed. Cambridge, Mass.: M.I.T. Press, pp. 23–63.

Ledger, H. P.
1963 "Animal Husbandry Research and Wildlife in East Africa," *East African Wildlife Journal* 1:18–29.

Leopold, A.
1933 *Game Management.* New York: Charles Scribner's Sons.

Letcher, O.
1911 *Big Game Hunting in North-Eastern Rhodesia.* London: John Long Ltd.

Lienhardt, G.
1961 *Divinity and Experience.* Oxford: Oxford University Press.

Livingstone, D.
1874 *The Last Journals of David Livingstone*, vol. 1, H. Waller, ed. London: John Murray.

Long, N.
1968 *Social Change and the Individual.* Manchester: Manchester University Press.

Lyell, D. D.
1910 *Hunting Trips in Northern Rhodesia.* London: Horace Cox.
1913 *Wildlife in Central Africa.* London: Horace Cox.

Mackenzie, D. R.
1925 *The Spirit Ridden Konde.* London: Seeley Service and Co., Ltd.

Mackworth-Praed, C. W., and Grant, C. H. B.
1962–63 *Birds of the Southern Third of Africa,* vols. 1 and 2. London: Longmans, Green and Co.

Malinowski, B.
1948 *Magic, Science, and Religion and Other Essays.* Garden City, N.Y.: Doubleday Anchor Books.

Marwick, M. G.
1965 *Sorcery in Its Social Setting.* Manchester: Manchester University Press.

Mech, L. D.
1966 *The Wolves of Isle Royale,* Fauna of the National Parks of the United States, series no. 7. Washington, D.C.: U.S. Government Printing Office.

Melland, F. H.
1923 *In Witch-Bound Africa.* London: Seeley Service and Co., Ltd.
1938 *Elephants in Africa.* London: Country Life Ltd.

Middleton, J., and Winter, E. H. (eds.)
1963 *Witchcraft and Sorcery in East Africa.* London: Routledge and Kegan Paul.

Miracle, M. P.
1962 "Aboriginal Trade Among the Senga and Nsenga of Northern Rhodesia," *Ethnology* 1:212–22.

Mitchell, J. C.
1949 "The Yao of Southern Nyasaland," *Africa* 19(2):94–100.

Moore, O. K.
1965 "Divinations: A New Perspective," *American Anthropologist* 59:69–74.

Moore, R. J. B.
1940 "Bwanga Among the Bemba," *Africa* 13:211–34.

Moubray, J. M.
1912 *In South Central Africa.* London: Constable & Co. Ltd.

Mpika District Notebooks and Tour Reports
Zambia National Archives, Lusaka.

Needham, R.
1967 "Right and Left in Nyoro Symbolic Classification," *Africa* 37(4):425–52.

Odum, E. P.
1959 *Fundamentals of Ecology.* 2d ed. Philadelphia and London: W. B. Saunders Company.

Pitman, C. R. S.
1934 *A Report on a Fauna Survey of Northern Rhodesia with Special Reference to Game, Elephant Control and National Parks.* Livingstone: Government Printer.

Radcliffe-Brown, A. R.
1948 *The Andaman Islanders.* Glencoe, Illinois: The Free Press.

Rappaport, R. A.
1963 "Aspects of Man's Influence Upon Island Ecosystems: Alteration and Control," in *Man's Place in the Island Ecosystem,* F. R. Fosberg, ed. Honolulu: Bishop Museum, pp. 155–70.
1967 *Pigs for the Ancestors.* New Haven: Yale University Press.

Richards, A. I.
1939 *Land, Labour, and Diet in Northern Rhodesia.* London: International African Institute.
1950 "Some Types of Family Structure Amongst the Central Bantu," in *African Systems of Kinship and Marriage,* A. R. Radcliffe-Brown and D. Forde, eds. London: Oxford University Press, pp. 207–51.

Robinette, W. L.
1963 "Weights of Some of the Larger Mammals of Northern Rhodesia," *Puku* 1:207–15.

Roth, H. H.
1965 "Observations on Growth and Ageing of Warthog *Phacochoerus aethiopicus* (Pallas)," *Zschr. Saugetierk* 30(6):367–80.

Rudebeck, G.
1950 "The Choice of Prey and Modes of Hunting of Predatory Birds with Special Reference to their Selective Effect," *Oikos* 2:65–88.
1951 "The Choice of Prey and Modes of Hunting of Predatory Birds with Special Reference to their Selective Effect (Continued)," *Oikos* 3:200–31.

Sachs, R.
1967 "Live Weight and Body Measurements of Serengeti Game Animals," *East African Wildlife Journal* 5:24–36.

Schaller, G.
1967 *The Deer and the Tiger.* Chicago: University of Chicago Press.
1968 "Hunting Behavior of the Cheetah in the Serengeti National Park, Tanzania," *East African Wildlife Journal* 6:95–100.
1972 *The Serengeti Lion.* Chicago: University of Chicago Press.

Schenkel, R.
1966 "On Sociology and Behavior in Impala," *East African Wildlife Journal* 4:99–114.

Scudder, T.
1962 *The Ecology of the Gwembe Tonga.* Manchester: Manchester University Press.
1971 *Gathering Among African Woodland Savannah Cultivators.* Lusaka: University of Zambia, Zambian Papers, no. 5.

Spinage, E. A.
1967 "Ageing the Uganda Defassa Waterbuck *Kobus defassa ugandae,*" Neumann. *East African Wildlife Journal* 5:1–17.

Stefaniszyn, B.
1964a *Social and Ritual Life of the Ambo of Northern Rhodesia.* London: Oxford University Press.
1964b "The Material Culture of the Ambo of Northern Rhodesia," *Occasional Papers of the Rhodes–Livingstone Museum*, no. 16.

Stevenson-Hamilton, J.
1947 *Wild Life in South Africa.* London: Cassell and Co. Ltd.

Taber, R., and Dasmann, R. F.
1954 "A Sex Difference in Mortality in Young Columbia Blacktailed Deer," *Journal of Wildlife Management* 18(3):309–15.

Thomas, F. M.
1958 *Historical Notes on the Bisa Tribe, Northern Rhodesia.* Lusaka: Rhodes-Livingstone Communication, no. 8.

Thompson, J. G.
1960 A description of the growth habits of mopane in relation to soil and climatic conditions. *Proceedings First Federal Science Congress.* Salisbury, pp. 181–87.

Thomson, B. P.
1954 *Two Studies in African Nutrition.* Lusaka. Rhodes-Livingstone Papers, no. 24.

Turner, V. W.
1957 *Schism and Continuity in an African Society.* Manchester: Manchester University Press.
1967 *The Forest of Symbols.* Ithaca, N.Y.: Cornell University Press.

Van Etten, R. C., Switzenberg, D. F., and Eberhardt, L.
1965 "Controlled Deer Hunting in a Square-Mile Enclosure," *Journal of Wildlife Management* 29(1):59–73.

Verheyan, R.
1955 "Contribution a l'ethologie de waterbuck *Kobus defassa*, et de l'antilope harnachee, *Tragelaphus scriptus*," *Mammalia* 19:309–19.

Walker E. P.
1964 *Mammals of the World*, vols. 1 and 2. Baltimore, Md.: The Johns Hopkins Press.

Wilson, V. J., and Roth, H. H.
1967 "The Effects of Tsetse Control Operations on Common Duiker in Eastern Zambia," *East African Wildlife Journal* 5:53–64.

White, C. M. N.
1956 "The Role of Hunting and Fishing in Luvale Society," *African Studies* 15(2):75–86.

White Fathers
1954 *Bemba-English Dictionary.* London: Longmans, Green, and Co.

Whiteley, W. H.
1966 "Social Anthropology: Meaning and Linguistics," *Man* (New Series) 1(2):139–57.

Wynne-Edwards, V. C.
1962 *Animal Dispersion in Relation to Social Behavior.* Edinburgh and London: Oliver and Boyd.

Index